THE
THEOLOGY OF
F. D. MAURICE

THE

THEOLOGY OF

F. D. MAURICE

ALEC R. VIDLER D.D.

S C M   PRESS   LTD
56 BLOOMSBURY STREET, LONDON   W.C.1

TO

J. H. OLDHAM

First published in Great Britain October 1948

Printed in Great Britain by Jarrold and Sons, Limited, Norwich.

CONTENTS

Preface

1. ONLY A DIGGER   7

2. THE HEAD AND KING OF OUR RACE   35

3. THE IDEA OF A CHURCH UNIVERSAL   64

4. THE SACRAMENT OF CONSTANT UNION   94

5. OTHER SIGNS OF THE KINGDOM OF CHRIST   121

6. THE BOOK OF THE WAYS OF GOD   155

7. A LIVING POLITICS   183

8. A UNITED CONFESSION OF THE NAME   207

Bibliography of Works by F. D. Maurice   234

The Hale Lectures   239

Index   242

PREFACE

I AM grateful to the Board of Trustees of Seabury-Western Theological Seminary both for the honour of being invited to deliver the Hale Lectures and for their agreement with my proposal to take the theology of F. D. Maurice as my subject. I heard of Maurice from my earliest theological teachers at Cambridge, the late Dr. J. O. F. Murray and Dr. S. C. Carpenter, now Dean of Exeter Cathedral. I have had some of his books on my shelves since my undergraduate days. I had gradually collected a considerable number of them, and from time to time had read one or more of them. But I had never been satisfied that I had discovered what he was really driving at, and at the same time I had felt more and more that it would be exceedingly worth while to make that discovery. Hence I welcomed an opportunity of embarking on a thorough study of his theological work.

I will say no more here than that the preparation of these lectures has been for me an illuminating experience, and that I hope their publication may be instrumental in communicating something of the same illumination to any who read them. It will be obvious that any virtue the lectures possess is due to the subject, and not to the lecturer.

It should be added that the lectures were published in America under the title of *Witness to the Light*.

ALEC R. VIDLER

St. Deiniol's Library,
Hawarden.

I

ONLY A DIGGER

*My sole vocation is metaphysical and theo-
logical grubbing.*—LIFE OF F. D. M., II, 295.

A BOUT a hundred years ago Walter Bagehot, who was
then a student at Lincoln's Inn, took his friend
R. H. Hutton to hear one of the afternoon sermons by the Chaplain of the Inn. "I remember
Bagehot's telling me, with his usual caution,"
wrote Hutton forty years later, "that he would not exactly
answer for my being impressed by the sermon, but that at
all events he thought I should feel something different went
on there from that which goes on in an ordinary church
or chapel."[1]

 On a Sunday in February, 1865, Lady Frederick Caven-
dish—the niece of Mr. Gladstone, and wife of the Lord
Frederick Cavendish who was to be murdered in Phoenix
Park—was taken by her husband to hear the same preacher.
That evening she wrote in her diary:

> We went to hear the famous Mr. Maurice in the
> morning. He preached most beautifully on Triumphant
> Hope; with a manner full of love and fervour. If one
> had not known of his startling, peculiar opinions, I
> think one would have seen nothing in his sermon but
> what any Christian might agree with. But alas! there is
> terrible difficulty and dispute all round one now, and

[1] R. H. Hutton, *Essays on Some of the Modern Guides of English Thought in Matters of Faith* (1887), p. 306.

7

one is unconsciously on one's guard and in a state of distrust.[2]

Lady Frederick was as keenly interested in ecclesiastical affairs as her uncle, and the comments upon them in her published diaries are generally discerning. Seven years later, when Maurice died, she wrote:

> The famous Mr. Maurice is just dead; the papers for the most part speak of him with great respect, and indeed I believe he was a true Saint, though perhaps with the misfortune, which seems to belong to some schools of thought, of inspiring his disciples with his errors rather than his truths.[3]

Except that she had once or twice heard Maurice preach, the diarist's impressions were second-hand. They convey the mid-Victorian ecclesiastical atmosphere ("At no period in the history of the Church of England," said Dean Rashdall, "have parties been more sharply distinguished than at about the middle of the nineteenth century"[4]); they also suggest an honest perplexity about Maurice. With none of the ecclesiastical parties was Maurice a *persona grata,* and Lady Frederick, like Mr. Gladstone, was a staunch High Anglican. But like her uncle she had an independent and a liberal mind, and though mystified by Maurice she could not refuse to own his spiritual greatness. Gladstone himself said that Maurice was "a spiritual splendour," while confessing that he found his intellectual constitution "a good deal of an enigma."[5]

The impression that Maurice was the leader of "a school of thought" was natural and widespread, but no one who knew him intimately or who really understood him would

[2]*The Diary of Lady Frederick Cavendish,* ed. by John Bailey (1927), I, 251.
[3]*Ibid.,* II, 131.
[4]Hastings Rashdall, *Principles and Precepts* (1927), p. 155.
[5]*Life of F. D. M.,* II, 207 f.

have let it pass. For Maurice abhorred the very idea of leading a school of thought, of forming a party, or of gathering a company of disciples. But hardly any one at the time did understand him. His friends and admirers were almost as much mystified by him as his critics and opponents, though in a different way. A recent writer speaks of "that tiresome genius Maurice with his almost perverse antagonism to those with whom he should have been found in agreement and his enthusiastic support of those who were embarrassed by his approbation."[6]

That the partisans of the various religious sects and schools of thought should have used violent or extreme language about Maurice is not at all strange. What is remarkable is the diversity of the opinions that were formed about him by men of eminence and comparatively independent judgment in his own lifetime and afterwards. Here are a few examples:

> Maurice has been petted and told he is a philosopher, till he naturally thinks he is one. And he has not a clear idea in his head. It is a reputation that, the instant it is touched, must go like a card-house. (J. B. Mozley, 1853.)[7]

> We venture with some confidence to assert, that for consistency and completeness of thought, and precision in the use of language, it would be difficult to find his

[6]G. L. Phillips, Art. on "Wilhelm Dilthey" in *Laudate*, June, 1946, p. 17.

[7]*Letters of J. B. Mozley* (1885), p. 222. Mozley is referring in particular to Maurice's *Theological Essays*. For a comment by Newman on why Mozley undervalued Maurice, see F. L. Cross, *John Henry Newman* (1933), p. 181. One may wonder of how careful a study of Maurice's teaching some adverse verdicts were the outcome. Hort reports in 1849 that Harvey Goodwin "used to employ all his wit in ridiculing Maurice, but that a lady of his relations who was an admirer of Maurice persuaded Goodwin to read his writings more carefully, and that for the last two years he has had a very high opinion of him." See A. F. Hort, *Life and Letters of Fenton J. A. Hort* (1896), I, 104.

(Maurice's) superior among living theologians. (James Martineau, 1856.)[8]

That man (Maurice) I never allow anything to be said against. (Tennyson, 1861.)[9]

He (Maurice) was misty and confused, and none of his writings appear to me worth reading. But he was a great man and a disinterested nature, and he always stood by any one who appeared to be oppressed. (Benjamin Jowett, 1872.)[10]

I am writing an article on Maurice for Morley! Of all the muddle-headed, intricate, futile persons I ever studied, he was about the most utterly bewildering. (Leslie Stephen, 1874.)[11]

I need not say that in my estimation no greater honour could be paid to any living man than to ask him to write upon Mr. Maurice. (J. H. Shorthouse, 1884.)[12]

When the religious history of the nineteenth century comes to be written, the leaders of great parties and schools of thought, the men who in their own age were most widely looked up to and followed, may not always occupy so large and important a place in it as we or they might expect. But however our estimates may be falsified by the judgement of posterity, there is one of whom it is safe to say that he must always stand out pre-eminently: Maurice the seer. . . . He was beyond question the greatest seer of the century. (W. E. Collins, 1902.)[13]

His work . . . is often obscure, not carefully studied, with no particular charm of style. . . . Maurice stands

[8]*Essays, Reviews, and Addresses* (1890), I, 258.

[9]E. Abbott and L. Campbell, *The Life and Letters of Benjamin Jowett* (1897), I, 350.

[10]*Ibid.*, II, 45. For Maurice's opinion of Jowett, see *What is Revelation?*, pp. 212 f.

[11]F. W. Maitland, *The Life and Letters of Leslie Stephen* (1906), p. 240.

[12]*Life and Letters of J. H. Shorthouse,* ed. by his wife (1905), I, 220.

[13]In *Typical English Churchmen from Parker to Maurice* (1902), pp. 327 f., 360.

to-day as the greatest thinker of the English Church
in the nineteenth century. (C. F. G. Masterman,
1907.)[14]

It would be interesting to inquire how these divergent
opinions were arrived at, but the result would probably
cast much more light upon their authors than upon Maurice
himself. What anyhow is evident is that a man who provoked such different estimates is not likely to prove easy
to understand. He cannot be satisfactorily classified, and
this is one reason why his teaching has been regarded as
mystifying. As he himself said, "a man will not really be
intelligible to you, if, instead of listening to him and sym-
pathizing with him, you determine to classify him."[15] None
of the labels that have been proposed really sticks to him.
The label that has come nearest to sticking in popular repu-
tation is "Christian Socialist." This is the aspect of Maurice's
career which is most remembered, and about which most
has been written. But it is necessary only to read his biography, or to scan the list of his published works, in order
to perceive that it was, however significant in its way, no
more than an incidental aspect.

The only label that really meets the case, if label there
must be, is the grand one—"Theologian." This is what he
himself felt to be his calling, and almost every page he
wrote bears it out. What he said about one of his works,
he could have said about all. "It will be evident to the
reader of any part of these volumes that I have felt as a
theologian, thought as a theologian, written as a theologian;
that all other subjects in my mind are connected with
theology, and subordinate to it."[16] But it was necessary
then to add, and it is necessary still: "I use the word in
its old sense. I mean by theology that which concerns the
Being and Nature of God. I mean the revelation of God

14C. F. G. Masterman, *Frederick Denison Maurice* (1907), p. 6.
15*Religions of the World*, p. 94.
16*Moral and Metaphysical Philosophy*, II, ix.

to men, not any pious or religious sentiments which men may have respecting God."[17]

Since this book has to do with Maurice as a theologian, it may be well at the outset to elaborate this point a little. "Theologians of the ordinary type," said R. H. Hutton, "coming to the study of Maurice are not only apt to be bewildered as to his real meaning, but to feel themselves reproached for that external and 'Notional' view of things divine which they find him rebuking as the lowest element in himself, whereas *they* had rather taken a pride in their masterly speculative apprehension of matters so transcendental."[18] For, according to Maurice,

> theology is not (as the schoolmen have represented it) the climax of all studies, the Corinthian capital of a magnificent edifice, composed of physics, politics, economics, and connecting them as parts of a great system with each other—but is the foundation upon which they all stand. And even that language would have left my meaning open to a very great, almost an entire, misunderstanding, unless I could exchange the name theology for the name GOD, and say that He Himself is the root from which all human life, and human society, and ultimately, through man, nature itself, are derived.[19]

And in the same letter (to J. M. Ludlow) he said:

> Let people call me merely a philosopher, or merely anything else, or what they will, or what they will not; my business, because I am a theologian, and have no vocation except for theology, is not to build, but to dig, to show that economics and politics . . . must have a ground beneath themselves, that society is not to be made anew by arrangements of ours, but is to be regenerated by finding the law and ground of its

[17]*Ibid.*
[18]*Aspects of Religious and Scientific Thought* (1899), p. 270.
[19]*Life of F. D. M.,* II, 136.

order and harmony, the only secret of its existence in God.[20]

It is God, then, God in Himself, God revealing Himself, God in His relation to the world and all that is in it, who is the subject matter of theology (if the use of the term "subject matter" is tolerable here)—and *not* religion, or religious experience, or religious dogmas, or men's thoughts or speculations about God. It is easy to pay lip-service to this indication of the theologian's work, and equally easy for any actual theologian to slip away from it as soon as he sets to work. Maurice knew this temptation and this tendency in himself, and knew how fatal it was to yield to it. Hence his warnings and his protests against it. The fundamental maxim of theology, he said, is this: "We cannot discover the Eternal and Infinite, but He discovers Himself, and in discovering Himself helps us to see what we are, what our relations to our fellow-creatures are, what we are to seek, what we are to hate."[21]

The task of the theologian is not to construct a system, but to look for and to witness to the light that God has made to shine and is ever making to shine. The whole of God's world is the theologian's province; he is concerned with all the great human questions.

What do we worship? A dream, or a real being? One wholly removed from us, or one related to us? Is He a Preserver, or a Destroyer? Has Death explained its meaning to us, or is it still a horrible riddle? Is it still uncertain whether Life or Death is master of the world, or how has the uncertainty been removed? What is the evil which I find in myself? Is it myself? Must *I* perish in order that it may perish, or can it be in any wise separated from me? Can I give myself up and yet live? What are these desires that I feel in myself for something unseen, glorious, and per-

[20]*Ibid.*, II, 137.
[21]*Friendship of Books*, p. 273.

fect? Are they all phantasy, or can they be realised?
If they can, by what means? Has He to whom they
point made Himself known to me? How am I connected with Him? Must I utterly renounce all the
things about me, that I may be absorbed into Him,
or is there any way in which I can devote them and
myself to Him, and only know Him the better by
filling my place among them? These are the great
human questions; distance in time and space does not
affect them; if we are not concerned with them it is
because we have not yet ceased to be savages, or be-
cause· we are returning, through an extreme civilisation, into the state of savages.[22]

But the theologian does not address himself to these
questions in general or in the abstract. He is concerned
with them as they press upon himself and his contemporaries in their own actual experience. "The highest
theology is most closely connected with the commonest
practical life."[23] Indeed, theology is a dead subject unless
it is speaking to the real condition of man in society. "I
am convinced that theology will be a mere *hortus siccus*
for Schoolmen to entertain themselves with, till it becomes
associated once more with the Life of nations and humanity; that politics will be a mere ground on which despots
and democrats, and the tools of both, play with the morality
and happiness of their fellow-beings, till we seek again
for the ground of them in the nature and purposes of the
eternal God."[24]

In all his practical activities, his participation in politics,
in social reform, in educational enterprises, Maurice was
simply practising what he preached; he was acting as a
theologian. His participation in the "Christian Socialist"
movement was the way in which he was led to apply his
principles at .one period of his life. But to single this out

[22]*Religions of the World*, p. 63.
[23]*Acts of the Apostles*, p. 315. Cp. *Conscience*, p. 17.
[24]*Gospel of St. John*, p. 475.

as though it were the main thing about him, and to let the theological concern which prompted it drop into the background, is a monstrous perversion. This misunderstanding of Maurice's message has by now a long pedigree. We are told that Phillips Brooks in 1879 "noted with some surprise and regret, in his later visits to England, that the rising generation of clergy were turning aside from Maurice's theology in order to devote themselves more exclusively to social studies and methods of social reform."[25]

The theologian, Maurice knew, has a deeper ground of common interest with men in every sphere of life when he approaches them as a theologian than when he tries to transport himself into their special interests.

> If I consider what I say I believe, if I determine to hold that fast, I may discover that I have in theology a much broader as well as firmer meeting-ground with men as men, with men of all kinds and professions, of all modes and habits of thought, with men who attack my convictions, with men who are indifferent about their own convictions, than any maxims of trade, of convenience, of modern civilization, of modern tolerance, can supply me with.[26]

We may understand better what theology meant to Maurice and how he conceived the task of the theologian, if we look at what has been called his "system-phobia."[27] "When once a man begins to build a system," he said, "the very gifts and qualities which might serve in the investigation of truth, become the greatest hindrances to it. He must make the different parts of the scheme fit into each other; his dexterity is shown, not in detecting facts, but in cutting them square."[28] He regarded it as a great merit in Plato that he refused to build a system.

[25]A. V. G. Allen, *Life and Letters of Phillips Brooks* (1900), II, 224.
[26]*Conflict of Good and Evil*, p. 182.
[27]See *Life of F. D. M.*, II, 43.
[28]*Ecclesiastical History*, p. 222. Cp. *Kingdom of Christ* (Ev. ed.), I, 40.

Not to frame a comprehensive system which shall include nature and society, man and God, as its different elements, or in its different compartments, and which therefore necessarily leads the system-builder to consider himself above them all, but to demonstrate the utter impossibility of such a system, to cut up the notion and dream of it by the roots, this is the work and the glory of Plato.[29]

The Bible, the Church, the Creeds, the Book of Common Prayer, so far from propounding a system or furnishing materials for system-building, were man's great protection against systems. The Bible erects no theological system. "I hope you will never forget that the Bible is the history of God's acts to men, not of men's thoughts about God. It begins from Him. He is acting and speaking in it throughout."[30] The task of the theologian is to look at God acting, to listen to God speaking, to witness to and interpret what he sees and hears, not to work it all up into a system of which he is master. Likewise Maurice held "a Catholic *system* . . . to be one of the greatest enemies of the Catholic *Church*."[31] Of the Creed he said:

It is a creed for the people which the schoolman cannot and dares not meddle with, and yet which he is obliged to confess says much more than he can say in hundreds of folios. It is a tradition—often it has been called *the* tradition of the Church. As such we receive it, and rejoice in it. But on this ground especially, that it is a continual protection against traditions, that when they try to force themselves upon us, we can always put this forward as a declaration that what we believe and trust in is not this or that notion, or theory, or scheme, or document; but that it is the Eternal Name into which we are baptized, and in

[29]*Moral and Metaphysical Philosophy*, I, 150 f. Cp. *Conscience*, p. 147.
[30]*Ecclesiastical History*, p. 2.
[31]*Life of F. D. M.*, I, 308.

which the whole Church and each member of the Church stands.[32]

And of the Book of Common Prayer he said:

> I do not want to force any one to like it; nor do I care a sixpence for it as a piece of fine composition. I never called it "an excellent liturgy" in my life, and hope I never shall. But it has helped me to see more of the love of God and of the bonds by which men are knit to each other, and to feel more hope as to those whom I should naturally regard as foes, than any other book except the Bible. It is my protection and the protection of the Church against Anglicanism and Evangelicalism and Liberalism and Romanism and Rationalism, and till these different evils cease to torment us, I will, with God's help, use this shield against them.[33]

What he meant will become plainer as we proceed. But Maurice did not carry his distrust of systems to the point of refusing to learn anything from them. He recognized that even wise and good men have an inveterate propensity for system-building. Moreover, it is almost certain that any system that has wielded influence in the world and has stood the test of time has some important truth at the bottom of it. The theologian ought to dig down beneath the superstructure and discover this truth. "I cannot believe that any system is permitted to exist which is not working some good."[34] "Fanaticism and even consciously dishonest quackery cannot produce any results unless they have some true principle to work with."[35]

Further, it would be entirely to misunderstand Maurice

[32]*The Prayer-Book and the Lord's Prayer*, p. 147. *Cp.* pp. 124–27, *infra*.

[33]*Life of F. D. M.*, I, 512.

[34]*Kingdom of Christ* (Ev. ed.), I, 72. Cp. *Lectures on National Education*, p. 12.

[35]*Kingdom of Christ* (Ev. ed.), I, 145.

to suppose that, in attacking system-mongering, he was opposing order, logic and method in theology.[36] What he maintained was that logic is one of the handmaids, and not the mistress, of theology.[37] No man was more intent on examining the meaning of words and tracing them to their roots.

> The cure for the extreme lust of distinction is certainly not found in overlooking distinctions or denying their importance. It is not found by shrinking from the severe examination of words and of their shades of meaning. The more carefully that examination is pursued, the more we are led to feel the significance and sacredness of words, the less we are likely to play dishonest tricks with them. That words are things, mighty and terrible things, was the special lesson which the middle ages had to learn, and which they had to impart.[38]

Dean Church observed that Maurice himself had learned this lesson, and was also able to impart it.

> We always rise (he said) from the perusal of one of Mr. Maurice's books with the feeling that he has shown us one great excellence, and taught us one great lesson. He has shown us an example of serious love of truth, and an earnest sense of its importance, and of his own responsibility in speaking of it. Most readers, whatever else they may think, must have their feeling of the wide and living interest of a theological or moral subject quickened by Mr. Maurice's thoughts upon it. This is the excellence. The lesson is this—to look into

[36]See *Sequel to the Inquiry*, pp. 196 ff.
[37]See *Life of F. D. M.*, II, 496. He instanced the controversy between Nominalism and Realism as a case of logic leaping into the throne of theology, and with dry skeleton hands swaying her awful sceptre. See *Subscription No Bondage*, pp. 63–68. Cp. *Kingdom of Christ* (Ev. ed.), II, 72, concerning eucharistic controversy, and *Claims of the Bible*, pp. 58 ff.
[38]*Moral and Metaphysical Philosophy*, I, 577. Cp. *Subscription No Bondage*, pp. 46–59.

the meaning of our familiar words, and to try to use them with a real meaning.[39]

In so far as logic means using words carefully and significantly, no one was a keener logician than Maurice.

While he suspected system, he greatly esteemed method. "To me," he said, "these words (*system* and *method*) seem not only not synonymous, but the greatest contraries imaginable: the one indicating that which is most opposed to life, freedom, variety; and the other that without which they cannot exist."[40] And he illustrated the difference from the Bible, which baffles and defies the systematizer, but manifests the order and method of God's dealings with the world, a "harmony, not in the words but in the history."[41] It is for the theologian to discover and follow this order and method, and to let this harmony speak for itself.

What Maurice meant by *system* and *method* may also be illustrated from what he says of his aim in his *Moral and Metaphysical Philosophy*:

> From first to last I have kept one object before me. I have not aspired to give an account of systems and schools . . . I take no interest in the subject. I should have wearied myself and my readers if I had endeavoured to pursue it. But to trace the progress of the thoughts that have contributed to form these schools and systems; to connect them with the lives of the men in whom they originated; to note the influence which they have exerted upon their times, and the influence which their times have exerted upon them; this I take to be an altogether different task.[42]

In *The Claims of the Bible and of Science* he describes

[39]R. W. Church, *Occasional Papers* (1897), II, 309 f.

[40]*Kingdom of Christ* (Ev. ed.), I, 238. Cp. *Kingdom of Christ* (1838), I, xxv; *What is Revelation?*, p. 280.

[41]*Ibid.* (Ev. ed.), I, 238.

[42]*Moral and Metaphysical Philosophy*, II, vii. Cp. *ibid.*, I, 31; *What is Revelation?*, pp. 51 f.

what he considers to be "the conditions which are required for arriving at the knowledge of divine truth."

> Surely they are stern conditions! It is a straight and narrow way which leadeth to life! There must be a continual waiting for light; a distrust of our own assumptions; a readiness to be detected in error, certain that God's meaning is infinitely larger than ours, and that other men may perceive an aspect of it which we do not perceive; a belief that He is fulfilling His promise "that all shall be taught of Him," in ways which we cannot imagine; a dread of shutting out any truth by our impatient notion that it must contradict some other; a determination to maintain what little has been given us in the hope of its expansion, and never to contradict, if we understand ever so little, what may have been given to another; a resolution to hold the ground on which we stand, without judging him if he cannot yet see what this ground is. Hard is it to form these habits of mind; I covet them more than I can express, and believe in my sane moments that the Spirit would educate us all into them if we would but submit.[43]

Because Maurice believed that all men really have a divine teacher, whether they follow His guiding or not, he felt that at all events he must try to follow it. He must be ready to learn what God had been teaching every man, including the men who had built systems. The theological method is "the method of the Creeds and of the Bible, where all things descend from God to the creature, instead of ascending from the creature to God."[44] "The theological method," he said, "is the oldest of all methods. The Bible begins with it in the first Chapter of Genesis. God speaks, Man hears. But it is a new method to you, to me, to a great part of the Christian world."[45] Were the belief that

[43]*Claims of the Bible,* pp. 30 f.
[44]*Sequel to the Inquiry,* p. 231.
[45]*Tracts for Priests and People* (1862), No. XIV, p. 61.

there is one divine teacher of all men unfounded, this method would no doubt land whoever followed it in mere eclecticism—Liddon said that Maurice's mind "throughout its career was before all things eclectic and self-reliant"[46]; but if the belief is justified, it will be the only way of keeping the mind open to receive all the truth that God has to impart. Maurice vigorously rebutted charges of eclecticism. "Oh, there is nothing so emasculating as the atmosphere of Eclecticism! Who that has dwelt in it has not longed for the keen mountain misty air of Calvinism, for anything, however biting, that would stir him to action?"[47]

These considerations will also have suggested the method that ought to be followed in studying Maurice's own teaching. We shall not attempt to find in his writings a theological system; we shall not attempt to extract one from them, or to build one out of the materials which he supplies. We shall be prepared to believe that he had a divine teacher, and that a light was shining upon him to which it was his aim to bear a faithful witness. Our object therefore will be to discover the truths that he believed he was taught, and that were given to him to communicate to others. His method was to reflect earnestly upon what was happening in the world, and to ask what God was doing and saying in the events of his own time. "No man, I think, will ever be of much use to his generation, who does not apply himself mainly to the questions which are occupying those who belong to it."[48] Or, he might better have said, to the questions which ought to be occupying them. "I believe my business . . . is to take advantage of passing occasions, and to treat them with something of

[46]*Life of E. B. Pusey* (1893), I, 350.

[47]*Life of F. D. M.*, I, 339. Cp. *ibid.*, I, 358; *Moral and Metaphysical Philosophy*, I, xxxiii f. On "eclecticism" see also *Kingdom of Christ* (Ev. ed.), I, 180–84, 186 f., II, 316; *ibid.* (1838), I, 161–65; *Methods of Supporting Protestantism*, p. 16.

[48]*Kingdom of Christ* (Ev. ed.), I, 10.

2

the earnestness and principle which are generally reserved for what belongs to all times."[49] "The thought was always present to his mind," says his son, "What are we to learn from this? What truth is there here?"[50]

This circumstance combines with his peculiar style, which many (though not all) readers seem to find difficult, and about which I shall have something to say presently, to make his books uncongenial reading for posterity. They were written *ad hoc* and *ad hominem*. They deal with the questions and controversies of the period, and require for their full understanding a fairly close acquaintance with the period. Yet because Maurice brought all those questions and controversies to the light of God's self-revelation, and penetrated to their core, his books are full of permanent instruction for any who have the patience to search diligently. They are full of hints—a favourite word of his— which can help subsequent generations to understand their own questions.

In other words, Maurice was a seminal theologian, or a generative thinker. What he wrote of Boehme might be applied to himself:

> His books may not hold at all honourable places in libraries; his name may be ridiculous. But he *was* a generative thinker. What he knew he knew for himself. It was not transmitted to him, but fought for. And, therefore, however small his faculty for making himself intelligible to the many, he has made himself intelligible to a few, in a sense which Grotius, with his clearness of utterance and command of language,

[49] *Life of F. D. M.*, I, 271.
[50] *Ibid.*, II, 68. Cp. *ibid.*, II, 67: "This desire to consider whatever came before him in the 'spirit of a learner' is the key-note of my father's life. This constant condition of his mind, that of a man looking up to a divine teacher, his Father . . ." *Cp.* also what Bishop Ewing said of Thomas Erskine: "His abiding attitude of soul is that of one who is ever listening and saying, 'Speak, Lord, for Thy servant heareth.'" A. J. Ross, *Memoir of Alexander Ewing* (1887), p. 311.

never made himself intelligible to any. He spoke to the
hearts of those few. He made them feel that they were
in the midst of a very strange world, or rather of two
strange worlds, full of problems which demand a solution, and which no mere maxims or formulas can
solve.[51]

Of the lessons which Maurice had to impart some have
been assimilated. This is true of the best-known theological
controversy in which he was involved, the controversy
about the meaning of eternal life and eternal punishment,
which resulted in his expulsion from King's College, London. To a large extent it is true also of his other great
controversy with Mansel about the meaning of revelation.
It would be hazardous to claim that theologians today
would generally agree that Maurice was right; they would
however generally agree that Mansel was wrong. It is
natural that in such accounts as have been given of
Maurice's theological teaching attention should chiefly have
been fixed on these two subjects.[52] But the effect has been
to obscure the possibility that he has many more lessons to
teach, which have yet to be learned.

That this is so was suggested by Bishop Collins, and
those who read this book will have an opportunity of judg-
ing for themselves how far the suggestion is warranted.
"Many elements of his (Maurice's) teaching," wrote Collins, "have been so generally assimilated amongst us that
this very fact stands in the way of our realizing our debt
to him; we neither know whence we derived them nor
who it was who brought them forth, but assume that our
fathers were as familiar with them as we are. On the other
hand, it may be doubted whether we have yet begun to
assimilate some of the most essential elements of his teach-

[51]*Moral and Metaphysical Philosóphy*, II, 325.

[52]L. E. Elliott-Binns, *Religion in Victorian England* (1936), p.
144, says that Maurice's "great achievement was to make men
realize that eternity was not time extended, but time abolished."

ing."[53] The object of this book is to discover some of these essential elements, and to provide the reader with means of estimating whether they ought to be assimilated.

To this end it is necessary that Maurice should be allowed to speak freely for himself, and I make no apology for the number and extent of my quotations from his writings. Just because it is unlikely that his numerous books— with the exception, perhaps, of *The Kingdom of Christ, Theological Essays,* and a few others—will ever be widely read, it is important that those who are willing to learn from him should be given access to his own words, and not only second-hand impressions of his teaching which run, every risk of distorting his meaning. And even if his books are tedious to read *in extenso,* they nevertheless afford ample material for informative and pregnant quotation.

There remain three matters about which I want to say something in this introductory chapter—Maurice's style, his consistency, and his indebtedness to other teachers.

(1) The best comment on his style that I know is that of C. F. G. Masterman:

> Here is little grace or beauty of style. Maurice will often give his readers the pregnant phrase, and at intervals his passionate eloquence will sweep forward with a kind of swing and fury of indignation or appeal. Sometimes he is almost terrible in his denunciation of meanness or cruelty. Sometimes he is filled with the vision of things present and to come in a kind 'of inspiration. Sometimes he is gazing over the great city in a kind of tenderness and longing: "If thou hadst known . . ." But there is none of that solemn intensity and delicate charm of style which

[53]W. E. Collins in *Typical English Churchmen from Parker to Maurice* (1902), p. 328. In 1856 James Martineau said he suspected that there was more of the future contained in Maurice's teaching "than in any talking theology whose cry is heard in our streets." *Essays, Reviews, and Addresses* (1890), I, 265.

has made such a writer as Newman appeal to successive generations, nor of the clear light and simplicity of Church, nor of the pomp and marching music of Ruskin and the magic splendour of Carlyle.

Much of his work is dictated matter, and bears all the evidences of dictated matter. . . . It repeats itself. It sprawls over chapters and pages. It is often extraordinarily tangled and obscure.[54]

His son has told us of his curious mode of literary composition.

It was a very great relief to him to compose his books by dictation and to avoid the labour of mechanical writing. His usual manner of dictation was to sit with a pillow on his knees hugged tightly in his arms, or to walk up and down the room still clutching the pillow, or suddenly sitting down or standing before the fire with the pillow still on his knees or under his left arm, to seize a poker and violently attack the fire. . . .[55]

It is true that subsequently he did a great deal of work upon the manuscripts,[56] but they do not seem ever to have recovered from this strange origin. It is to be remembered too that most of his books consist of what were sermons or lectures in the first place, and what is designed to be heard is seldom so effective when it falls to be read.[57] But I suspect that his lack of ease in writing was largely due to his isolation. He had no public on which he could rely to understand him or with which he could feel at home; and on the other hand there were plenty of controversialists waiting in the distance to pick up and misrepresent what-

[54]*Frederick Denison Maurice* (1907), p. 219.

[55]*Life of F. D. M.*, II, 286.

[56]Though if Hort's experience with the sheets of *Kings and Prophets* (sic) was typical, Maurice sent his mss. to press in a very unfinished state. See Hort's *Life and Letters*, I, 232.

[57]For descriptions of Maurice's preaching, see *ibid.*, I, 154; *Letters of J. R. Green* (1901), pp. 128 ff.

ever he said. This atmosphere was not calculated to encourage easy, fluent or confident composition. Still, the difficulty of his style may easily be exaggerated. It was naturally felt at the time because he was wrestling with ideas that were both unfamiliar and unacceptable to most of his contemporaries. Any one who reads him now with sympathy and some measure of understanding will find little relish in Disraeli's crude witticism in his speech in the Sheldonian Theatre at Oxford in 1864, when he alluded to "the lucubrations of nebulous professors, who seem in their style to have revived chaos, and who if they could only succeed in obtaining a perpetual study of their writings would go far to realise that eternal punishment to which they object."[58]

(2) The question about the consistency of Maurice's theological teaching is more important for our purpose, since, if his teaching changed at different periods of his life or underwent substantial modification, it would be necessary for us to take this fact into account, to distinguish clearly between what he said at one period and at another, and to trace the evolution of his thought. But happily the question can be given a definite, if curious, answer. The remarkable thing about Maurice is that, from the time when the confusions and uncertainties of his youth were resolved by his adhesion to the Church of England in 1831, his teaching was consistent and substantially the same until the end of his life. In the case of many men this would not be in the least remarkable. It is remarkable in the case of Maurice both because he disowned the very idea of a fixed system of thought, and because he claimed always to be learning, and indeed was learning, from the great and rapid changes that were taking place around him. "Maurice's theology," said Principal Tulloch, "was

[58]G. E. Buckle, *The Life of Benjamin Disraeli* (1916), IV, 372. A footnote points out, what is obvious enough, that the allusion is to Maurice.

virtually complete from the outset of his career as a clergy-man."[59] His son points out that the germ of nearly all his later thought was contained in a letter of 1831 to his father.[60]

R. H. Hutton brings out the paradox well:

> I should say that never was there a man who studied the events and characters which came within his ken more patiently and with a more ardent desire to learn from them and understand them; that never was there one who did apprehend them better, so far as the lead-ing convictions and general bias of his own character enabled him to enter into them; but that never was there a character so little altered by the events and persons with whom he came into contact from the opening of his life to its close.[61]
>
> There never was, perhaps, a great and good man who was so completely the same from his earliest to his latest day.[62]

Hutton says that there were only three subjects on which Maurice changed his mind (*Subscription No Bondage*, the use of the Athanasian Creed, and democracy),[63] but this is an exaggeration. On the other hand, his son inclines to exaggeration in the opposite direction when he says that Maurice "modified his position on many questions as he found reason to believe that certain of his ideas and thoughts had been proved not to be in accordance with the will of God as it revealed itself in the progressive history of the time."[64] The truth is that his leading convictions hardly

[59] John Tulloch, *Movements of Religious Thought in Britain during the Nineteenth Century* (1885), p. 284.

[60] *Life of F. D. M.*, I, 131. *Cp.* Tulloch, *op. cit.*, p. 267: "There are few, even of his after controversies, the germs of which can-not be found in these letters" (his early letters to his parents).

[61] R. H. Hutton, *Criticisms on Contemporary Thought* (1894), p. 81.

[62] *Ibid.*, pp. 80 f.

[63] *Ibid.*, p. 82.

[64] *Life of F. D. M.*, II, 68.

seem to have changed at all, but that in some instances he came to see that they could be realized or applied only by a different policy from what he had once advocated. Our aim must be to unearth his leading convictions.

(3) But were his leading convictions original, or were they derived from others? To what extent, or in what way, was Maurice indebted to other teachers? The exercise involved in detecting the sources of an author's ideas may be engrossing, but it is less profitable than the exercise involved in inquiring what his ideas actually were, how he held them together, and whether they were true. Obviously every teacher is indebted to others. The important question here is whether he is simply reproducing ideas which he has taken over from others, and purveying second-hand goods, or whether he has so made what he has learned from others his own, and so tested in his own experience what he has learned, that his own teaching has genuine originality and a first-hand character. Before we take the trouble to discover what an author was concerned to say, it is an advantage to know whether he spoke as a scribe or with authority. For if he was merely one of the scribes, our time will be better spent in going to the sources behind him.

Now, Maurice disclaimed all originality in the vulgar sense. There was nothing really new in his writings, he said. "But while I utterly disclaim *novelty* . . . there is a sense in which I earnestly desire to be original. . . . An original man is not one who invents—not one who refuses to learn from others. I say, boldly, no original man ever did that. But he is one who does not take words and phrases at second hand; who asks what they signify; who does not feel that they are his, or that he has a right to use them till he knows what they signify. The original man is fighting for his life; he must know whether he has any ground to stand upon; he must ask God to tell him, because man cannot."[65]

[65]*Doctrine of Sacrifice,* pp. x f.

There is no doubt that in this sense Maurice was an original theologian. He spoke with authority. He had tested everything he said on his own pulses. What he said of his central conviction, he could have said of all that he learned: "I can say, I did not receive this of man, neither was I taught it. Every glimpse I have of it has come to me through great confusions and darkness."[66] At the same time, no one was readier to acknowledge that, under God, he had been taught of men. A great part of his genius lay in his capacity to learn from all sorts and conditions of men, and not only from those whom he found temperamentally congenial. Any one who seeks confirmation of this has only to read the great work on *Moral and Metaphysical Philosophy*, which occupied him during the greater part of his life. He makes it plain that he had learned something from each of the philosophers—and he interprets the term liberally—with whom he deals. Bishop Collins summed the matter up admirably when he said that Maurice "had the great gift of being able to accept from teachers of the most diverse kinds whatever elements of good they had to offer, without either following them in every ramification of their teaching, or repudiating them on account of what he could not receive. The Fathers, the Schoolmen, later theologians and philosophers and poets, are all laid under contribution. There can be few who have studied with so catholic a mind as he."[67] Here we can all learn much from the example of his method, whatever we may think of his conclusions.

Yet it is true of course that there were certain teachers to whom he was particularly indebted. To the Bible, first and foremost, and all the time. It is not due to a pulpit convention that so many of his books consist of sermons which expound passages or texts of Scripture. Nor was he one of those preachers who adopt a text as a motto, and

[66]*Life of F. D. M.*, II, 16.
[67]In *Typical English Churchmen*, p. 343.

then proceed to air opinions otherwise derived. Next doubt-
less Plato should be named. "I never have taken up any
dialogue of Plato," he said, "without getting more from
it than from any book not in the Bible."[68] If every thinker
is to be labelled either an Aristotelian or a Platonist, then
certainly Maurice must be labelled "Platonist." But he
would have cared for this label as little as any other. And
if it is taken to imply that Maurice was primarily an adherent of Platonism as a philosophical system, and that
he interpreted Christianity and everything else in the light
of it, it is manifestly absurd. It was the Platonic method
to which he felt himself to be vastly indebted.

Let us hear from his own testimony what he found in
Plato—and Socrates—and what he learned from them:

> It was the necessary consequence of Plato's situa-
> tion, and of the task which had been committed to
> him, that he was always seeking for principles. The
> most simple every-day facts puzzled him; nothing that
> human beings were interested in was beneath his at-
> tention: but then it was the meaning of these things,
> the truth implied in them, which he was continually
> inquiring after. He found the commonest acts that
> men do, unintelligible, except by the light which comes
> from another region than that in which they are
> habitually dwelling.

And he continues with regard to Aristotle:

> Of this feeling there are no traces in Aristotle. To
> collect all possible facts, to arrange and classify them,
> was his ambition, and perhaps his appointed function:
> no one is less tempted to suspect any deep meaning
> in facts, or to grope after it. In like manner, to get
> words pressed and settled into a definition is his highest
> aim: the thought that there is a life in words, that
> they are connected with the life in us, and may lead
> at all to the interpretation of its marvels, never was

[68]*Life of F. D. M.*, II, 37.

admitted into his mind, or at least never tarried there. In this disposition there may be a comfort and an advantage; but it certainly is not that upon which persons who are careful in the use of language would bestow the epithet "profound."[69]

Again, he thus differentiated between their attitudes to God:

It was a Being to satisfy the wants of men which Plato sighed for; it was a first Cause of Things to which Aristotle did homage. The first would part with no indication or symbol of the truth that God has held intercourse with men, has made Himself known to them; the second was content with seeking in nature and logic for demonstrations of His attributes and His unity. When we use personal language to describe the God of whom Plato speaks, we feel that we are using that which suits best with his feelings and his principles, even when, through reverence or ignorance, he forbears to use it himself. When we use personal language to describe the Deity of Aristotle, we feel that it is improper and unsuitable, even if, through deference to ordinary notions, or the difficulty of inventing any other, he resorts to it himself.[70]

We have not here to discuss whether in these statements Maurice does more than justice to Plato and less than justice to Aristotle. The point is that they indicate what significance should be attached to his reputed Platonism. No doubt he shared with Plato a vivid sense of mystery and a deep conviction of the reality of the eternal and the

[69]*Moral and Metaphysical Philosophy,* I, 180. Cp. *Subscription No Bondage,* pp. 42–45. But see also *Worship of the Church,* pp. 13 f.: "You prefer Aristotle to Plotinus. Be it so. I am not the champion of either; I am glad to learn from both. I have gained much more from the ethics of the elder teacher than of the latter; there is in him, I think, for most of us, a better praeparatio Evangelica"; and *Social Morality,* pp. 18 f.
[70]*Moral and Metaphysical Philosophy,* I, 218.

invisible. If Jowett was right in saying that germs of all ideas are to be found in Plato,[71] it will not be difficult .to find many other points of connexion. It was not, however, his doctrines but his method which Maurice directly derived from Plato. It was in sifting his own words and thoughts that he received help from Plato and Socrates.[72] Beyond that, Maurice was no more, though surely no less, of a Platonist than the Fathers or than St. Paul and St. John.[73] If we bear this in mind, we shall not be misled when we find one of his critics speaking of Maurice as "Platonism in gown and cassock."[74]

In view of what has been said, no attempt need be made to list all the teachers to whom Maurice was indebted; it would be an endless task. But mention ought to be made of two of his contemporaries, to whom he acknowledged an extraordinary debt—Coleridge and Erskine of Linlathen. Coleridge he never saw,[75] but he was one of the many young men of the time for whom Coleridge played the part of a living Platonist, in the sense that has just been

[71] Abbott and Campbell, *Life and Letters of Benjamin Jowett* (1897), I, 261.

[72] *Life of F. D. M.*, II, 134. And he found that this was the method of Christ Himself; *e.g.*, see *What is Revelation?*, p. 29: "I find Him beginning His pilgrimage on earth as a questioner. I find Him astonishing the upholders of a long and safe tradition by that method. I find Him sanctioning that as His own sound method of detecting falsehood and laziness, and of urging men to seek truth that they may find it."

[73] Cp. V. F. Storr, *The Development of English Theology in the Nineteenth Century 1800–1860* (1913), pp. 343 f. On Maurice's view of the accusation of "Platonizing" brought against some of the Fathers, see *Kingdom of Christ* (Ev. ed.), I, 59; cp. *Sequel to the Inquiry*, p. 291; *Doctrine of Sacrifice*, pp. xix f. For some just observations concerning this accusation, see H. de Lubac, *Catholicisme: les aspects sociaux du dogme* (1938), pp. 15 f. Maurice deals with the relation between Hebraism and Hellenism in *Social Morality*, pp. 202 ff.

[74] J. H. Rigg, *Modern Anglican Theology*[2] (1854), p. 159.
[75] See *Life of F. D. M.*, I, 178.

specified.[76] And if on its theological side the three characteristics of the Coleridgean movement were, as Principal
Tulloch suggested, a renovation of Christian ideas, an advance in Biblical study, and an enlarged conception of the
Church, then Maurice was in it heart and soul. But he
was in many ways critical of Coleridge's own teaching,
especially of his disregard of facts.[77] Any one who wishes
to know more about the relation between Maurice and
Coleridge should consult the detailed inquiry into the subject in C. R. Sanders' recent book on *Coleridge and the
Broad Church Movement*.[78]

Maurice's relation to Erskine was different. While he
was helped by Erskine's teaching, it would be true to say
that the two men were led independently to similar theological conceptions, and delighted in one another's work
and company. They confirmed one another in the faith.
But neither should be described as a disciple of the other.
Of Maurice it can be said more than of most theologians,

> *Nullius addictus iurare in verba magistri.*

My aim in this book is not to trace the exact pedigree
of various points in Maurice's teaching, or even of his
leading convictions, but to show what these were and how
we may learn from them. We can say of his teaching what
he said of the doctrine of gravitation.

> It may be very desirable to know, whether the dis-
> covery of the doctrine of gravitation can be traced to

[76]On the nature and extent of Maurice's debt to Coleridge,
see his Dedication to *Kingdom of Christ* (Ev. ed.), I, 1–15.

[77]*Life of F. D. M.*, I, 203, 251, 510, II, 168; *Kingdom of Christ*
(1838), I, 141. Julia Wedgwood, in *Nineteenth Century Teachers
and Other Essays* (1909), disputes Maurice's own claim to reverence facts, but see R. H. Hutton, *Essays on Some of the Modern
Guides of English Thought in Matters of Faith* (1887), p. 322.

[78]Duke University Press, 1942. See also Cyril K. Gloyn, *The
Church in the Social Order: a study of Anglican Social Theory
from Coleridge to Maurice* (Pacific University, 1942).

Newton or Kepler, or any earlier thinker; but it is somewhat more important to know, whether the doctrine of gravitation is true or false; whether it will explain the facts of the universe; or, whether it is only contained in a book called "The Principia."[79]

[79]*Apocalypse,* p. 368.

2

THE HEAD AND KING OF OUR RACE[1]

I hope . . . by God's grace that no fear of offending my best and dearest friends will keep me from proclaiming that truth of Christ as the actual Head of Man, which I was sent into the world to proclaim, and which it seems to me that you have never taken in—or at least, which is a much smaller matter, have not apprehended my language on the subject.—F. D. M. TO MR. LUDLOW, 1853.[2]

I F we are looking for Christian apologetics—meaning by that the argumentative defence of Christianity—we shall turn to Maurice in vain. He will supply us with no freshly conceived or stated arguments for the existence of God, the divinity of Christ, etc. He disclaims any intention of doing so; in fact, he deplores "the unfortunate rage for apologetic literature in the Christian Church."[3] It was not for him to try to buttress Christianity with new defences, nor to safeguard it with chains of irrefragable argument. He supposed it to be the task of the theologian to set forth, to expound, to proclaim the truth

[1]"We are created to give up ourselves for the Son of Man, the Head and King of our race."—*Kingdom of Heaven*, p. 157.

[2]*Life of F. D. M.*, II, 161. His son speaks of "the central principle on which my father's faith was based—that Christ was the head of every man, not only of those who believed in Him.' *Ibid.*, II, 304.

[3]*Lincoln's Inn Sermons*, V, 114. Cp. *What is Revelation?*, pp 55 f.; *Social Morality*, p. 356.

which God had revealed, to which the Bible bears witness, which the Holy Spirit is seeking to teach every man. He claimed that this was the method of the Bible, of the Creeds, of the Book of Common Prayer, and even of the Thirty-Nine Articles. It was for him to declare the truth, and to trust to its own convincing power, or rather to trust in God to do His own convincing work.[4] He really believed, what it seems very difficult for theologians to believe, that "God can take care of His own cause."[5] And it seemed to him that it was proclamation, rather than arguments, that would bring men into the light. "Arguments about a Creator will fall dead upon them. A message from a Father may rouse them to life."[6]

What then was the message? What was its starting-point and its ground? Here it seemed to Maurice that the preaching and teaching of the religious world of his time started for the most part in the wrong place, took a false ground from the beginning, and so perverted the Gospel. Divines and preachers began by declaring that men were evil, and that they belonged to a fallen and depraved race, and then proceeded to declare that God had provided through Christ a means by which some men—either the baptized or the believers—might be rescued from this condition.

Romish and Protestant divines, differing in the up-shot of their schemes, have yet agreed in the con-

[4]See *What is Revelation?*, pp. 232 f.

[5]*Apocalypse*, p. 40. Cp. *What is Revelation?*, p. 459.

[6]*Life of F. D. M.*, II, 428. Cp. *Gospel of St. John*, p. 8. In the Introductory Dialogue to *Kingdom of Christ* (Ev. ed.), I, 29, the Quaker says: "Assertions which proceed from deep conviction do often affect me more than elaborate and logical proofs"; and the author agrees with him. In 1865 Maurice wrote to Kingsley: "People send me books about final causes, primary beliefs, and so on. I gaze at their covers, wish I could read them, and some-times actually contrive to do it; but scarcely unless I can find some historical or biographical interest in them and can per-suade myself that a man has been fighting his way to some final cause, or that a nation is laying hold of some primary belief." —*Life of F. D. M.*, II, 496.

struction of them. The Fall of Man is commonly regarded by both as the foundation of Theology—the
Incarnation and Death of our Lord as provisions
against the effect of it. Now St. Paul speaks of the
Mystery of Christ as the *ground* of all things in Heaven
and Earth, the History as the gradual discovery or
revelation of this ground.[7]

Protestants and Romanists, even while they de-
nounce and excommunicate each other, yet appear to
recognize the fact of depravity, of Evil, as the fundamental fact of divinity. The fall of Adam—not the
union of the Father and the Son, not the creation of
the world in Christ—is set before men in both divisions
of Christendom as practically the ground of their
creed.[8]

Immensely valuable as I hold the Methodist preaching of the last age to have been, with the Evangelical
movement in the Church and among the Dissenters
which was the result of it—utterly dead as I conceive
the faith of the English Nation would have become
without this rekindling of it—I cannot but perceive
that it made the sinful man and not the God of all
grace the foundation of Christian Theology.[9]

Referring to one of his anonymous Evangelical critics, he
spoke of "the real issue upon which the dispute between
his school and me turns. It is the question whether the
Fall or the Redemption is the ground on which humanity
rests."[10]

Looking further back, he said that

In the Calvinistical bodies from the first, and in the
Lutheran so far as they caught the purely Protestant
complexion, the idea of the Incarnation was deposed
from the place which it had occupied in the older

[7] *The Prayer-Book and the Lord's Prayer,* pp. 118 f. Cp. *Kingdom of Christ* (1838), I, 279.
[8] *Conflict of Good and Evil,* p. 170.
[9] *Theological Essays,* p. xvi. Cp. *Sequel to the Inquiry,* p. 181.
[10] *Doctrine of Sacrifice,* p. xxxii.

3

divinity of the Church. The state and constitution of humanity was determined by the fall; it was only the pure, elect body, which had concern in the *Redemption;* that redemption therefore could only be contemplated as a means devised by God for delivering a certain portion of His creatures from the law of death, to which the race was subjected.[11]

The habit of contemplating the fall of Adam as the starting point of divinity, or if not the starting-point, as only subsequent to a divine arrangement which provided a means for curing the effects of it, necessarily put him (Milton) out of sympathy with the old creeds of the Church, which do not allude to the fall, but which at once set forth the only-begotten Son, who was with His Father before all worlds, as the perfect manifestation of God, and as the object of faith and trust to all men.[12]

Was Maurice right in regarding this as the real issue in dispute between him and most of his contemporaries? Did they in fact treat the fall of man as the ground of theology? Whether or not they would have so stated their position, it can hardly be denied by any one familiar with the literature of the period that in effect it was so. It was a commonplace of the pulpit. W. Moore Ede, the late Dean of Worcester Cathedral, in an article on Maurice written in 1933, thus recalled the impressions of his youth.

Few today realize how the theology which starts from human depravity prevailed at the time. I am old enough to remember how crude theories of the Atonement dominated popular theology, and can recall many weary hours in which I wrestled with the doctrine of the Fall, as commonly expounded, which I felt to be untrue, but from which I could see no way of escape, till I came under the influence of those who had themselves been influenced by Maurice.[13]

[11]*Kingdom of Christ* (Ev. ed.), I, 129.
[12]*Moral and Metaphysical Philosophy,* II, 341 f.
[13]*The Modern Churchman* (December, 1933), p. 530.

William Wilberforce in his *Practical View*—a book which had an extraordinary circulation and influence—had struck the note which was to be echoed again and again, when he wrote: "We should not go too far if we were to assert that (the corruption of human nature) lies at the very root of all true Religion, and still more, that it is eminently the basis and ground-work of Christianity."[14] That this was the prevailing theological emphasis could be readily confirmed from biographies and autobiographies.[15] And it was not of course peculiar to English Christianity.

Doctor E. Clowes Chorley's Hale Lectures on *Men and Movements in the American Episcopal Church* supply evidence that the same state of things existed in the U. S. A. "The starting point of Evangelical theology," he says, "was the fact of sin—both personal and inherited. Their favorite word was 'depravity.' " And again: "Speaking broadly, the Evangelicals and the High Churchmen were at one in their teaching of the fundamental doctrines of the Gospel. Both built on the foundation of the depravity of the human race. Hobart said of the Church that 'her whole system of doctrine is founded on the truth of the defection of man from original righteousness.' " And he refers to Devereux Jarratt, prophet and exponent of the Evangelical Movement in the American Church, who said: "I began my ministry with the doctrine of original sin . . . instead of moral harangues . . . I endeavoured to expose, in the most alarming colours, the guilt of sin, the entire depravity of human nature."[16]

Subsequently, we all know, there was a general reaction from this emphasis on the fall of man and on human de-

[14]*A Practical View &c.* (1797), p. 24.

[15]For the effect of popular Roman Catholic teaching, see the chapter on "Eternal Punishment" in M. D. Petre, *My Way of Faith* (1937).

[16]E. Clowes Chorley, *Men and Movements in the American Episcopal Church* (1946), pp. 61, 168, 7. On the Evangelicals in Germany, see *Life of F. D. M.*, I, 450.

pravity. This was due to a number of factors—the difficulties that arose in accepting the traditionally assumed history of the fall of Adam, the confidence engendered by science and invention in man's limitless capacity for progress, and a humane revulsion against the notion that the majority of mankind could be doomed to eternal punishment. None of these factors weighed much, if at all, with Maurice. Though he was not afraid of Biblical criticism or of any facts that science might disclose, he himself had no difficulty in accepting the historicity of the Book of Genesis,[17] including Archbishop Ussher's chronology.[18] So far from being sanguine about human progress, or confiding in the spirit of the age, he was moved by its characteristics to ask, "Is it not true . . . that the time which boasts to have outlived the evil spirit is the one which is most directly exposed to his assaults? May it not be that our progress, which is not to be denied, and for which we are to feel all gratitude, has brought us into a closer conflict with the spiritual wickedness in high places than our forefathers were ever engaged in?"[19] His revulsion against current doctrines of eternal punishment was far from being merely humane or sentimental. It was not negative at all; it was produced by the positive conviction that they were based on a denial of the truth about both God and man.

What then was the truth to which Maurice bore witness, and which he conceived it to be his mission to declare? "My desire," he said, "is to ground all theology upon the Name of God the Father, the Son, and the Holy Ghost; not to begin from ourselves and our sins; not to measure the straight line by the crooked one. This is the method which I have learned from the Bible. There everything proceeds from God; He is revealing Himself, He is

[17]"The Fall is a fact in history, just as the Bible presents it to us."—*Doctrine of Sacrifice*, p. 287.
[18]Maurice frequently speaks of the history of mankind as having lasted for six thousand years.
[19]*Lincoln's Inn Sermons*, I, 289. *Cp.* pp. 221–26, *infra*.

acting, speaking, ruling."[20] Whereas the Evangelicals "seem to make sin the ground of all theology . . . it seems to me that the living and holy God is the ground of it, and sin the departure from the state of union with Him, into which He has brought us. I cannot believe the devil is in any sense king of this universe. I believe Christ is its king in all senses, and that the devil is tempting us every day and hour to deny Him, and think of himself as the king. It is with me a question of life and death which of these doctrines is true; I would that I might live and die to maintain that which has been revealed to me."[21]

The truth from which he started was that God has created and redeemed mankind *in Christ*. God's union with our race in the Person of a Mediator is to be received as the interpretation of all other facts, as the kernel mystery of the universe.[22] "Mankind stands not in Adam but in Christ."[23] It is in the relation of adopted sons that men have always stood to God, whether or not they knew and acknowledged it. "This relation is fixed, established, certain. It existed in Christ before all worlds. It was manifested, when He came in the flesh. He is ascended on high, that we may claim it."[24] "The proper constitution of man is his constitution in Christ."[25] This is how God looks upon mankind, and we should do so too. "If by the very law and constitution of His universe God contemplates us as members of a body in His Son, we are bound to contemplate ourselves in the same way."[26] We are to look

[20]*Doctrine of Sacrifice*, p. xii.

[21]*Life of F. D. M.*, I, 450.

[22]See *What is Revelation?*, p. 102.

[23]*Life of F. D. M.*, II, 358. Cp. *Sequel to the Inquiry*, pp. 246–49. Marcus Dods well said that the fundamental difference between Maurice's theology and current Evangelical orthodoxy would be brought out by their respective answers to the question: "Is Adam or Christ the root of humanity?"—*Erasmus and Other Essays* (1891), p. 222.

[24]*The Prayer-Book and the Lord's Prayer*, p. 378.

[25]*The Church a Family*, p. 46.

[26]*Gospel of St. John*, p. 500.

upon Christ's death and resurrection "as revelations of the Son of God in whom all things had stood from the first, in whom God had looked upon His creature Man from the first."[27]

Sin, the condition of separation from and rebellion against God, is' not then man's true state; his evil nature is due to his departure from his true state. Maurice's teaching does not at all mitigate the horror and disaster of sin. It has been said that he used language which suggested the unreality of evil,[28] but that is a very superficial impression. It is difficult to believe that any one could rise from reading his books or the letters contained in his *Life* without having a deeper sense both of the reality of evil and of the power and range of sin in himself. Speaking of the clause in the Lord's Prayer, "Deliver us from evil," Maurice said:

> How hard, when evil is above, beneath, within, when it faces you in the world, and scares you in the closet, when you hear it saying in your own heart, and saying in every one else, "Our name is Legion," when sometimes you seem to be carrying the world's sins upon yourself, and then forget them and yourself altogether—which is worse and brings a heavier sense of misery afterwards—when all schemes of redress seem to make the evil under which the earth is groaning more malignant, when our own history, and the history of mankind, seems to be mocking at every effort for life, and to be bidding us rest contented in death; oh how it is hard, most hard, to think that such a prayer as this is not another of the cheats of self-delusion in which we have worn out existence.[29]

No, there was no minimizing of the reality of evil, and

[27] *Unity of the N. T.*, p. 367.
[28] R. H. Hutton, *Criticisms of Contemporary Thought and Thinkers* (1894), p. 88. Cp. his *Essays on Some of the Modern Guides of English Thought in Matters of Faith* (1887), pp. 318 f.
[29] *The Prayer-Book and the Lord's Prayer*, pp. 381 f.

no making light of the fact of sin, in Maurice's teaching, for the sufficient reason that they were intensely real to him in his own experience, far more dreadful and oppressive than to most men. That is why it seemed to him of crucial importance to know whether the devil or Christ was the actual Lord of mankind. That is why the Gospel that Christ is the Head and King of our race was good news indeed. It was because Maurice knew so keenly in himself the temptation to declare that all is vanity, that the revelation of Christ as the Lord of every man spoke to his condition and set him on his feet.

> The Gospel of Jesus Christ—the Gospel, as He called it, of the Kingdom of Heaven—does profess to show why the life of man is not vanity, and how it becomes vanity. The life of man, so the Gospel declares, is not vanity, for it is derived from the life of the Son of God. He is the Lord of every man. In Him is life, and His life is the light of men. The life of a man becomes a vain show, just because he does not confess his relation to this Fountain of Life; just because he seeks that life where it is not to be found—in the things which he is to rule, not in the Lord who rules him.[30]

Sin consists in refusing to acknowledge our relation to God in Christ, in forgetting it, in trying to live apart from Him and independently of Him. But we deny the truth if we regard our sinfulness, our separation from God and from one another, as our true state.

> We are very apt to think thus, "We belong to a guilty race; God looks upon us all as sinners. But perchance *I* may get Him to treat me differently; *I* may procure a separate pardon." No! that will not do. There is selfishness, there is separation from *thy* brother, there is the very essence of sin in that thought. St. John strikes at the root of it when he says, "*Your*

[30]*Lincoln's Inn Sermons*, III, 90.

sins are forgiven you for His Name's sake." You are
not looked upon as a sinful race; you are looked upon
as a race of which Christ the Son of God is the head.
When He offered Himself to God, He took away the
sin of the world. We have no right to count ourselves
sinners, seeing we are united in Him. We become sinners when we separate from Him, when we forget His
Name, and resume our own miserable separate name.[81]

If we have taken in the truth of this,

we shall no longer say, as we have been tempted to
say, "The power of evil is supreme over the universe;
only there has been a special deliverance vouchsafed
to us"; we shall, from our hearts, abjure such blas-
phemous Manicheism; we shall say boldly to all people
among whom we go, "The devil is not your master,
he has no right to your worship; the God, in whom is
light and no darkness at all, has claimed you and the
whole creation for His own. His marvellous light is as
much for you as for us. We only enjoy it upon the
condition of renouncing all exclusive claim to it, upon
the condition of bidding you enter into it."[82]

No man has a right to say, "My race is a sinful,
fallen race," even when he most confesses the greatness
of his own sin and fall; because he is bound to contemplate his race in the Son of God . . . I can, with
the most inmost conviction, assert that in me—that is,
in my flesh—dwelleth no good thing, just because I
feel that all good which is in me, or in any one, is
derived from the perfect humanity of Christ, and that,
apart from that, I am merely evil.[83]

We are very evil, each part is so; separate from God
the whole is so, but in Him all is redeemed, and raised,
and reconstituted, and if we desire to abide in Him,
and to remember His love and to love by the spirit
He gives us, we shall find how it is that He looks upon

[81]*Epistles of St. John,* p. 110.
[82]*Religions of the World,* pp. 238 f.
[83]*Life of F. D. M.,* II, 408.

us as very good, in spite of what we seem to ourselves, and in spite of the unbelief which makes us so unlike our own true form and image.[84]

Maurice never wrote a systematic treatise on Christ as the Head and King of the race. Otto Pfleiderer complained that he "failed to reduce his convictions to a consistent logical whole."[85] But that, after the manner of German theologians, is what Maurice never designed or attempted to do. The doctrine of the universal Headship and King-ship of Christ, however, runs throughout his theological teaching as a dominating conviction. It comes out especially in his expository works on the Bible. For he claimed that this doctrine was central to the Biblical testimony, and he found Scriptural witness to it everywhere.

I shall have something to say in a later chapter about Maurice's Biblical exegesis. Here I will remark only that, while obviously this doctrine does not lie on the surface of the whole Bible, and while Maurice cannot be acquitted of seeing "everywhere his favourite ideas"[86] (though this was the last thing he intended to do),[87] yet his main con-tention is a much stronger one than may appear at first sight to Christians who are accustomed to suppose that Christ is, strictly speaking, the Head only of believers or of the baptized or of the Church as distinguished from the race. The question is whether we can rightly take the affirmations about Christ's relation to the whole order of creation which the Bible ends by making, particularly in the Pauline and Johannine writings, as culminating insights which we are to use in interpreting the whole divine revela-

[84]Ibid., I, 514.

[85]The Development of Theology in Germany since Kant, and in its progress in Great Britain since 1825 (1890), p. 373.

[86]J. Tulloch, Movements of Religious Thought in Great Britain (1885), p. 278.

[87]See, e.g., Gospel of St. John, p. 4; Kingdom of Christ (Ev. ed.), I, 301.

tion. This is what Maurice did,[38] more consistently perhaps than any theologian has yet done. I believe that in principle he was right; but in practice, while he confessed that the universal Headship of Christ was revealed and discovered gradually, he inclined to find direct testimony to it too readily in all parts of the Bible. This was partly due to his unconscious disregard of the canons of historical criticism. But it does not invalidate the principle. His own application of it may arouse suspicion or prejudice in the minds of those who study the Bible with all the resources of modern criticism at their disposal, but this may be only to say that much yet remains to be done in carrying through a theological interpretation of the Bible that makes full use of those resources.

It was not only to the Bible that Maurice appealed. He thought that the early Church and the Fathers had had a grasp of Christ's relation to the whole race and of the universal scope of the redemption, which had subsequently, especially since the Reformation, been relaxed, with the result that the Church's understanding of the range of the Gospel had been narrowed and impoverished.[39] That this was so is amply borne out by the patristic materials that are collected and commented on in Henri de Lubac's magnificent book, *Catholicisme: les aspects sociaux du dogme*, which was published in 1938.[40] Reading that book again after the preparation of this manuscript, I have been continually struck by the way in which it confirms, enforces,

[38]"In this passage (Ephesians I–III) it seems to me lies the key to the whole character of the dispensation, as well as of the books in which it is set forth."—*Ibid.*, I, 256. James Martineau said that at the approach of Maurice's characteristic thoughts "there are parts of Scripture, the Pauline Epistles eminently, and the Prophets in no slight degree, where a darkness readily breaks away." See his *Essays, Reviews, and Addresses* (1890), I, 265.

[39]See *Kingdom of Christ* (1838), I, 108 f., II, 2; (Ev. ed.), I, 111, 311, II, 16, 30; *Three Letters to the Rev. W. Palmer*, pp. 9, 64; *Epistle to the Hebrews*, p. cxv; *Theological Essays*, p. 6; *Moral and Metaphysical Philosophy*, I, 499.

[40]Les Éditions du Cerf, Paris.

enriches and sometimes refines Maurice's leading convictions, particularly that of the universal Headship of Christ. Nor is that book an isolated phenomenon in contemporary theology. I shall point in a moment to some other evidence of attention that is now being paid to truths which Maurice was asserting and applying a century ago.

I have said that, after Maurice's time, there was a general reaction from treating the Fall and human depravity as the ground of theology, but this reaction was mainly due to adventitious circumstances. It was not the result of a rigorous or popular reckoning with what Maurice declared about the true ground and starting-point of theology, though the teaching of, *e.g.*, Westcott and the Lux Mundi school certainly took that direction. Now however another reaction or swing of the pendulum has supervened. A generation, which has had so many and such dreadful signs of the Fall and of human depravity thrust upon its notice, has rediscovered the dogma of original sin, and is disposed to assign to it that fundamental position in theology from which it had been not so much dethroned as allowed to disappear.

"Just because Christ is born, we have to regard the world as lost in the sight of God," is a characteristic dictum of a very influential theologian of our own day (Karl Barth).[41] I am far from wishing to suggest that such a saying gives a fair impression of the whole tenor, of the main emphasis, or of the final conclusion, of Doctor Barth's theological teaching; but when a master permits himself to say things like that, what is to be expected of the disciples?[42]

On the other hand, signs are multiplying in contemporary Western[43] theology, Protestant, Anglican, and Romanist,

[41]In *Natural Theology*, by E. Brunner and K. Barth (1946), pp. 116 f.

[42]*Cp.* Lady Frederick Cavendish's observation, quoted on p. 8, *supra*.

[43]On the characteristics of the Eastern Orthodox tradition, see M. J. Congar, *Divided Christendom* (1939), chap. VI.

of dissatisfaction with individualist conceptions of salvation and sectional conceptions of the nature of the Church—and of emphasis on the solidarity of the human race, on the doctrine of the mystical Body of Christ, on Christ's Lordship over all men and His relation to the whole created order, and on the promise of a universal restoration of all things grounded in the fact that the universe was created and has been redeemed in Christ. These signs are evident in the work of both Biblical and dogmatic theologians. Here, for example, are a few passages from Professor C. H. Dodd's recent book, *The Bible To-day,* that may show which way the wind is blowing in Biblical exegesis.

These claims (to the realization of the Kingdom of God) are not made (by St. Paul) for individual members of the Church . . . they are not made for the Church so far as it is an exclusive body with a limited membership; but for the Church as "catholic" or universal, ideally identified with the whole human race as "redeemed" through Christ (p. 71).

As Adam is all mankind, so is Noah all mankind; and the story (of the Deluge) stands as witness that God's covenant, though historically it was made with Israel, is applicable to the whole human race, and indeed to all created life—a truth finally established in the universal Gospel of the New Testament (p. 114).

The Last Judgement is universal. The logic of the biblical revelation seems to demand an equal universality for the final "restoration of all things." One New Testament writer alone explicitly draws the conclusion. Paul brings to a close his penetrating analysis of the biblical history, in Roman ix–xi, with the pregnant sentence, "God hath shut up *all* unto disobedience, that He might have mercy upon *all.*" As every human being lies under God's judgement, so every human being is ultimately destined, in His mercy, to eternal life (p. 118).[44]

[44]Dodd adds this footnote: "This 'universalism' has never been generally accepted in the Church, though it has been held by some theologians of credit in antiquity and in modern times."

A man stands before God simply as a man, a son of Adam, sharing Adam's tragic fate, but entitled to a higher destiny in Christ, who is called the "Second Adam"—the Representative of man under God's mercy as Adam represents him under God's judgment (p. 159).[45]

And here are some statements from a recent work of dogmatic theology by Fr. E. L. Mascall, *Christ, the Christian, and the Church.*

It is not just a matter of re-created men, but of a re-created human race (p. 79).

In the coming of Christ, everything that was good in the fallen world was claimed by him to whom it belonged and was brought beneath the radiance of his redeeming activity. The Creator of the world is also its Redeemer (pp. 150 f.).

With the Incarnation something new has begun to be, namely human nature hypostatically united to the Person of the Word of God; and, while the organic communication of this re-created human nature to men and women as their personal possession is (at any rate normally) brought about by baptism, its radiance and healing power are shed upon the whole of the created order (p. 151).

And here, most remarkable of all and nearest, it would seem, to Maurice, are some of the things that Père Emile

[45]*Cp.* these statements in *The Apostolic Ministry* (ed. by K. E. Kirk, 1946): "In St. Paul's thought . . . Christ as the Beginning is both source and sphere of creation . . . God's only Son is the source and Lord of both creations, and therefore their end and goal. . . . But He is also the sphere of both creations" (L. S. Thornton, C. R.); Jesus "is the originating Head of the whole redeemed race as 'the Second Adam,' in whom all His posterity are in some sort contained. He is these things with a plenitude which knows no limitations; in no way do they depend upon human acknowledgement of them for their validity" (Gregory Dix, O. S. B.) —*Op. cit.,* pp. 78 f., 299. *Cp.* Thornton, *The Common Life in the Body of Christ,* pp. 141 f.: "We receive the Spirit, not as individuals, but as partakers of the Christ, as members of the One Man in whom the whole purpose of God has been fulfilled."

Mersch says in his posthumously published *La Théologie du Çorps Mystique.*

> Le christianisme est la reprise de tout l'univers humain dans l'unité de Dieu par l'unité du Christ (I, 44 f.).

En bien des endroits, et des plus importants, où elle parle de l'incarnation, l'Écriture la montre comme une union qui est propre au Christ sans doute, mais aussi comme un événement qui concerne la création tout entière, un événement cosmique. Ne la décrit-elle pas comme une seconde création, et plus réelle que la première; ne montre-t-elle pas le Christ comme le second ˙Adam dont le premier ne soit que la figure? (I, 164).

Pendant les premiers siècles, le dogme du péché originel n'a guère d'autre formule que celle du dogme de la rédemption. La rédemption est universelle; c'est donc qu'il y a une universelle déchéance (I, 181).

L'incarnation n'est pas un événement qui ne concernerait que l'humanité assumée; elle est, et par elle-même, l'événement humain par excellence, l'événement universel et mondial, non seulement par sa sublimité, mais par son efficacité (I, 239).

Premier, dernier et total dans l'humanité régénérée, le Christ comme homme la reprend toute en lui, comme il la récapitule en lui; l'emplissant toute . . . comme Dieu remplit tout (I, 277).

Dès l'instant où il existe—en fait ou dans les décrets divins—l'union de Dieu et tous les hommes est réalisée en lui (le Christ) (I, 288).

Le Christ est chef d'un corps mystique, qui, selon la vocation divine, comprend toute l'humanité (I, 354).

C'est en effet par le perfectionnement qui se réalise, à cause de l'union hypostatique, dans l'humanité du Christ, et qui rend cette humanité immensément et comme universellement humaine que le Christ atteint tous les hommes, les contient par grâce tous en lui et les élève ainsi en lui à l'état surnaturel (II, 354).

Nous penserions volontiers . . . que, dès la promesse du rédempteur le genre humain tout entier a reçu avec cette qualité de race du Sauveur, de souche de l'Homme-Dieu, une élévation intrinsèque qui l'adaptait à être vraiment ce que Dieu voulait qu'il fût. . . . S'il est ainsi, tout homme, depuis la création telle qu'elle a été, ou depuis la promesse qui a suivi la chute, a en lui quelque commencement qui l'habilite, en quelque manière, à préparer le formation du Christ en son âme, comme l'humanité entière a en elle la semence divine, qui la constitue humanité où se forment, par un travail séculaire, le corps and l'âme du Christ (II, 385).[46]

I do not say that these writers would endorse all Maurice's teaching. In any case their theological idiom is not the same as his, and at some points they are obviously paying a closer regard to traditional theological definitions than he was inclined to do, though at the same time they are seeking to expand those definitions to their utmost limits. I have quoted these passages in order to indicate that there are trends in contemporary theology,[47] which suggest that Maurice's teaching may receive a more sympathetic and favourable hearing than it did in his own time, and it is possible that he may be able to show us more than has yet been seen of what will be involved in a recovered insight into Christ's universal Headship of the race.

In the succeeding chapters we shall be considering what light this conviction, when it is accepted as paramount, throws upon the Church and sacraments, upon Christian institutions and ordinances, upon politics and lastly upon the calling of the Anglican Communion. I propose in the

[46]Mersch also asks whether there are any souls who have no rudimentary *lien avec le Christ* (I, 115), evidently expecting the answer, No.

[47]See also art. "De la prise en charge de l'humanité par Jésus-Christ" by H. Bouëssé, O. P., in *Nouvelle Revue Théologique* (April, 1947).

remainder of this chapter to glance at Maurice's hints[48] about how certain main themes of the Bible should be interpreted with a governing reference to Christ's universal Headship. (1) The relation between the Creation, the Fall and the Redemption, and the First and Second Adams; (2) The doctrines of Election and Predestination; (3) Man's justification.

(1) The truth about the creation can be clearly seen only in the light of the redemption. There had been many and increasing intimations of it before Christ came in the flesh, but only when He had been manifested, could it be plainly read. Thus the author of the Fourth Gospel, in the Prologue, was able to gather up "in one distinct statement, one full revelation, that which it had taken ages to spell out."[49]

Man is created in the image of God—not just a first man, but mankind, the human race, every man. "It is not the separate man who is in the image of God; it is man as a kind, it is the individual man so far as he is the member of a kind."[50] But how can we tell what this "image of God" means, and where are we to look for it? It is manifested in Christ, who is the Son of God and the Son of Man, in the Word made flesh. The Bible "assumes man to be made in the likeness of God, because the Man is His perfect likeness."[51] We are "not to think that the world was created in Adam, or stood in his obedience; for the Scriptures of the New Testament, illustrating those of the Old, teach us that it stood and stands in the obedience of God's well-beloved Son; the real image of the Father,

[48]Of *The Kingdom of Christ*, his most orderly and methodical theological work, Maurice said: "It will never, I hope, be regarded as any thing but as a collection of Hints."—*Op. cit.* (*Ev. ed.*), I, 17.

[49]*Gospel of St. John*, p. 19.

[50]*Lincoln's Inn Sermons*, II, 51. Cp. *Kingdom of Christ* (1838), III, 7.

[51]*Lincoln's Inn Sermons*, III, 31. Cp. *Doctrine of Sacrifice*, pp. 215 f.

the real bond of human society and of the whole universe, who was to be manifested in the fulness of time, as that which He had always been."[52] That is to say, we arrive at the Man who is the image of God by going straight to Christ, not by attributing to Adam and Eve "what we please out of our fancies about their transcendent knowledge, or their seraphic virtues. Nothing of it is to be found in the Bible. No hint of any vast endowments, or wide-reaching thoughts, or great projects."[53] It is Christ who was the Head of mankind from the beginning.

> Men are told that they are made in the •image of God: how it could be they knew not. Here is His express image, not shewn in the heavens above, nor in the earth beneath, but in a man. In Him creation has subsisted, in spite of all the elements of confusion and discord within it. *"He has upholden it by the word of his power."* In Him we find how humanity has been a holy thing, though each man felt himself to be unholy.[54]

Maurice's exposition of the opening chapters of Genesis in *The Patriarchs and Lawgivers of the Old Testament* is handicapped by his conservative adherence to the view that they are a record of actual history. He tries to expound them as testimony both to the truth about mankind and to the history of the first man.[55] His exposition would be freed from confusion and would gain in illumination if the latter element were discarded, as it ought to be. Then the story of Adam will be taken as a witness to the truth about mankind and about every man, a witness which interprets to every man the conflicting intimations of his

[52]*Patriarchs and Lawgivers*, p. 66. Cp. *Claims of the Bible*, p. 117.
[53]*Patriarchs and Lawgivers*, p. 53.
[54]*Epistle to the Hebrews*, p. 29.
[55]He regards Genesis I as referring to the creation of mankind (the Species) and Genesis II to the creation of an individual. *Patriarchs and Lawgivers*, pp. 34 f.

4

conscience about the meaning of his existence. And evidently this is what Maurice was most concerned to say.

> Every one verifies the truth of the Scripture narrative, in his own daily history. . . .
> The principle that man was made in the image of God, is not a principle which was true for Adam and false for us. It is the principle upon which the race was constituted and can never cease to be constituted. Adam's sin consisted, if we are to believe the Scripture account, in disbelieving that law, in acting as if he were not under it. . . . The sin of him and of us . . . is and must be the same. We have a right to justify the truth of the Scripture narrative, by that which we know of our own temptations and our own falls.[56]
> Brutal violence, men corrupting their ways upon the earth—this is just what we hear of everywhere. Scripture had nothing new to tell us about this. But it had a work of its own. It had to teach us how these facts are compatible with others—apparently quite at variance with them, which ordinary history and our own experience also make known to us. It had to show, how this natural corruption could co-exist with a perpetual witness in man's conscience, with a continual strife in his will, against it. And it does this work. It shows that man, yielding to his nature, resists the law which he is created to obey; that man, given up to himself, has yet God's Spirit striving with him. It shows us how man in himself can have no good thing, and yet how much good he may have; because there is One who is continually raising him out of himself—imparting to him that which in his own nature he has not.[57]

[56]*Ibid.*, pp. 55 f. James Martineau perceived that "'Original sin' . . . is not, in his (Maurice's) view, a *prior* condition giving way to 'reconciliation' as a *posterior;* but both exist together in all men." See his *Essays, Reviews, and Addresses* (1890), I, 263.

[57]*Patriarchs and Lawgivers*, p. 62. Cp. *Kingdom of Christ* (Ev. ed.), II, 28, and on the Deluge *Claims of the Bible*, p. 111.

Men, all men, therefore, are to be looked upon, and ought to look upon themselves, as created in Christ, and so as righteous beings. The Redeemer, who is also the Creator, restores men to their original state in the divine purpose. "It was signified in the word *Redemption*, that the partakers of it were not brought into some novel or unnatural state, but into that for which they were created, that which was implied in their human constitution."[58] From this point of view, the Second Adam is prior to the First Adam. The First Adam, the fallen Adam, stands for man asserting his independence of the Head of the race in whom he was created, and rebelling against the true law of his being. For Christ "was the Lord of all before He came in the flesh; therefore God must have looked upon mankind in Him . . . therefore there must have been always One near men who was speaking to them, and revealing God to them, whom they might fear and obey, in whose strength they might work righteousness."[59] Whatsoever is good in any man is derived from Christ who is the Head of all men, the bond of society, and the root of all righteousness. "There is a selfish evil nature in every man, let him call himself Churchman or man of the world, believer or unbeliever, which cannot bring forth good fruit—which is utterly damnable; and . . . there is a Divine root of humanity, a Son of Man, whence all the good in Churchman or man of the world, in believer or unbeliever, springs—whence nothing but good can spring."[60] "Each right and true man has had some grace, denoting him to be of divine origin. In (Christ) dwelt that fulness of grace and glory, of which these were the scattered rays."[61]

Is there no difference between the believer and the

[58]*Religions of the World*, p. 220.

[59]*Acts of the Apostles*, p. 158. Cp. *Theological Essays*, pp. 171, 202.

[60]*Kingdom of Heaven*, pp. 124 f.

[61]*Gospel of St. John*, p. 36.

unbeliever? Yes, the greatest difference. But the difference is not about the *fact,* but precisely in the belief of the *fact.* . . . Though tens of hundreds of thousands of men live after the flesh, yea, though every man in the world were so living, we are forbidden by Christian truth and the Catholic Church to call this the real *state* of man. . . . The truth is that every man is in Christ; the condemnation of every man is, that he will not own the truth; he will not *act* as if this were *true,* he will not believe that which is the truth, that, except he were joined to Christ, he could not think, breathe, live a single hour.[62]

The preacher of the apostolic Gospel is commissioned to make this proclamation to all men:

The state which (God your Father) always intended for man, his original state, his real state, the state of members of one family, united in one head, contemplated, loved, only in Him, this estate He now permits and calls upon you to assert for yourselves, and to renounce for ever that vile independence which your first father set up when he disobeyed the command of his Creator, and which it is the nature of each one of you to claim for himself.[63]

"It was the business of Christ's ministers to proclaim that there could have been no families, no nations, no social impulses, no laws, nothing to resist the selfish, self-seeking tendencies which each of us is conscious of in himself and complains of in his neighbours, if there had not been one living centre of the whole body of Humanity, one Head of every man."[64] "The Gospel . . . is the full discovery of Him who is the Living Centre of the Universe, the assertion that all men are related to Him; the destruction of every wall of partition between Man and Man;

[62]*Life of F. D. M.,* I, 155.
[63]*Christmas 'Day,* p. 78. Cp. *Epistles of St. John,* p. 307.
[64]*Lincoln's Inn Sermons,* IV, 9.

the admission of all who desire it into fellowship with the Father of the whole family in Heaven and Earth."[65] "If in making this proclamation we appear to assume that a communion between God and Man is not merely the rare privilege of a few, but is the foundation on which the very existence of our race stands; that without it there would have been no thought, memory, hope, no feeling of kinsmanship, no possibility of friendship or affection—we are only reaffirming the doctrine of the Bible, as well as confirming the anticipation of all nations; we are cutting down human pride, that the Lord alone may be exalted."[66]

If we are going to speak of human depravity,

> it is better, safer, truer language to speak of individual depravity than of universal depravity. By individual depravity I mean my own. I find it out in myself; or rather, He who searcheth me and trieth my ways, finds it out in me. That sense of depravity implies the recognition of a law which I have violated, of an order from which I have broken loose, of a Divine image which my character has not resembled. It is the law and the order which are universal. It is this character of Christ which is the true human character. It is easy enough to own a general depravity; under cover of it you and I escape.[67]

(2) The theme of divine election and predestination to salvation and eternal life is firmly embedded in the Scriptures and in the Christian tradition. I do not know how it may be in America, but in England there is a popular notion that this theme is a peculiarity of Calvinism. This, however, is due to the fact that Calvinism prominently asserted a particular form of the doctrine, which was the subject of long and acute controversy. When Calvinism went out of fashion, the theme of divine election and pre-

destination went out with it, and little has been written about it by our theologians and still less, if that is possible, has been said about it by our preachers. It is now no doubt being revived where the influence of Neo-Calvinism is spreading, but there is little noticeable change yet, in this respect at least, in Anglican divinity and preaching.

Nevertheless, we shall find that we have to take this theme seriously if we are going to deal faithfully with the Biblical testimony as a whole. And we may discover that Maurice has some valuable hints to offer us. He could not ignore the subject as we have found it easy to do, since it was being pressed upon him from his early days in his family,[68] and in his maturity by his theological critics. Moreover, his determination to expound the whole Biblical message anchored him to it.

He would say that the doctrine of divine election and predestination had fallen into discredit, not because it was unscriptural or untrue, but because as developed in Calvinism it had been interpreted not only in an exclusive but in an individualistic[69] way and therefore contrary to the Biblical testimony. According to the Biblical testimony the Elect of God is Christ Himself, the beloved Son in whom the Father is well pleased. Election and predestination signify not the arbitrary picking out of privileged individuals from a lost and perishing race, but the Father's good pleasure to restore the race itself to its foreordained state by incorporating its members in the body of which Christ is the Head. "He chose us in him before the foundation of the world" (Ephesians I, 4). Men are elect inasmuch as they are in Christ; they forfeit the divine election in so far as they refuse to confess Him in whom it is grounded.

Since, according to the doctrine of this chapter

[68]His mother and some of his sisters were converted from Unitarianism to Calvinism, and in the family circle there was much heart-searching discussion of the issues involved.
[69]See *Kingdom of Christ* (Ev. ed.), I, 101, 111.

(Ephesians I), the adoption to Sonship on earth corresponds to the election in the heavenlies, cannot be more extensive than that, it must follow that what St. Paul asserts on behalf of himself and the little band of those who had turned to God and believed in Christ, was a share in the privileges of humanity as that is created, elected, known by God in Christ. For the original purpose before the foundation of the world must be that of which Adam's sin and the sin of every descendant of Adam is the contravention and denial; every man trying to stand by himself, and not to stand upon God's election, is on a fallen, rebellious, false ground; every man claiming the privilege of God's election, now manifested to all in Christ, affirms that neither Adam's sin nor the sin of the world, has been able to defeat the design of the Creator.[70]

It is quite true that in history there is what appears to be a divine election of some men and not others, of Israel under old covenant, of the Christian ecclesia under the new covenant. But this election should be understood as arising out of an inclusive and not an exclusive purpose. It is in each case an election on behalf of the whole race, the election of a special body for the purpose of bearing witness to the universal election of mankind. "That the Jewish people were brought to know that they were under the guidance of a Divine Word—their ever-present Teacher, and King, and Judge—is what I mean when I speak of God calling out that nation, of God ruling it and educating it, of God making it a blessing to all the families of the earth."[71] And the same was true of the election of the new Israel. "It was no formal election of a set of favourites of Heaven, who were to earn rewards from which the rest of the world were excluded. It was the election of a people to know what are the rights of men,

[70]*Unity of the N. T.*, pp. 526 f. Cp. *Doctrine of Sacrifice*, pp. 201 f.
[71]*Gospel of St. John*, p. 470.

that they might be witnesses to all men of *their* rights."[72]
I would refer to the Hulsean Lectures of J. O. F. Murray,[73] a theologian who was deeply influenced by Maurice, for a careful examination of the Biblical testimony on this subject and an elaboration of Maurice's hints.

It may be suspected at first sight that this interpretation of the idea of divine election and predestination is an attempt to evade difficulties, particularly the difficulty of believing that God has predestinated some men to damnation. But Maurice and Murray would contend that it is really implied in the Biblical testimony, which in any case does not assert the negative or exclusive doctrine of election that was worked out by St. Augustine[74] and, above all, by Calvin and his successors. The nearest approach in the New Testament to a statement that implies predestination to reprobation is I Peter II, 8: "They stumble at the word, being disobedient: whereunto also they were appointed." But most commentators (*e.g.,* Hort,[75] Bigg,[76] Selwyn[77]) do not regard this interpretation as correct; Wand[78] is more doubtful.

On the other hand, Maurice held that Calvinism witnesses, though in a perverse way, to the fundamental truth that salvation is grounded in God's choice of man and not in man's choice of God. "If man is held to choose God,

---

[72]*What is Revelation?*, p. 118.

[73]*The Goodness and the Severity of God* (1924).

[74]As Lord Eustace Percy says, "this narrowing of human destiny to a bare choice between heaven and hell, a stark contrast between the 'elect' and the 'reprobate' was not, of course, peculiar to Calvinism. It had been the universal assumption of the Church for at least a thousand years, ever since the early Christians' hope of Christ's second coming was blotted out by the terrors of the Day of Judgment."—*John Knox* (1937), pp. 108 f.

[75]F. J. A. Hort, *The First Epistle of St. Peter* (1898), pp. 123 f.

[76]Charles Bigg, *A Critical and Exegetical Commentary on the Epistles of St. Peter and St. Jude* (1902), p. 133.

[77]E. G. Selwyn, *The First Epistle of St. Peter* (1946), p. 165.

[78]J. W. C. Wand, *The General Epistles of St. Peter and St. Jude* (1934), pp. 64 f.

and not God to choose man, I see no deliverance from
the darkest views of His character and of our destiny."[79]
And Maurice was not a universalist, as that term is commonly understood.[80] Bishop Alexander Ewing recorded that
Mcleod Campbell of Row differed from Erskine of Linlathen "in one respect, feeling it possible that a free human
will *may* eternally escape the Divine longings, which Erskine
thinks incredible."[81] In this respect Maurice was nearer to
Campbell than to Erskine.

(3) Maurice also taught that the acknowledgment of
Christ's universal Headship makes all the difference in our
understanding of man's justification. "Justification by faith
is surely a most wholesome and complete doctrine when
it means faith in a Justifier, in one who is righteous, and
who makes righteous; but is it not a pestilent doctrine if it
means that we are justified by faith in our difference from
those who are not justified?"[82] We are justified by the
fact that Christ is the Head of our race, not by our belief
in the fact. According to St. Paul, the resurrection of Christ

just as much asserted that God judges the race to be
righteous, as the expulsion of Adam from Paradise
proved that He judges them to be sinners. The assertion puzzles and baffles us if we determine that Adam
is Head of our race, if we deny that Christ is the
Head of it. The assertion puzzles and baffles us, if we
suppose that Christ only became the Head of it when
He was shown by His death and resurrection to be the
Head of it. But if that was the manifestation of an

[79]*Theological Essays*, p. 123. Cp. *What is Revelation?*, pp.
382 f.

[80]See *Life of F. D. M.*, I, 208, II, 15–20. In *The Word "Eternal,"* p. 14, Maurice says: "I have said distinctly that I am *not*
a Universalist, that I have deliberately rejected the theory of
Universalism, knowing what it is; and that I should as much
refuse an Article which dogmatised in favour of that theory as
one that dogmatised in favour of the opposite."

[81]A. J. Ross, *Memoir of Alexander Ewing* (1887), p. 448.
[82]*Life of F. D. M.*, II, 575.

eternal truth—if that showed who holds the race in one, while the act of Adam showed what rends it in pieces—we must be wrong when we speak of a universal Fall without speaking also of a universal Justification. We must be departing from the lesson of Scriptures, if we teach that each man comes into the world with a nature that is ready to sink into selfishness and death, without adding that he is related to a righteous and living Lord who would raise him to righteousness and life.[83]

The rediscovery of justification by faith at the time of the Reformation was originally a rediscovery of Christ as man's Justifier, and implied both the need and the possibility of growth in sanctification. It was only afterwards that it was "turned from a living principle into an empty shibboleth,"[84] which separated the faithful from the faithless according to their subjective condition, teaching men "to believe in justification by faith instead of to believe in a Justifier."[85] Luther "did not call upon men to·acknowledge either a new doctrine or an old one, to believe either in a certain opinion concerning justification or in a certain opinion concerning the atonement. He called upon them to believe in God the Father Almighty—in Jesus Christ His only Son our Lord, and in the Holy Ghost."[86] Later, however, the doctrine of justification by faith was elaborated into an exclusive dogmatic system.[87] The object

[83]*Lincoln's Inn Sermons,* V, 265. On the saying of St. Paul "Therefore, as by the offence of one judgment came upon all men to condemnation, so by the righteousness of one the free gift came upon all men unto justification of life," Maurice comments: "It is an obvious remark, that whatever is affirmed of the race of men in one of these clauses, is also affirmed of that same race in the other. It is not said that all were condemned and some were justified, but that all were condemned and all were justified." *Ibid.,* V, 264.

[84]*Kingdom of Christ* (Ev. ed.), I, 277.

[85]*Ibid.,* I, 218.

[86]*Ibid.,* I, 98.

[87]*Ibid.,* I, 115–19.

of faith and the person who exercises it were forgotten in
"endless controversies about the nature, mode, effect, signs,
attributes, qualifications of a living or dead faith."[88]

What the doctrine meant for Luther, and what it ought
to be taken to mean for all men, Maurice sought to bring
out in these words:

> The justice or righteousness of God, a living justice
> and righteousness, was proclaimed as the deliverance
> from the bitter curse of the divine law; as that with
> which the man clothes himself by faith, just as all
> the grandeur and beauty of the outward. firmament
> become his by sight. What a vision to be presented
> to poor earthly grovellers at the very moment when
> they were made most conscious of their degradation!
> If there was immediate delight and satisfaction in the
> discovery of a state which was theirs by the highest
> title, it was evidently a satisfaction involving the idea
> of a continual progress, a continual ascent. The good
> was close at hand, close to the beggar and the outcast;
> but it was an unfathomable good; something to be
> found and sought for, and found again for ages upon
> ages.[89]

[88]*Ibid.*, II, 10.
[89]*Moral and Metaphysical Philosophy*, II, 122. Cp. *Kingdom of Christ* (Ev. ed.), I, 87.

3

THE IDEA OF A CHURCH UNIVERSAL

*There rose up before me the idea of a
CHURCH UNIVERSAL, not built upon human inventions or human faith, but upon the
very nature of God Himself, and upon the union
which He has formed with His creatures.—*
KINGDOM OF CHRIST (EV. ED.), I, 14.

*As he became convinced that God has Him-
self established a great and universal fellowship,
from which no one, except by his own act, is
excluded, he was necessarily more indifferent to
human means for securing this great end—more
impatient of those who wish to divert the stream
of God's mercy into canals and tanks of their
own manufacture—more anxious to persuade all
not to choose these in preference to the full and
all-embracing ocean of the Catholic Church.—*
MEMOIR BY J. A. STEPHENSON IN LIFE OF F. D. M.,
I, 151.

FROM what has been said in the preceding chapter
some might infer that, since according to Maurice
Christ is the Head of the whole human race (and
not only of a portion of it), since all men are
created in Christ and have been redeemed by Him,
and since Christ is the Head of every man, no place is
left for what the New Testament calls the Ecclesia or
Church as a distinct society. Does not the Church on this

view become coterminous with humanity? Are the Church and the world then simply alternative names for humanity?

But this is of course very far from being the case. I want now to begin to fill in Maurice's teaching about the Church in its distinction from the world, on the one hand, and in its contrast to sects, on the other. We can best begin with a passage from the *Theological Essays*.

The world contains the elements of which the Church is composed. In the Church, these elements are penetrated by a uniting, reconciling power. The Church is, therefore, human society in its normal state; the World, that same society irregular and abnormal. The world is the Church without God; the Church is the world restored to its relation with God, taken back by Him into the state for which He created it.[1]

Maurice refused to think or speak of the world in the way that religious people often did in his day and still do, as though it were an alien society from which the Church is separate and ought to keep itself aloof, and to which it must be hostile. In the first place, he condemned that Manicheism, which indeed the Church has condemned, although churchmen have been apt to fall into it, the Manicheism which says: "This visible world . . . is accursed, the work of an Evil Spirit; almost given up to him. Christ came into it that He might deliver His elect out of it. While they dwell in it they are to regard it with suspicion, with a kind of horror. Its beauty is worse than its deformity; 'touch not, taste not, handle not' any of its treasures. The devil told our Lord that they were his, that he gives them to those who worship him."[2]

There is, however, a more common and a more subtle form of anti-worldliness, which regards the Church and

[1] *Theological Essays*, p. 403. Cp. *Three Letters to the Rev. W. Palmer*, p. 8.
[2] *Lincoln's Inn Sermons*, I, 246 f. Cp. *Kingdom of Christ* (Ev. ed.), II, 178; *Theological Essays*, p. 245.

the world or what is called the secular order as inveterate and inevitable rivals, as though the Church were purely celestial and the world purely terrestrial, and which says in effect:

> Christ . . . has built up a Church, has endowed it with various gifts, has pronounced it altogether good. And the world sets itself up as a rival to this divine body, is jealous of its prerogatives, wishes to enslave or to destroy it. The outward world of trees and flowers may be good enough; the things of the world, its silver and gold, may be turned to high purposes. It is the world of men from which the Church is separated, against which it exists to protest. In baptized nations she has a right to claim these men as her own. But her power over them is disputed by kings who want them as their citizens, by parents who want them to transmit their names. With these the Church finds herself in conflict. She may enter into terms with them; may make use of their services, may consent, for her own ends, to receive their honours or their wealth; but they constitute a world-order; they belong to this earth: her polity is celestial. She must always be suspecting their maxims, always devising means for exalting her own in contrast to them.[3]

The temptation of religious people to think thus of the world and of its relation to the Church is, I fancy, in some respects stronger now than it was a century ago. The number of baptized nations has diminished. Kings, or their modern counterparts—dictators, social engineers, planners—exercise more power over men and are less inclined to share their power with the Church. Everywhere, in Europe anyhow, the cleavage between the Church and the world, thus regarded, threatens to become sharper. In several countries already the Church has taken the position of a resistance movement and may yet do so in others. It is

[3]*Lincoln's Inn Sermons*, I, 248.

seasonable for us then to attend to Maurice's warning against the perils in this cleavage, a warning which was, it will be perceived, radically theological. The passage just quoted continues thus:

> The Church which I read of in the Bible is baptized into the name of the Father and the Son and the Holy Ghost. This name is its foundation. But if I adopted the report of the relation between the Church and the world which this theory gives, I should be obliged to suppose that the Church had nothing to do with this Name, that it existed to contradict all which that Name expresses. For it is written, that the Father loved the world, and sent His only begotten Son into it, that He might save it. It is written, that the Son came into the world, not to condemn the world, but that the world through Him might be saved. It is written, that the Holy Ghost the Comforter comes to convince the world of sin, because it believes not in Christ its Saviour; of righteousness, because He is gone to the Father; of judgment, because the Prince of this world is judged. The Father loves the world, the Son dies for the world, the Holy Ghost convinces the world that it has a Deliverer and a Righteous Lord, and that He has taken it out of the hands of a usurper; and the Church, which is sealed with His name, is not to love the world, not to save the world, not to convince the world, but to set itself up as a rival competitor to the world, to plot against the world, to undermine the world![4]

The world, to Maurice, meant not the State or the secular order opposed to, and set over against, the Church. The Church is the witness to the only true foundation of States, nations, families, and all human order. They become the world in an evil sense (as the Church itself may become a world) only in so far as they set themselves up to pursue their own ends, in so far as they become organized

[4]*Ibid.,* I, 249.

selfishness, refusing to confess that they have one foundation, one centre, one bond. This is the great refusal and
the great rebellion, in consequence of which the world
becomes a scene of discord and confusion. That, however,
is not its true state.

> The Universal Church, constituted in its Universal
> Head, exists to protest against a world which supposes
> itself to be a collection of incoherent fragments with-
> out a centre, which, where it reduces its practice to a
> maxim, treats every man as his own centre. The
> Church exists to tell the world of its true Centre, of
> the law of mutual sacrifice by which its parts are
> bound together. The Church exists to maintain the
> order of the nation and the order of the family, which
> this selfish practice and selfish maxim are continually
> threatening.[5]

Similarly, commenting on John XV, 17–20, he said:

> The one difference which we have already discov-
> ered between the world and those whom He chooses
> out of it, is that they confess a Centre, and that the
> world confesses none; that they desire to move, each
> in his own orbit, about this Centre, and that the world
> acknowledges only a revolution of each man about
> himself. The world, indeed, cannot realize its own
> principles. It must have companies, parties, sects,—
> bodies acknowledging some principle of cohesion, as-
> piring after a kind of unity. Still, as a world, this is
> the description of it; and therefore, as a world, it must
> hate all who say, "We are a society bound together,
> not by any law of our own, not by an election of our
> own, but by God's law and election."[6]

About the world in this sense Maurice could use very
anti-worldly language.

[5]*Ibid.*, I, 251.
[6]*Gospel of St. John*, pp. 392 f.

The world, considered as apart from God—considered as a society which frames its maxims and its practice without reference to Him—this world is condemned to a very hopeless kind of darkness. Its members cannot see any light which should guide their footsteps, for they confess no light but what proceeds from themselves. They are always stumbling against each other, never doing justice to each other, for the same reason.[7]
    The Church is the witness for the true constitution of man as man, a child of God, an heir of heaven . . . the world is a miserable, accursed, rebellious order, which denies this foundation, which will create a foundation of self-will, choice, taste, opinion . . . in the world there can be no communion . . . in the Church there can be universal communion; communion in one body by One Spirit.[8]

The world is humanity trying to base itself on a falsehood, on a denial of its true constitution. It "would have been torn in pieces by its individual factions,"[9] did not this true constitution lie beneath it, this unconfessed bond of peace and fellowship. The world does not denote a society or an organization that is separate from the Church. It denotes a principle on which men are naturally inclined to organize their lives, a principle which is opposed to, and a contradiction of, the order which has been prepared for them by God. This false principle is at work everywhere and always, in the Church itself as well as in the nation and the family, but it is the special office of the Church to witness against it by witnessing to the truth.

    The principles of the world exist in the heart of every family and of every nation . . . they are precisely the natural tendencies and inclinations of men . . . they are always threatening to become predominant. . . . When they become predominant there

[7]*Lincoln's Inn Sermons,* II, 182.
[8]*Life of F. D. M.,* I, 166.
[9]*Kingdom of Christ* (Ev. ed.), I, 40.

5

ceases to be any recognition of men as related to a
Being above them, any recognition of them as possessing a common humanity. . . . The Church, being
especially the witness for these facts which it is natural
to us to deny, must be a *distinct* body. In losing its
distinctness it loses its meaning, loses to all intents and
purposes, though the words may at first sound paradoxical, its universality.[10]

What then are the principles to which the Church must
bear witness, the principles which it must confess and realize?
Maurice will maintain that these principles are not abstract
notions or ideals, but facts, facts that are expressed in the
visible signs by which the common life of the Church is
marked, visible signs through which its universal character
becomes articulate. Such are the sacraments of Baptism
and the Eucharist, the Creeds, the Liturgy, the Ministry,
and the Scriptures, and these we shall consider in the
following chapters. But before we inquire how these ordinances and institutions bear their witness, we need to
see what is, according to Maurice, the truth about the
nature of the Church to which they may be expected to bear
witness.

> Does it occur to you that because Christ died for all
> mankind, therefore no particular body can look upon
> themselves as now in covenant with Him? You might
> as well say that because all men are in truth the
> servants of God, the Jews might not look upon them-
> selves as taken into His covenant and recognised as
> His people. Where, I ask you, would be the blessing
> to mankind of Christ's death, if there were none to
> bear witness of it, none to claim the universal fellow-
> ship which it is meant to establish? We see that the
> world is not united in the acknowledgment of God or
> of the Mediator, not united to each other in one Lord
> or one faith. How, think you, can it be shown to them

[10]*Ibid.*, I, 260 f.

that there is such a Lord, such a Mediator, such a bond between all men, unless there be some who feel themselves successors to more than Jewish privileges, taken into covenant with God, His appointed witnesses? And who must these be? I answer, all nations who, through God's mercy, have heard the Gospel of Christ, and have confessed it to be true; all who by baptism have claimed the privilege of belonging to His Church.[11]

The witness of the Church to the unity of mankind in Christ is not exclusive but inclusive, not inward-looking but outward-looking, and outward-looking because upward-looking. The Church does not say: "There is unity for us, but not for you." It says: "There is unity in Christ for all; do you come and claim it with us, and share it with us." The truth of this witness does not depend on the number or impressiveness of those who are bearing it, or on the size of the Church at any given place or time.

If there be one man in any county of England who declares that the Lord is his God, who says, "I was baptized into His name, I am taken to be His child, and His Spirit dwells with me," that man says what is true of him and true of all the men and women in that county, and true of all the members of Christ's Church in every part of the world. If they do not think so, that is their misery. If they make the spirit of evil their Lord and God, that is their lie. But though every man be found a liar the thing is true; we have been taken to be God's children, and He is our Father. And as every true man in the Church is a witness of what every other man in the Church has been made, so the Church itself is a witness to all mankind of what God has done for them, and what they really are, created in Christ, and redeemed by Christ, and capable, but for their disbelieving this truth, and not taking their

[11]*Christmas Day*, pp. 126 f. *Cp.* Thomas Erskine, *The Brazen Serpent* (1831), pp. 230 f.

position as members of His body, of shewing forth His character and His glory.[12]

What Maurice was saying was put in different and perhaps plainer words by Westcott:

In Christ all men are brethren. . . . Our relationship one to another does not depend on any remote descent: it is not imperilled by any possible discovery as to the origin or the antiquity of man: it is not bound by the conditions of the outward life: it is not measured by the course of days and years: it is not closed by death. The brotherhood of men seen in Christ is a question not of genealogy but of being. It rests upon the present and abiding fatherhood of God, Who in His Son has taken our common nature to Himself. We may acknowledge this God-made kinsmanship or we may reject it; but none the less we all are not only brethren in constitution, brethren in death, but brethren in Christ, brethren for evermore.[13]

[12]*Christmas Day*, p. 180.
[13]B. F. Westcott, *Social Aspects of Christianity*[2] (1888), pp. 9 f. W. Moore Ede in *The Modern Churchman* (December, 1931, p. 527), says Westcott told him that he never read Maurice. "I did read one thing he wrote, and I purposely never read any more, for I felt that his way of thinking was so like my own that if I read much of Maurice I should endanger my originality." *Cp.* J. Adderley, *In Slums and Society* (1916), p. 106, who says that Westcott "never read more than one book by" Maurice. A more adequate account of the relations between Westcott and Maurice is given by J. Llewellyn Davies in the Appendix to J. Clayton's *Bishop Westcott* (1906). It is true that Westcott avoided reading Maurice in the period when his thought was being formed, but he was at that time in other ways exposed to the influence of Maurice's teaching. And later he certainly read some of Maurice's books. In 1892 he wrote of *Social Morality* as "one of my very few favourite books." See Arthur Westcott, *Brooke Foss Westcott* (1903), II, 160. See also Hort's *Life and Letters*, I, 222. The subject of this note is discussed by L. E. Elliott-Binns in his *Religion in the Victorian Era* (1936), pp. 296 f. He does not, however, allude to the Appendix to Clayton's book. Nor do I think he can be right in concluding that *Social Morality*, which was not published till 1869, was the "one thing" Westcott referred to when speaking to Moore Ede.

The Church is the body in which this God-made kins-manship is acknowledged, and where the effectual signs of its reality are at work. Those whom God has brought into His visible Church are a "kind of first fruits of His crea-tures." "The open consecration of a part marks the destiny of the whole."[14]

It seemed to Maurice that the *articulus stantis aut cadentis ecclesiae* is "that God has claimed us all in Christ as His sons,"[15] and that "the baptized Church is not set apart as a witness *for* exclusion, but against it."[16] It seemed to him that the Biblical descriptions of the Church, which may at first sight give it an exclusive colour, are on a deeper view universally inclusive and uniting.

Let us look, for instance, at what he said about the theme of the covenant. "Every one who reads the Old Testament must perceive that the idea of a covenant of God with a certain people is that which presides in it."[17] "The fundamental principle of the Old Covenant" was "that the choice of one people was to be for the blessing of all."[18] It appears first in the story of Noah. God's covenant with Noah was a pledge and assurance to man that he is in relation to God, "a pledge of God's care of the world, of God's special care of him his chief minister in and over the world."[19] But it is Abraham who is "the

[14]B. F. Westcott, *The Victory of the Cross* (1888), pp. 50 f.; cp. *ibid.*, p. 119.

[15]*Life of F. D. M.*, II, 357. *Cp.* Bishop Ewing: "The truth that God the Son 'hath redeemed me and all mankind.' *That is the rock on which the Church of England is built.*" A. J. Ross, *Memoirs of Alexander Ewing* (1887), p. 355.

[16]*The Prayer-Book and the Lord's Prayer*, p. 10.

[17]*Kingdom of Christ* (Ev. ed.), I, 239. Maurice assumed the historical accuracy of the O. T. records; but his theological in-terpretation of their significance is not thereby discredited. The witness of the O. T. to the divine covenant is not dependent on any particular reconstruction of the historical process by which Israel came to bear that witness.

[18]*Patriarchs and Lawgivers*, p. 269.

[19]*Ibid.*, pp. 76 f.

beginner of the Church on earth."[20] The covenant with Abraham, "like the covenant with Noah, was one not of bargain, but of blessing. It was an assurance, that he who entered into it was called, chosen, set apart by God. He had not taken up the position himself; his business was simply to acknowledge that it was his, and to act as if it were."[21] The Bible is the witness to the gradual manifestation of the blessings into which men are received, first through the family relationship, then through a national community, and finally through a universal society. The Bible "is telling us what the will and purpose" of the living God "is towards us and towards the universe. It is telling us what His method is in dealing with the creatures whom He has formed in His image. It is telling us how He forms them into societies, and deals with them as belonging to a society; how it is their continual tendency to act as if they were selfish creatures having no relation to each other."[22]

The covenant with Abraham was a covenant with a family. "The fact of his relationship to God is interpreted to him by the feeling of his human relations, and his capacity of fulfilling them arose from his acknowledgement of the higher relation."[23] "The Abrahamic family, though cut off by their covenant from other families of the earth, was so cut off expressly that it might bear witness for the true order of the world."[24] The Bible "tells us how a family is called out to show forth the true divine law of society, and to strive against the false and destructive perversion of it. It tells us how the members of the chosen family are just as prone to that perversion of it as any other men —and exhibit it in a new and more pernicious form—pretending that God has set them up against His other creatures, not as blessings to them."[25]

[20]*Kingdom of Christ* (Ev. ed.), I, 240.
[21]*Patriarchs and Lawgivers*, p. 91.
[22]*Ibid.*, p. 151.
[23]*Kingdom of Christ* (Ev. ed.), I, 239 f.
[24]*Ibid.*, I, 241.   [25]*Patriarchs and Lawgivers*, pp. 151 f.

The covenant with Moses was a covenant with a nation. "The God of Israel is declared to be the God of all the nations of the earth; the Israelites are chosen out to be witnesses of the fact."[26] God declares Himself to be their appointed guide and deliverer by "that name upon which the Jewish covenant stands, which is the foundation of all law, I AM THAT I AM."[27] This covenant is a manifestation of the absolute sovereignty of God, and also of the derivation of national institutions as well as of family relationships from Him and of their dependence on Him. "The Jewish institutions, as they are described in the Pentateuch . . . led the thoughts of the Jews above the bonds of family and of law, though they were inseparably intertwined with both."[28]

> That there was an awful self-existent Being from whom all law came, was declared by the commandments: the Tabernacle affirmed that this Being was present among His people, and that it was possible in some awful manner to approach Him. The family covenant bore witness that there was a relation between Him and His worshippers; the Priesthood from generation to generation witnessed that this relation might be actually realised, that it might be realised by the whole people, in a representative.[29]

They learned that "no king, no priest, no judge, has a right to look upon himself as possessing intrinsic power; that he is exercising office, under a righteous king, a perfect priest, an all-seeing judge. . . . As then in the patriarchal period the Divine Being manifested Himself in the family relations, and by doing so manifested on what these relations depend, how they are upheld, and wherein their worth consists: so in the national period He was manifested to

26*Kingdom of Christ* (Ev. ed.), I, 243.
27*Ibid.*, I, 241.
28*Ibid.*, I, 242.
29*Ibid.*, I, 242.

men through all national offices; thereby explaining their meaning and import, how they are upheld, and wherein their worth consists."[30]

But the nation like the family is by definition an exclusive and limited society.[31] The Old Testament contains the promise of a new covenant and of a universal society, which would not displace the old covenant with the family and the nation, but which would adopt it into itself.[32] Could this be realized in any way but through a universal empire? The Old Testament cannot tell. The answer was given in the manifestation to which the New Testament bears witness. It was the manifestation of the kingdom of Christ, the God-man, the universal Mediator, reconciling men to God and one another by His death, resurrection and ascension, who is now and for ever the invisible Head of all nations and all families, in whom they are at once preserved in their distinctness and bound together in unity. "That they all may be one, as thou, Father, art in me, and I in thee, that they may be one in us." "Either those words," says Maurice, "contain the essence and meaning of the whole history, or that history must be rejected as being from first to last the wickedest lie and the most awful blasphemy ever palmed upon the world."[33]

The Church of the new covenant is the permanent witness to the full manifestation of this universal and spiritual kingdom which God had ever intended for men, and which was implicit and indeed present, though only partially revealed, from the first. "We must never forget that while this universal society, according to the historical conception of it, grew out of the Jewish family and nation, it is, according to the theological conception of it, the root of both. 'That,' says Aristotle, 'which is first as cause is last in discovery.' And this beautiful formula is translated into

[30]*Ibid.*, I, 243 f.
[31]See *Social Morality*, p. 107.
[32]See *Kingdom of Christ* (Ev. ed.), I, 247.
[33]*Ibid.*, I, 254.

life and reality in the letter to the Ephesians, when St. Paul tells them that they were created in Christ before all worlds, and when he speaks of the transcendent economy as being gradually revealed to the Apostles and Prophets by the Spirit."[34] The difference established by the new covenant was "that whereas heretofore God had declared Himself to the King of one nation, now He would own Himself the Father of all in His well-beloved Son; that whereas He had admitted the Jews to call themselves His servants, He would now invite men to look up to Him as sons . . . that instead of merely reigning over them He would dwell in them."[35]

The Church was the new Israel, the continuation and expansion of the old Israel. "The baptized men who were scattered in little bodies through the cities of Greece and Asia were not supplanting the old commonwealth of Israel, they were the continuation and expansion of it."[36] Likewise the Old Testament description of God's people as His bride is not superseded but fulfilled in the Church of the new covenant.

> There is One in whom the whole Church is presented as a chaste bride to the Father, in whom it is holy, in spite of all the corruptions and abominations which its members commit when they forget their calling and live as if they were separate creatures. Their unbelief cannot destroy the reality and perfection which it has in God's eyes; which it does not derive from itself, but from Him; which it only understands when it turns from itself to Him.[37]

The Church is the permanent witness to the true constitution of humanity.

All the Churches throughout the Roman Empire

[34]*Ibid.*, I, 256.
[35]*Christmas Day*, p. 126.
[36]*Lincoln's Inn Sermons*, II, 271.
[37]*The Prayer-Book and the Lord's Prayer*, p. 250.

were so many witnesses that the Incarnation has established human society upon this deep and eternal basis, and that there is none other upon which it can be established. Jerusalem fell, the Roman Empire fell, and still the baptised family went on in different lands, testifying by its very existence, that this is our true human constitution, and that all changes in governments, all convulsions—moral, political, physical, till the final one—will prove it to be so.[38]

Thus all men are related to the Church of the new covenant, whether they acknowledge it or not. To all men the preacher of the Gospel can say: "Of your relation to this Church you cannot rid yourselves, any more than you can change the law under which your natural bodies and the members of them exist. It is one which you must confess along with us, because you are human beings as well as we are."[39] For the covenant presupposes an actual relation between mankind and God in Christ. The covenant does not constitute the relation. It makes it manifest. It is the way in which men enter into, and realize, the relationship with God and their brethren, which is still the law and constitution of their being, even if they practically deny it by refusing to enter into it. To enter into the covenant is to be drawn out of separation or individual isolation into a body in which the universal relationship can be realized.

> Without a covenant we are not members of a body; the Spirit dwells in the Body, and in each of its members *as such,* and not as individuals. The Spirit in an individual is a fearful contradiction. The difference as to preaching seems to be—You declare forgiveness of sins as belonging to man-kind, and invite them to become (which they have not been hitherto) portions of the kind—the Church; to the others (*i.e.,* to those

[38]*The Church a Family,* p. 29.
[39]*Lincoln's Inn Sermons,* V, 241.

who are already members of the Church) you say—
"You are forgiven, you have the Spirit."[40]

Yet of course no man ever is a sheer individual in complete isolation or separation; no man therefore is without
some foretaste or premonition of what it means to share
in the unity of a body. The family and the nation, and
other human associations too, are partial anticipations of
the universal society. Wherever men are bound together
in a true fellowship, there is a work of the Spirit of unity,
but His work can attain its fullness and perfection only
in a universal Church. It will be evident by now that
Maurice did not accept that sharp differentiation between
nature and grace, or between the natural and the supernatural, or between humanity and the redeemed humanity,
that seems to underlie much received theology.[41] He would
attribute the goodness in any man and in all men to the
grace of Christ and the inspiration of His Spirit, and so
claim it for the Church. He thus interpreted the XIIIth
Article of Religion, "Of Works before Justification." This
Article

> cannot, of course, refer to the works done before Christ
> died for men's sins and rose again for their justifica-
> tion; it does not concern one period of the world's

[40]*Life of F. D. M.*, I, 209. Cp. *Kingdom of Christ* (1838), I,
119: "Nothing is clearer, I conceive, from the language of Scripture, and the very idea of Christianity, than that we enjoy the
presence of the Spirit, His teachings and illuminations, not as
individuals, but as living portions of a living body."

[41]For evidence of dissatisfaction with the received system in
contemporary French Roman Catholic circles, see an article entitled "La nouvelle théologie où va-t-elle?" in *Angelicum* (July-
December, 1946), pp. 126–45. The article is the sounding of an
alarm by one who is confessedly *un théologien traditionnel*, Fr.
Reg. Garrigou-Lagrange, O. P. Henri de Lubac, one of the French
theologians, whom Garrigou-Lagrange refers to with disapproba-
tion, speaks of "la véritable et pleine idée chrétienne (de la
nature et de la raison), que nos siècles modernes ont de plus en
plus perdue." See his book, *Surnaturel* (1946), p. 437.

history more than another. . . . "The grace of Christ, the Inspiration of His Spirit" must, it says, be the spring of every good act. Most inwardly do I accept that teaching. I know not how far the compilers of the Articles meant it to be carried. They may not have recognized the length and breadth of their own proposition. But I cannot see how we can safely take it in any limited sense. If we do and must attribute virtues to heathens, then we do and must suppose that their virtues had their source "in the grace of Christ and the Inspiration of His Spirit." Those who regard Christ as merely a man born at a certain time into this world, and the head of a sect called Christians, may stumble at such an assertion. But I need not tell you that this is not the orthodox faith; not the doctrine of these Articles. They set forth Christ "as the Son, the Word of the Father, begotten from everlasting of the Father." They say "that everlasting life is offered to mankind by Christ in the Old Testament"; when He had not taken flesh. There is every reason therefore in the tenor of the Articles for giving this one its full import.[42]

That there is no salvation outside the Church should not be taken to mean that none can be saved beyond the limits of the visible Church, but that all salvation is within the Church and all who are saved will find when their eyes are opened that they belonged to the Church even though they knew it not.[43] Maurice knew that the work of the Holy Spirit was not confined to those who were orthodox in belief. "I have found in many of the Unitarian body whom I have known and do know, Divine graces which I have not found in myself."[44] He held that God is in a living relation with all men, that no man is merely "natural."

[42]*Faith of the Liturgy*, pp. 41 ff. Cp. *The New Statute and Mr. Ward*, pp. 22 f.
[43]*Theological Essays*, pp. 404 f. Cp. my book, *The Orb and the Cross* (1945), p. 121; H. de Lubac, *Catholicisme*, pp. 174 ff.
[44]*Life of F. D. M.*, II, 412.

Between the notions that our union to a Spiritual Being is not *real* and that it is *natural,* men's minds, if I may judge by my own, are continually liable to oscillate. The first begets feeble and desponding exertions to produce it; the second, a vain wonder that the happy feelings which it should suggest do not come of their own accord into us. When we once assure ourselves, that *it is so,* for us and for all men, whether we believe it or not, and yet that it is something above our nature; then I think faith and peace begin.[45]

In the Church the relationship of humanity to God in Christ is visible, asserted, articulate; but the relationship itself is not restricted to baptized or believing members of the Church. Speaking of the three collects for Good Friday in the Book of Common Prayer, Maurice said: "That (the second) was for Christ's Church, and this (the third) is for those who will not belong to it. By using the first, we declare that we believe Christ's death to be the bond of a great family; by the other (the third), we declare that we do not believe its blessing to be confined to those who are members of His family now."[46] If we are thinking of the Church in the final and complete sense of the word, it is best for us to say that we cannot and ought not to set any limits to its membership. "What is this Catholic Church? If you mean by that question, what are its limits? who have a right to say that they belong to it? I cannot answer the question; I believe only One can answer it; I am content to leave it with Him."[47]

It will not now be difficult to see why Maurice all through his life was waging war against every tendency that he detected to substitute the conception of a sect for that of a Church. By a sect he meant a society of which the characteristic feature was that it stood for certain peculiar opinions. It consisted of men who were bound together because

[45]*Ibid.,* I, 198.
[46]*Christmas Day,* p. 209. [47]*Epistle to the Hebrews,* p. cxxiv.

they willed to hold and to propagate those opinions. It was a voluntary society; it was grounded on the will of men and on the belief of men. The Church, on the other hand, was a body called into being by God, grounded on His will, representing the unity of the race in Christ, binding men together because of their unity in Christ and in spite of the peculiar opinions they might hold.

Christendom in Maurice's time was riddled with sectarianism. "The religious world," it seemed to him, was "trying to reduce all Churches into a Babel of sects."[48] The sectarian temper may appear to be less rife today, because there has been a large abatement of fanaticism among Christians, a growth of toleration, a spreading aspiration after some kind of unity. But sectarian notions are still widely taken for granted, though the fact that they have lost much of their sting may make them appear comparatively innocuous. The denominations may increasingly call themselves "Churches," and resent being called anything else. They may express their desire to be united in one Church. But is not what is often intended by this only a vast collection or federation of sects, which will acquiesce in one another's peculiarities while cultivating their own?

It is no part of my intention to survey our contemporary Christendom, and to distinguish between those Christian bodies which are entitled to be called Churches and those which ought to be styled sects. For I should say that all across Christendom the conception of the Church and the conception of the sect are present and in at least implicit conflict. Maurice's strong utterances on this subject may therefore still have much to teach Christians generally, and Anglicans in particular. For the sectarian principle may be as much displayed within a single communion as between separated societies. Let us first, however, consider the question in general terms, and then look at the way in which it presses, or ought to press, on Anglicans.

[48]*Doctrine of Sacrifice,* p. xi.

It is one of the melancholy results of a divided Christendom that every part of the separated Church has for practical purposes to be given, and indeed has itself to make use of, a name, title, or label which will distinguish it from every other part. That is to say, every part of the Church has to become, for certain purposes at any rate, a "denomination." Even those parts of the Church which claim to be the whole Church and would deny to any other body the status of a Church, for example the Roman Church, cannot escape from being regarded as denominations, or being treated as such by civil governments, cannot dispense with the need to attach some epithet or epithets to the word "Church" in order to mark their separation from other claimants to the title, and cannot avoid in practice referring to other claimants as Churches. Thus, Romanists in England seldom scruple to speak of "the Church of England," though it is open to them there to substitute the opprobrious title "Establishment"; in Wales and elsewhere not even this escape is open to them.

The effect of this inevitable affixing of denominational labels to Churches, which has us all in its grip, is to induce in our minds sectarian conceptions of the nature of the Church, however firmly and indignantly we may reject them when they are brought into consciousness and their implications unfolded. Just because we are accustomed to speak complacently about the Roman Catholic Church, the Presbyterian Church, the Episcopal or Anglican Church, the Baptist Church, etc., we can hardly fail to be influenced by the notion that a Church is a society that is separated from other societies on the ground of certain peculiar opinions or practices which constitute its *raison d'être*. It may be the exaltation of the Roman see, or the Presbyterian or Episcopalian form of church government, or an insistence on believers' baptism, and so on. Without prejudice to whatever may be said on behalf of these distinguishing features of particular Churches, must

we not confess that this usage involves speaking of Churches
as though they were sects? Even if Christians themselves
could resist the infection which this mode of speech is calculated to produce, it is bound to make this impression on
the world at large, which is a scarcely less disastrous consequence.

Maurice acknowledged the good intentions by which the
founders of sects are often inspired, and the good work
that had been done by sects, at least in their youth.

> Sects, schools, orders, have been . . . established
> in the Christian Church. They have been established
> generally by earnest and devout men, conscious of some
> great task which has been forgotten, of some great
> duty which has been neglected, eager to assert the one
> and perform the other. They have flourished; they
> have drawn proselytes and devotees to them, for the
> truth and the duty have been felt to be divine. But
> the counsel and the work were of men; therefore, the
> strength of the society decayed often as its outward
> prosperity increased; at last it came utterly to nought.[49]

But the counsel and the work were not only of men. We
must own that it has sometimes been the work of the Lord
to rend the Church by schism, or to raise up sects to witness
against it. Speaking of England after the Reformation,
Maurice said:

> We must not shrink from the acknowledgment, that
> the different sects which rose up in this land, seemingly
> to rend the body of Christ more completely asunder
> than it had been already, were from the Lord.[50]

Yet the result was to jeopardize the idea of a Church
Universal.

The Church since the Reformation has had one

[49]*Acts of the Apostles*, p. 69.
[50]*Prophets and Kings*, p. 102; see the whole passage, pp. 100–4.
Cp. on Scotland, *Kingdom of Christ* (1838), III, 180.

of the direst of its old enemies to fight with. The idea
of it as a great sect or a small sect, a great collection of
sects, a great machine for converting the nations, has
more and more driven out the old faith, has led people
to think that the Church must be either a mere world,
or else a narrow, self-willed confederation; that it must
either cease to be a spiritual body, or cease to be a
universal one.[51]

The belief that a great or inclusive Church must be corrupt, whereas a small or narrow sect can be pure, which
is commonly entertained by the promoters of sects, is fal-
lacious.

> You must acknowledge that a holy body can con-
> tinue to exist, though a multitude of its members com-
> mit acts which are most unholy. . . . Every experi-
> ment to make bodies holy by cutting off the supposed
> holy portions from the rest, has proved the more un-
> successful and abortive, the more consistently and per-
> severingly it has been pursued.[52]

And the sects have a graver record of bigotry and cruelty
than the Church. "I am sure you will find every sect narrower and more cruel than the Church. I am sure that the
Church is only narrow and cruel when she apes the sects,
and assumes the character of a sect."[53]

It is the law of sects, however much they may witness
for positive truth and unity in their beginnings, in the long
run to foster negation and division, and the perpetuation
of obsolete controversies.

> You know, from the records of history, what has
> happened when any sect or school has become domi-
> nant; that it has changed from a witness for Christ
> into a witness for itself; that the vital convictions

[51]*The Church a Family*, pp. 14 f.
[52]*Lincoln's Inn Sermons*, II, 23.
[53]*Life of F. D. M.*, II, 444.

6

which were dear to its founders pass into dead notions
and an unmeaning phraseology; that the opposition to
other schools becomes the chief token that it retains
any energy of its own.[54]

And after all was not sectarianism the sin of the Jews in
the time of our Lord, which His passion and death manifested in its true colours?

> I believe that the great misery and sin of the Jews,
> in the time when our Lord appeared among them in
> the flesh, was that they had lost the feeling of national
> unity—that they had become mere covetous individuals,
> herding together in sects, knit to each other by opinions
> and antipathies, not by the sense of a common origin,
> a common country, a common Lord. Jesus came to
> gather together the lost sheep of the House of Israel
> under their true Shepherd.[55]

No doubt Maurice's opposition to sectarianism tended
to become something like an obsession, and he was liable
to exaggerate and over-simplify. But can it be denied that
he had grasped a fundamental truth when he asserted, as
he did in season and out of season, that "the bond of
churchmanship is an altogether different bond from that
which holds the disciples of a school together."[56] It is a
truth that everywhere in Christendom, whatever may be
professed, is always in danger of being forgotten, especially
in the West, where the separation of the Church into denominations has inevitably given it the appearance of a
collection of sects. Let me repeat that nothing I have said
has been intended to draw a line through the denominations
and to set those that have the character of a Church on
one side and of a sect on the other. For I conceive that
the elements of, and the forces that make for, both true

[54]*Ibid.*, II, 374 f.
[55]*Gospel of St. John*, p. 188.
[56]*Life of F. D. M.*, II, 374.

churchmanship and sectarianism are universally present and at work, though mingled in different proportions and in diverse modes in the various Christian bodies. "I can well conceive," said Maurice, "how galling it is to a Dissenter to be told that he is a member of a Sect, and that we are not members of one. Moreover, the words seem to me unjust. I think he claims to be a member of Christ's Church as I do. I think I am as liable to sink into a Sectarian, and to be only that, as he is."[57] Here is a case, if ever there were one, where it behoves us to cast the beam out of our own eye, before trying to cast the mote out of our brother's eye. Therefore let us look now upon the way in which this question ought to press upon Anglicans.

In 1841 Doctor Hook, the Vicar of Leeds, who had not been a member of the Tractarian party, though he had broadly sympathized with the Tracts for the Times, was so provoked by the condemnation of Tract XC at Oxford that he published a letter in which he said that the act of the Hebdomadal Board had made it absolutely necessary for him and others to take sides and to join a party in the Church.[58] In reply to this, Maurice, who was then Chaplain of Guy's Hospital, published an open letter entitled *Reasons for not joining a Party in the Church*. Hook had a little lost his head in the excitement of the moment, and he afterwards wrote and told Maurice that he had been wrong, and Maurice right, in this matter.[59] Nearly thirty years later Maurice could thank God that He had not suffered him to join a party in the Church in his youth, or manhood, or old age.[60]

[57]*A Few Words on Secular and Denominational Education*, p. 12.

[58]See W. F. Hook, *Letter to the Right Reverend the Lord Bishop of Ripon on the State of Parties in the Church of England* (1841), p. 5.

[59]See *Life of F. D. M.*, I, 239.

[60]See *ibid.*, I, 240.

Just as the violence of sectarian animosity is now much abated if compared with its state a century ago, so has the violence of party hostility within the Anglican Communion. Yet parties are still with us; they have their rival organizations, their newspapers, their propaganda. There are still Anglicans who call themselves "Catholics" not on the ground that they have been baptized and are members of the Church but because of certain opinions or practices which differentiate them from other members of the Church. There are still Anglicans who call themselves "Evangelicals" not on the ground of the Gospel whose blessings they share with the whole Church but because they wish to distinguish their own mode of proclaiming it and to protest against other modes.

The *odium theologicum* is far from dead, even if it excites little of the public interest that it excited in the nineteenth century. The fact that our parties today are less powerful and less prominent, and have far fewer devotees, if it is partly due to a spread of the conviction that there ought not to be parties in a Church, is, I suspect, more due to the obsolescence of the causes which the surviving parties represent. If a new movement or movements started in our Communion, it is by no means certain that a fresh party or parties would not be formed, with all the consequences that Maurice pointed out. The parties that are still with us, although weak and decadent except in their own estimation, are able to diffuse a good deal of poison throughout our Communion. If Maurice were able to convince us "that the words *Party* and *Church* are essentially hostile to each other; that he who says, 'I will be a Churchman,' says, in effect, 'I will *not* be a Party man'; that he places himself under bonds and conditions with which those other bonds, and conditions are, in principle as in practice incompatible,"[61]—he would be doing us a good service.

---

[61]*Reasons for not joining a Party in the Church,* pp. 7 f.

It happened that Maurice had a closer and larger acquaintance with the sects and parties of his time than almost any one else can have had. It was before the days of the Student Christian Movement, of interdenominational co-operation, and ecumenical conferences; it was a time when sects and parties kept as much as possible to themselves. Maurice was brought up among the Unitarians and Quakers; through changes of conviction which occurred within his own family he was brought into touch with the Baptists and the Independents. He knew the Irvingites well. In the Church of England he was successively associated with the Evangelicals, the Liberals and the Oxford Movement. As his biographer says, "there was . . . no considerable body of English dissenters, or of English parties, which he had not known from within."[62] What he had to say about this matter was therefore the outcome of an unusual range of experience.

One thing that this experience impressed upon him was that every party and sect had got hold of some truth, and was witnessing to some truth, but that in each case it was a partial or one-sided truth, and the trouble was that the members of an organized party or sect almost inevitably treated their truth as the whole truth and very soon began to attack every one else for not agreeing with them. He "came more and more to hold that there was something to be learnt from everything 'positive' . . . in each one's faith, and that the mischief lay in the 'negative,' that is, in the denunciation of imperfectly understood truths held by others."[63] It seemed to him that the idea of a Church Universal, founded on men's relationship to God in Christ, and not on the particular truths that they had succeeded in grasping, was the great deliverance from this mischief, and the God-given way in which all these truths were to be reconciled. He conceived it to be the calling of the

[62]*Life of F. D. M.*, I, 337.
[63]*Ibid.*, I, 127.

Church of England, and if he had looked further afield
he would have said of the Anglican Communion everywhere, to witness to this idea of the Church. I shall have
more to say about this in my last chapter. Our present
concern is with Maurice's message about parties in the
Church.

Let it be said at once that he was keenly aware of the
danger of a merely negative attitude to parties, and of the
insidious temptation to form a "no-party" party to oppose
parties! "I would rather be the most vehement and mad
partisan," he said, "than one of those cold contemners of
all parties and of all men."[64]

> Above all, we must never be tempted to that greatest
> of all sins, the forming of a new party for the sake
> of displacing or overcoming existing parties. That
> temptation will present itself in ten thousand forms.
> The Evil Spirit will come as an Angel of Light. He
> will tell us that it is not a new party we are to con-
> struct—that would be very wicked—but a protest
> against all parties; in fact, a larger Church, a freer
> and more expansive Christianity. Accursed sophist!
> *We* construct a Church! *We* lay a broader foundation
> for Humanity than God has laid in His Son! *We* in-
> vent a more comprehensive Gospel than the Gospel
> of the Ascension, that He has gone up on high, leading
> captivity captive, glorifying our Nature at the right-
> hand of His Father! Such an experiment would con-
> centrate all the arrogance and unbelief of former sects
> into one grand, devilish scheme for our self-exaltation.
> The Society we assisted in forming would be the
> Society of AntiChrist. No, brethren! In this sense of
> attempting to compete with parties, or imitate them,
> or supersede them, we must let them wholly alone. In
> another sense, we must never let them alone; we must
> be continually tormenting them. The Apostles did not

[64]*Friendship of Books*, p. 291. Cp. *Kingdom of Christ* (Ev. ed.),
II, 332.

uproot the sect of the Pharisees, but they preached the corner-stone of Humanity.[65]

What he would have us do is to concern ourselves not with parties but with principles. He was always trying to bring out the principles which were contained, and perhaps concealed, in the witness of each party or sect as well as of each individual theologian. "The real germinant principle (of each thinker) is often hard to discover amidst the multitude of mere notions and opinions with which it has environed itself."[66] *A fortiori* the principles which a party is organized to represent get buried beneath the propaganda and the shibboleths of the efficient organizers who usually replace the original proponents of the principles and assume control of the machine.

Maurice described what happened in the history of the Evangelical party, and he saw the same tendencies at work in the Tractarian party. Indeed is not this the paradigm of religious parties?

> The Evangelical school under its first teachers was perhaps more narrow than it is at present: but what an amount of spiritual strength there was in it; what courage, what self-sacrifice! It became a party; it had its coteries; its consistories; its newspapers. It began to produce an effect; the press said it was so respectable and successful, that notice must be taken of it; the divines clapped their hands, and declared that the Gospel was spreading everywhere; editors were becoming believers in troops; the millenium was at hand. Alas! what a shrivelled thing has this popular system become. The holy and pious-minded men who are spoken of as maintaining it, do not really represent it. They are determined not to part with the principles which their forefathers bequeathed to them, and which they feel to be necessary to their own spiritual life; but

[65]*Lincoln's Inn Sermons*, IV, 12 f.
[66]*Moral and Metaphysical Philosophy*, I, 113

they are by no means certain that these are the only important truths; they wish to acknowledge good men who have started from a different point; they like better to call themselves Churchmen than Evangelicals. But the *system* has become a newspaper, cheap book, lecture machinery; not for propagating certain principles, but for attacking and slandering those who are supposed not to hold them, or to hold others different from them. . . .

Why is the quack machinery of the age less offensive, when it is employed in support of "Catholic Consent," than when it is used to support the principles of the Bible? But when was a *party* ever able to disclaim those who resort to these weapons? When has it ever been able to prevent them from acquiring supremacy? The talkers in streets and clubs, for all the purposes of a party, must be more important than the men who live in closets, and keep lonely vigils. And what is more sad, the first do exert an influence over the others: there is a pressure from without to which they unconsciously yield; their pure and noble thoughts take a taint from the vulgar men who call themselves by their names, and bedaub them with their flattery; their big manly voices shrink into childish treble.[67]

Obviously there always have been groups and movements in the Church which have aimed at bringing to light principles that had been neglected. Maurice was not foolish enough to deplore this; he welcomed it.[68] "The Spirit of God has guided them to the perception of particular truths, and these it is their province, their vocation, to maintain."[69]

[67]*Reasons for not joining a Party in the Church*, pp. 19 ff. Cp. *Kingdom of Christ* (Ev. ed.), II, 317 f.; *The Church a Family*, pp. 137 f.; and Mark Pattison's *Essays*, ed. by R. L. Nettleship (1889), II, 276 f.

[68]*E.g.*, see his appreciation of the initial work of the Evangelical and Catholic movements in England in *Methods of Supporting Protestantism*, pp. 6, 10.

[69]*Subscription No Bondage*, pp. 108 f. Cp. *Kingdom of Christ* (1838), I, 213.

But is it necessary for these groups or movements to be organized as parties? Later experience made Maurice pessimistic about this; it seemed that parties were inevitable and that his was bound to be a lonely role. "It may be good, here and there," he said in his farewell sermon at Vere Street, "to have a man who holds himself more aloof from every school and party, than it is perhaps possible or right for most to do, not because he wishes to see the faith of any one of them crushed or weakened, but because he believes there is a stronger faith, which they all profess, and which their hostilities are undermining. I feel keenly how difficult it is to maintain this ground without an appearance of arrogance."[70]

The appearance of arrogance would be less if more churchmen were trying to maintain that ground. It will be less difficult to maintain it, if the whole idea of parties in the Church is renounced, if men of principle will refuse to allow their principles to be degraded into party labels, and if they will be as eager to defend the right of other men to witness to the truths they see as they are on their own behalf. In this respect Maurice set a noble example. He was always ready to come to the defence of any unpopular group or individual in the Church that was being attacked by a temporarily dominant party. Thus he chivalrously defended R. D. Hampden against the Tractarians and W. G. Ward against the Evangelicals, although he agreed with neither.

May we not be more sanguine than he was about the inevitability of parties in the Church? Need we despair that through our Anglican experience of their bitter effects we may learn to abhor them? May we not believe that the idea of a Church Universal, which is the fact beneath our attempts to provide substitutes for it, will be welcomed, not only at last but *in via*, as the divine way of deliverance from all sects and parties?

[70]*Life of F. D. M.*, II, 595 f.

4

THE SACRAMENT OF
CONSTANT UNION

I was led to consider the meaning of this or-dinance of Baptism as a key to the nature of ordinances generally.—KINGDOM OF CHRIST (EV. ED.), I, 13.

Announce the Gospel, tell men that their Baptism is a reality and not a fiction.—THE PRAYER-BOOK AND THE LORD'S PRAYER, p. 7.

SINCE the subsidence of the Gorham controversy in the middle of the nineteenth century—which shed little fresh light upon the subject—the doctrine of baptism or Christian initiation has received hardly any considerable attention in Anglican theology, and I do not know that it has received much more elsewhere. During recent years, however, there have appeared what may be the first drops of a coming shower of fresh essays about it. *Magna opera* have yet to come, but there is already a substantial collection of Convocation Reports, review articles, pamphlets, and newspaper correspondences. Since I have been editor of the review *Theology*, I apprehend that more manuscripts have been submitted to me concerning this than any other theological topic.

The chief spur to this new interest, which is keenest among the younger parochial clergy, has been a practical one. The Church of England is waking up to the vast disproportion between the number of English citizens who are baptized in their infancy through its offices and the number who subsequently become in any degree active members of the Church. The problem presses most upon the parochial clergy in the large centres of population, because it is they who, as things are, are expected week by week to baptize infants about most of whom there is no reasonable assurance that they will be brought up as members of the Church. Thus the question is propounded whether the continuation of this custom is not turning the sacrament of baptism into a mockery or a superstition.

Wherever the parochial clergy foregather, the question of what is called "indiscriminate baptism" is being canvassed. Yet it is much easier to observe that the present custom is anomalous than to say what ought to be done to put it right. The newly fledged curate, upon his first encounter with the problem, may jump to the conclusion that the problem is quite simple and admits of a simple solution. What the Church of England must do, he may say, is to adopt the baptismal discipline of the Churches in the mission field, since England itself is now to all intents and purposes a mission field. None but the children of practising or communicant members of the Church should in future be baptized. This and similar things are often said, but little discernment is needed in order to see that the problem is more complicated. To call England a pagan country or a mission field does nothing to eliminate the profound difference between a pre-Christian and a post-Christian society. Any scheme for a strict, or even a rational, baptismal discipline for the Church of England is found upon investigation to involve the whole question of the Church's past, present and future relation to the national society, of which the question of "establishment" is only one aspect. In other words, the problem of what is to be done about baptism cannot be settled by itself. It will be possible to deal with it satisfactorily only as part of a general readjustment of the relations between the Church and society, and while this readjustment may be overdue there are few signs yet that the Church or the State or public opinion is ready for it.

But that is only one of the difficulties with which considering churchmen find themselves confronted when they begin to take Christian initiation seriously and cease to take it for granted. There is also a more definitely theological difficulty. The practical question about baptismal discipline can hardly be canvassed for long without some attention being given to the subject of baptismal doctrine. This is in fact what has happened in England, and the doctrinal question is in a fair way to putting the practical question in the shade for the nonce. For it is becoming apparent that there is an extraordinary diversity of belief in the Church about the meaning and effects of baptism and about its relation to the rite of confirmation. Moreover, disconcerting arrays of fact and theory are being produced[1] which seem to show that the history of the theology and practice of Christian initiation is compassed about with many confusions. I am not going here to participate in the various debates which have as yet only begun among our English divines, nor shall I try to anticipate the conclusions to which the Church may be led. From the present state of the discussion it looks as though it will be far from easy to reach any agreed conclusions.

The fact, however, that the whole subject is up for reconsideration may serve to win for Maurice's teaching about it a hearing which it did not receive in his own time. I will not say that his teaching cuts the ground from under much of the debate that is now proceeding; but it will, I think, be found to set much of it in a fresh light. Maurice was greatly occupied with the meaning of baptism. In view

[1]*E.g.*, see Gregory Dix, O. S. B., *The Theology of Confirmation in relation to Baptism* (1946); T. W. Manson, Art. on "Entry into Membership of the Early Church" in *The Journal of Theological Studies* (January-April, 1947), pp. 25–33.

of his convictions about the universal Headship of Christ
and the nature of the Church it was bound to be for him
a crucial question. It is a subject that had been forced
upon him in his youth by the controversies in his own
home, and by the circumstance that three of his sisters
underwent a second baptism under Baptist influences.[2]
Maurice himself also, though for different reasons, was rebaptized when he entered the Church of England.[3] In infancy he had been baptized by his father, who was a
Unitarian minister, but who used the Trinitarian formula.[4]
Maurice's motives in this case are not altogether clear, and
unfortunately the letter in which he explained them to one
of his sisters, and which is referred to in his biography, is
missing. But I presume he came to regard his father's baptism as baptism into a sect and not into the Church.[5] Anyhow, it is evident that his own experience impelled him
to give much more thought to the meaning of baptism
than most theologians are impelled to give.

[2]*Life of F. D. M.*, I, 20.

[3]*Ibid.*, I, 123. The biography does not say where this took
place. It was in the church of St. Mary Magdalen, Oxford. See
W. Tuckwell, *Reminiscences of Oxford* (1907), p. 89.

[4]*Life of F. D. M.*, I, 122.

[5]It appears that at this period doubts among Anglicans about
the validity of baptism in the dissenting sects, even when the
Trinitarian formula was used, were not uncommon. E. Clowes
Chorley in *Men and Movements in the American Episcopal
Church* (1946) tells of some Americans who were baptized in
England because they had "grave doubts whether baptism among
the Presbyterians was valid" (p. 135). Charles Kingsley uses the
expression "episcopally-baptized," which in its context implies
that High Churchmen were dubious about non-episcopalian baptism. See *Charles Kingsley: his letters and memories of his life*,
edited by his wife (1877), I, 254.

It is not without interest to note that Phillips Brooks, who was
in close sympathy with Maurice's teaching about baptism, had
also been baptized as an infant by a Unitarian minister who
used the Trinitarian formula, but that he did not follow Maurice's
example. The question came up at the time of his election to
the bishopric of Massachusetts, but he refused to be conditionally
rebaptized. See A. V. G. Allen, *Life and Letters of Phillips Brooks*
(1900), II, 848.

It is certain that Maurice had no doubts about the rightfulness of baptizing infants. He thought that in a Christian nation or in a Christian family men were bound to claim the rights and privileges of church membership for their children as well as for themselves. His teaching supposes that the baptism of infants is normal. It is sometimes supposed that because Christian initiation was originally received only or mainly by adults, and it is doubtful whether in the New Testament there is reliable evidence of the initiation of children, therefore infant baptism, however justifiable, entails a departure from what must be theologically normative. But it is equally possible, and perhaps more reasonable, to regard the New Testament period as in this respect abnormal and exceptional. Not until families and nations were Christian could Christian initiation assume its normal form. The Biblical testimony as a whole supplies no warrant for excluding children from church membership. On the contrary, the fact that infants were received into the old covenant by the rite of circumcision argues, unless there is some new principle to require their exclusion, that they ought also to be received into the new covenant.

There is indeed much doubt about what the exact form and sequence of the rite of Christian initiation in the New Testament period, and for some time after, actually were. All agree that water-baptism formed part of it, but whether it also invariably included the laying on of hands and/or anointing with oil is uncertain. It is also uncertain whether during this period a clear differentiation was made between the significance of the different parts of the rite, whether, for example, water-baptism was thought to signify the remission of sins and the new birth in sharp distinction from the laying on of hands or anointing which signified participation in the Holy Spirit. Theories about this may be confidently put forward, but their foundations are more or less conjectural, and there does not appear to be sufficient evidence available to support definite conclusions. May we not regard this as providential, and as designed to leave the Church free to adapt the form of the rite and to interpret its details in various ways—a freedom which in point of fact has been liberally exercised? Attempts sharply to separate the effects of Christian initiation, and to tie one effect to one part of the rite exclusively, may be consistent with certain types of sacramental doctrine, but it is another question whether they are consistent with the manner of God's gracious activity in His Church. The doctrine of concomitance as regards the eucharistic elements seems to be reasonable and a wholesome rebuke to scruples of this sort, however much Anglican divines in the past have felt themselves obliged to defend the necessity of communion in both kinds.

Maurice did not of course deal with this aspect of the matter, since the theories to which I have been alluding had not then been propounded. It was not until 1891 that A. J. Mason's *Relation of Confirmation to Baptism* was published which first called attention, though without much success, to this aspect of the problem. Maurice had no scruples in going to work with the teaching of the Book of Common Prayer that those who are baptized are sanctified and regenerated with the Holy Spirit and incorporated into the Church. He could have had no objection to any addition to the rite of baptism in the Church of England which would make it even more clear that this is its significance; but he would have objected absolutely to any interpretation of the rite which had the effect of denying that baptized infants were members of the Church and participated in the Holy Spirit. So much it seemed necessary to say in view of the controversies that have now arisen. We can proceed to consider what Maurice's teaching was about "the sacrament of constant union."

His teaching concerning the meaning of baptism is consistent with, and follows from, his interpretation of the

Gospel. The Gospel is the good news that mankind has been taken into communion with the ascended Christ. Christ is the universal Head of humanity, the Head of every man; every man is related to Christ, who is the Elder-Brother of all, whether or not he is conscious of and confesses the relationship. In Christ mankind is righteous; the sin of man is that he will not believe in this the true constitution of humanity and will not act upon it, but tries to set himself up in separate independence. Humanity which is made to be a Church is thus turned into a world. But the Church, which is the kingdom of Christ on earth, has been established; it is the universal society in which the blessings of the new covenant are received and confessed, whose outward signs and ordinances witness to the true state of mankind and bind its members together in the fellowship of the Holy Spirit.

Baptism is the first of these signs. It is the witness, the pledge, the assurance, to every man and to every child who receives it that he is a member of Christ, the child of God, and an inheritor of the kingdom of heaven. It is the sacrament of initiation into the new covenant. It is the enacted proclamation and assertion that what is true for mankind is true for this man and for that man. Maurice attached a high value to sacraments; he regarded them as the witness that men's union with God in Christ and their communion with one another in the Holy Spirit are grounded in God's grace and not in their belief. "Outward signs and tokens have a great worth. They attest the reality and the universality of God's gifts, as in the case of the water in baptism and the bread and wine in the Lord's Supper. They prevent men from fancying that their thoughts, and impressions, and beliefs, create the blessings which are bestowed upon us by God's free grace."[6] Ordinances are signs to the whole human race, signs of the existence of a universal body and of a universal kingdom; they are "indis-

[6]*Acts of the Apostles,* p. 188.

pensable in a higher sense than those dream of, who seem
to value them chiefly as means of exclusion; they are the
very voice in which God speaks to His creatures; the very
witness that their fellowship with each other rests on their
fellowship with Him, and both upon the mystery of His
Being."[7]

Baptism interprets to a man his true state,[8] the true law
of his being, and warns him of the power of evil that is
striving within him against the true law of his being.

> Baptism tells me that I am God's child, and may
> live as if I were; and that I have that within me
> which will not be subject to the law of God, which
> will not own Him as a Father, which will not have
> fellowship with any of my human brethren. This does
> not confound the evil with the good. It is a perpetual
> sign to me that God will not confound them, but will
> put all the width of heaven and hell between them.[9]

We should take our baptism and our children's baptism
"as a witness and pledge that our growth and theirs does
not depend ultimately upon us or them; that God's Holy
Spirit plants in us the first seeds of intelligence, of affection,
of belief; that He causes them to ripen; that He is nigh
at hand to destroy what is hindering them from springing
up and bearing fruit."[10] Baptism implies

> that God is the source and spring of all that is good
> in you; of the pricking in your hearts, of your re-
> pentance, of your faith, of every movement towards
> heaven now going on in you, or that has gone on in
> you at any time, of all moral and spiritual acts what-
> soever, of any kindly affection you have ever mani-

[7]*Kingdom of Christ* (Ev. ed.), I, 14.
[8]"The Baptismal Covenant . . . interprets our existence to us
. . . it interprets the condition of mankind."—*Lincoln's Inn Sermons*, V, 76.
[9]*Life of F. D. M.*, II, 242.
[10]*Acts of the Apostles*, p. 169.

fested towards a child or towards a parent, of every
wish and hope that has not been selfish and shameful.[11]

It is an act "for the remission of sins; which declares
that God puts them from you, that He does not treat you
as a servant, but as His child in Christ."[12] "By your baptism you have been admitted into the family of God; the
right of calling God your Father has been conferred upon
you; the right of believing that He has redeemed you and
reconciled you to Himself; the right of approaching Him
at all times and in all places through His well-beloved
Son."[13]

What Maurice was saying may become clearer if we
compare it with what seemed to him to be the teaching
about baptism of the two most vocal schools in the Church
at that time—orthodox Evangelicalism and Tractarianism.
The Evangelicals regarded baptism simply as admission
into the visible Church; the thing that really mattered happened when a man was converted, was consciously justified
by faith. It was then that he became a member of Christ
and a partaker of the Holy Spirit. Before that he was not
a child of God, unless it were in some vague and dubious
sense. "The Evangelical party say, if there be such a thing
as conversion, it cannot be that a man, previous to conversion, was a child of God, a member of Christ."[14] "If
men are not children of God," Maurice pointed out, "then
they have no right to confess their sins to God as their
Father; they have no right to believe that He pardons them
their sins for Christ's sake. If they are not children of God,
all their prayers, thanksgivings, adorations, confessions, are
downright mockery."[15] He spoke severely of those who
tried to escape from this difficulty by saying that all men
are in a certain sense, though not in the full sense, God's

[11]*The Church a Family*, p. 29.
[12]*Ibid.*, p. 29.
[13]*Christmas Day*, p. 26.
[14]*Kingdom of Christ* (1838), I, 83.   [15]*Ibid.*, I, 116.

children. "How commonly do we say, 'Oh, yes; in a general sense, all of us are God's children.' That general sense is *no* sense. The word 'children' is used to signify *creatures*. We say men are His, as we say the cattle are His."[16]

The Evangelicals were uneasy with the language of the baptism service and the Catechism in the Prayer-Book on account of its assertion of baptismal regeneration, etc.[17] Against them Maurice cited Luther, and quoted passages from his sermons which affirmed that justification by faith was grounded on baptismal regeneration.[18] To the Evangelicals Maurice summarized his own teaching as follows:

> I have maintained that Christ, by whom, and for whom all things were created, and in whom all things consist, has made reconciliation for mankind; that on the ground of this atonement for mankind, God has built His church, declaring men one family in Christ; inviting all men to consider themselves so; assuring them that only in Christ they are or can be one family; that separate from Him they must be separate from each other. Therefore we, believing there is such an atonement, and that such a declaration has gone forth, and that it is a sin for men to account themselves separate from Christ, and separate from each other, when God has, by such a wonderful act, declared them to be one body in Him; and believing that the mark of that universal body or fellowship, appointed by God Himself, is Baptism, do, without fear or scruple, asseverate of ourselves, and of all others who will come to this holy Baptism, of all who bear the marks and impress of that nature which Christ took, in His birth, of the blessed Virgin; that they are admitted into these high and glorious privileges; that they are brought into a state of salvation; that they are made sons of God

[16]*Gospel of St. John*, p. 249.
[17]*E.g.*, see J. T. Holloway, *Baptismal Regeneration and Sacramental Justification not the Doctrine of the English Church* (1842), pp. 69–76.
[18]See *Kingdom of Christ* (1838), I, 84–87, and (Ev. ed.), I, 277.

and heirs of everlasting life; and that for this they are
to give thanks to God unceasingly, and to look to Him
who has introduced them to such a dignity to keep
them in it even to the end. And in saying this, we
contend that we give honour to the free grace and
redemption of God; that we give faith, the faith of the
child, the faith of the boy, the faith of the man, a
ground upon which to stand, and which otherwise it
cannot have.[19]

The Evangelicals, he said, had got hold of the true principle that men could be children of God and reconciled
to the Father only *in Christ*. Their mistake lay in supposing
that men's relation to Christ depended on their consciousness of it or their belief in it. Children have been rightly
taught that

the Absolute and Eternal God has taken them to be His
own children, the members of Christ, the inheritors of
the Kingdom of Heaven. Surely that old English education is based not upon notions, but upon the assumption that we are actually united to the Father of all
in His Son; that He is actually guiding us by His
Spirit to a consciousness of our wants; at last, to a
knowledge of Him who is the satisfier of them. Such
education assumes an actual relation to be the ground
of all consciousness of it; an Actual and Living Being
to be the ground of the relation. That assumption
brings our common human life into harmony with
our life as connected with the Kingdom of Heaven;
each illustrates the other. The relation to the father
and the mother precedes all consciousness of it; the
father and the mother have a life of their own, besides their relation to us.[20]

[19] *Ibid.* (1838), I, 88 f. See the whole passage.
[20] *What is Revelation?*, p. 390. Cp. *Gospel of St. John*, p. 99,
where, commenting on John III, 18–21, Maurice says:
"Our Lord's words . . . show that our consciousness is not in
any sense the foundation of God's kingdom, that His Love is
the foundation of it. They make us understand that the revela-

Maurice had welcomed the reassertion of the Catholic doctrine of the Church and sacraments by the Tractarians. In 1843 in an open letter to Lord Ashley, protesting against "a certain proposed measure for stifling the expression of opinion in the University of Oxford," he said:

> I am bound to express my conviction, though I may seem to be uttering a paradox, that the Catholic movement which has taken place in this university within the last ten or twelve years was not a movement towards formalism but away from it. It arose, I believe, from a strong and deep feeling, that if forms exist at all they must have a meaning in them, otherwise they are shams and delusions. They did exist; by the Evangelical party they were regarded as useful accessories to personal devotion, in Oxford (*i.e.*, before the Tractarian movement) they were regarded with antiquarian and traditional homage. The acknowledgement of them, as possessing present worth, as being the witnesses of an actual connection between man and the invisible world, of an actual fellowship between man and man, was wanting to both.
>
> To recover this conviction was to recover that which is the great principle of a social faith, the principle that we exist in a permanent communion which was not created by human hands, and cannot be destroyed by them.[21]

---

tion of that Love is in very deed the reconciliation and regeneration of the world; that we may claim all as included in that reconciliation and regeneration; that our baptism of water and the Spirit, while it gives all warrant for conscious repentance and faith, must comprehend the unconscious, must declare upon what their consciousness is to stand. They *are* sons of God. God's Spirit is given them, that they may grow into the knowledge of their sonship, that they may be able to live in conformity with it."

[21]*Methods of Supporting Protestantism*, p. 10. Cp. *Life of F. D. M.*, I, 236: "The new form of churchmanship which was set forth in the Oxford Tracts had so far an attraction for me that it appeared to treat of a regeneration as dependent on the will of God and the death of Christ, not the individual faith of men." See also *Kingdom of Christ* (Ev. ed.), II, 310.

It was Pusey's Tract of Baptism[22] that opened Maurice's eyes to the fact that he could not go along with the Tractarians. For it seemed to him that Pusey's teaching, so far from acknowledging baptism as the witness to a permanent communion between God and man, made out that baptism was an instantaneous event which took a man out of his relation to Adam and made him a member of Christ. But this relation to Christ was not permanent; it was severed by post-baptismal sin. The teaching of the Tractarians struck Maurice thus:

> They, looking at Baptism as an act done in an instant, and accomplishing its purpose in an instant, and not rather as the witness of an eternal truth, the sacrament of constant union, the assurance of a continual living presence, are driven to this conclusion—that the moment after it has been performed is a period of ideal purity and excellence, from which the future life even of a saint is a deflection, and which those who have wandered far into sin cannot hope to recover;—these must be content, by much prayer and fasting, to seek for God's mercy, which may perhaps, though there is no certain promise to uphold the flattering expectation, once again redeem them out of sin and hell.[23]

The nerve of his mission as a minister of the Gospel would be cut by teaching such as this, Maurice thought.

> Where is the minister of Christ in London, Birmingham, or Manchester, whom such a doctrine, heartily and inwardly entertained, would not drive to madness? He is sent to preach the Gospel. What Gospel? Of all the thousands whom he addresses, he cannot venture to believe that there are ten who, in Dr. Pusey's sense,

[22]Tracts for the Times, No. 67. Published in 1835. In a second edition this tract was expanded into a treatise, and it is in this form that it is included in most editions of the Tracts for the Times. It was the first edition which made the profound impression on Maurice.

[23]Kingdom of Christ (1838), I, 96 f.

retain their baptismal purity. All he can do, therefore, is to tell wretched creatures, who spend eighteen hours out of the twenty-four in close factories and bitter toil, corrupting and being corrupted, that if they spend the remaining six in prayer—he need not add fasting—they may possibly be saved. How can we insult God and torment man with such mockery?[24]

Not so had Maurice read the teaching of Prayer-Book when ministering in his country curacy or as Chaplain of Guy's Hospital.

> I had been much impressed in my Bubbenhall curacy among labourers and farmers; I was still more impressed in the midst of this London population of sick men and women, with the language of our Catechism—that language which caused most offence to the Evangelical school. It seemed to me that except I could address all kinds of people as members of Christ and children of God, I could not address them at all. Their sin, it seemed to me, must mean a departure from that state; it must be their true state, that which Christ had claimed for them. I thought I had no Gospel for the sufferers in Guy's Hospital, if it was not that.[25]

Maurice alleged that "change of nature" expressed Pusey's teaching about the effect of baptism.[26] Pusey privately pointed out to him that he had not used that expression,[27] and anyhow Pusey and Maurice would not use the term "nature" in the same sense, and there was little prospect of their understanding one another.[28] The

[24]*Ibid.*, I, 97. Cp. Ev. ed., II, 321.
[25]*Life of F. D. M.*, I, 236.
[26]See *Kingdom of Christ* (1838), I, 92. On p. 175 Maurice says that he had not meant that the words "change of nature" were used by Pusey.
[27]*Life of F. D. M.*, I, 214.
[28]On the ambiguity of the term "natural" in this connexion, see *Theological Essays*, p. 232. See also the later correspondence between Maurice and Pusey in *The Times* newspaper, which is

point of Maurice's objection may be gathered from the
following passage:

> A man does not . . . by Baptism, by faith, or by
> any other process, acquire a new nature, if by nature
> you mean, as most men do, certain inherent qualities
> and properties. He does not by Baptism, faith, or by
> any other process, become a new creature, if by these
> words you mean anything else than that he is created
> anew in Christ Jesus, that he is grafted into Him, that
> he becomes the inheritor of His life and not of his
> own. That, being so grafted, he receives the Spirit of
> Christ, I of course believe. But I contend that the
> operation of this Spirit upon him is to draw him con-
> tinually out of himself, to teach him to disclaim all
> independent virtue, to bring him into the knowledge
> and image of the Father and the Son.[29]

His point is that baptism should be thought of as drawing a man into the new creation which is his true state,
not as imparting something to him as a separate individual.
It does not mean that an individual, considered in himself,
acquires a separate portion of grace. For the work of the
Holy Spirit is always to bring a man out of separation
into union; it is to bring him into relationship with God
and into communion with Christ, to sustain and build him
up in that relationship, which is the ground of his being.

> If Baptism . . . gives one and another the filial
> name and the filial privilege, it does so because Christ
> had first vindicated that name and those privileges for
> all human beings, by taking their flesh. It cannot do
> less or more than the charter from which it derives its
> force authorizes it to do. It can confer no separate or

---

reproduced in H. P. Liddon, *Life of E. B. Pusey*[2] (1897), IV, 57–
62. There is a paper by Maurice "On the Words 'Nature,' 'Natural,' and 'Supernatural' " in the Metaphysical Society's Papers
(privately printed), November 21, 1871, which however leaves
off just when it is becoming interesting.
   [29]*Kingdom of Christ* (Ev. ed.), I, 289.

independent grace upon any creature. It can only say: "Thou belongest to the Head of thy race; thou art a member of His body; thou dost not merely carry about with thee that divided nature which thou hast inherited from the first Adam—a nature doomed to death, with death stamped upon it—thou hast the nature of the Divine Son, thou art united to Him in whom is life, and from whom the life of thee and of all creatures comes."[30]

"Every person and every thing is good when it is taken into relation and union with God; every person and every thing is evil out of that relation. . . . The very word Sacrament would assert the principle; in its most general sense it is whatever God uses as an expression of His relation to the creature."[31] It seemed to Maurice that the Tractarians, like the Romanists, made sacraments transitory, and treated grace as a thing or property which could be imparted and lost and imparted again instead of as an enduring personal relationship, although he acknowledged that the two ideas had been present in Catholic theology side by side from early days. "Whenever any great spiritual principle has been strongly revealed to men, a material counterfeit of that principle has always appeared also . . . they have dwelt together in the minds of the best and wisest men."[32] In this case, according to the material counterfeit,

it is supposed that the man acquires something for himself in the instant of Baptism, that *he* is endowed with heavenly virtues, that he is in himself, separately considered, a new creature. By this opinion the Romanist supposes that he exalts Baptism. He seems to me utterly to degrade it and rob it of its meaning. He turns a *sacrament* into an *event*. He supposes the re-

[30]*Lincoln's Inn Sermons*, I, 81.
[31]*Epistle to the Hebrews*, p. cxv.
[32]*Kingdom of Christ* (Ev. ed.), I, 292. Cp. *Epistle to the Hebrews*, pp. cxv f.

demption of Christ to be exhausted by a certain gift, while the Bible represents it as bringing men into an eternal and indissoluble relationship. . . . He makes it appear that the blessing of Baptism is not this, that it receives men into the holy Communion of Saints, but that it bestows upon them certain individual blessings, endows them with a certain individual holiness.[33]

Baptism is a sacrament of constant union not only with God but with the whole people of God.

Baptism asserts for each man that he is taken into union with a Divine Person, and by virtue of that union is emancipated from his evil *Nature*. But this assertion rests upon another, that there is a society for mankind which is constituted and held together in that Person, and that he who enters this society is emancipated from the *World*—the society which is bound together in the acknowledgement of, and subjection to, the evil selfish tendencies of each man's nature. But, further, it affirms that this unity among men rests upon a yet more awful and perfect unity, upon that which is expressed in the *Name* of the Father, the Son, and the Holy Ghost. Lose sight of this last and deepest principle, and both the others perish.[34]

Maurice applauded the Tractarians for bringing out the social meaning of the sacrament, but they did not go far enough. They interpreted the witness of the sacrament in an exclusive manner, as though it asserted that those who were not baptized were not members of Christ, as though Christians were sons of God *only* because they were baptized men, and as though their sonship was a sentence upon all the world before them and around them.[35] Whereas, this is what ought to be said:

We tell all men, those who are most incredulous

[33]*Kingdom of Christ* (Ev. ed.), I, 290 f.
[34]*Ibid.*, I, 284.
[35]See *Gospel of St. John*, p. 13.

of our message, most hostile to it, that this Name is about them, that they are living, moving, having their being in it. They do not acquire this privilege by baptism; we baptize them because they have it.[36]

Those who are baptized into the Name of the Father and of the Son and of the Holy Ghost become the heralds of a common life and a divine kingdom to all nations.[37]

Our baptism is the simplest and fullest witness of a redemption which covers and comprehends those who are not baptised.[38]

The language which is true for all men is true in the highest sense for the baptized. They are witnesses to all men how true it is. Their profession solemnly declares that there is no light in any human being but what comes to him from Christ, the Head and Lord of Man.[39]

Maurice's interpretation of the meaning of baptism was not peculiar to himself, though, even if we leave out of account the Evangelical and Tractarian parties, it was not common in the Church at the time; that is to say, it was not explicitly taught. Maurice would be the first to allow, and to give thanks, that many churchmen acted upon an interpretation of the meaning of the sacrament which they did not formally profess. We may note, however, that F. W. Robertson and Phillips Brooks, who were, I suppose, the two greatest Anglican preachers of the nineteenth century, were both perfectly explicit and emphatic in the same sense as Maurice. Baptism, said Robertson,

is an authoritative symbol of an eternal fact; a truth of eternity realised in time, and brought down to the limits of the "then and there"; then and there made

[36]*Conflict of Good and Evil,* p. 179.

[37]*Prophets and Kings,* p. 444. Cp. *Hope for Mankind,* pp. 73 f.
[38]Art. on "The Revision of the Prayer Book and the Act of Uniformity" in *Macmillan's Magazine* (April, 1860), p. 424.
[39]See *Lincoln's Inn Sermons,* III. 150.

God's child: but it is only the realisation of a fact true before baptism, and without baptism: the personal realisation of a fact which belongs to all humanity, and was revealed by Christ; in other words, it is redemption applied.[40]

The Christian Church, said Phillips Brooks,

is the body of redeemed humanity. It is man in his deepest interests, in his spiritual possibilities. It is the under life, the sacred, the profounder life of man, his regeneration. Every human being in very virtue of birth into the redeemed world is a potential member of the Christian Church. His baptism claims and asserts his membership. . . .

I cannot think, I will not think, about the Christian Church as if it were a selection out of humanity. In its idea it is humanity.[41]

In the course of one of his sermons on baptism, the teaching of which closely harmonizes with Maurice's teaching, Robertson makes use of an illuminating comparison.

The Catechism . . . says: In baptism . . . I was *made* a child of God. Yes; coronation makes a sovereign; but, paradoxical as it may seem, it can only *make* one a sovereign who is a sovereign already. Crown a pretender, that coronation will not make a king. Coronation is the authoritative act of the nation *declaring* a fact which was fact before. And ever after,

---

[40]*Life and Letters of F. W. Robertson,* ed. by Stopford A. Brooke (1901), II, 62. See the whole passage and also *ibid.,* I, 329–36 and II, 288 ff. Christ, said Robertson, "was Humanity, and in Him alone my Humanity becomes intelligible" (*ibid.,* II, 36). "God's *idea* of Humanity is, and ever was, Humanity as it is in Jesus Christ" (*ibid.,* II, 113). "A man, as man, is the child of God" (*ibid.,* I, 164). Stopford Brooke says that Robertson "has been called a follower of Mr. Maurice; but though holding Mr. Maurice in veneration, he differed on many and important points from both him and Mr. Kingsley" (*ibid.,* I, 137; see also II, 181).

[41]A. V. G. Allen, *Life and Letters of Phillips Brooks* (1900), II, 625.

coronation is the event to which all dates back—and the crown is the expression used for all royal acts. . . .

Similarly with baptism. Baptism makes a child of God in the sense in which coronation makes a king. And baptism naturally stands in Scripture for the title of regeneration and the moment of it. Only what coronation is in an earthly way, an authoritative manifestation of an invisible earthly truth, baptism is in a heavenly way. God's authoritative declaration in material form of a spiritual reality. In other words, no bare sign, but a Divine Sacrament.[42]

What then is the meaning of regeneration? It certainly cannot mean just what, according to Maurice, the Evangelicals or the Tractarians took it to mean, though he would say that it asserts the ground of the principle with which each party was concerned. It appears that much of the controversy about regeneration since the Reformation has been the result of the use of the word in at least two different senses. W. F. Hook pointed this out.

Regeneration (he said) was the term applied to baptism by all the Fathers; by every writer, I believe, till the Reformation, and it was used to denote, not the final triumph of grace over the heart, but the primary operations of the Spirit in the scheme of man's redemption. The Puritans used the term to signify the final triumph of grace over the heart; and then, giving a new meaning to the term, abused the · Church for using the word in the old sense.[43]

But the regeneration that Maurice always had in mind[44]

[42]*Sermons by F. W. Robertson* (second series, 1898 ed.), pp. 56 f. See the whole of this and the following sermon.
[43]See W. R. W. Stephens, *The Life and Letters of W. F. Hook* (1878), I, 267. On the confusion between regeneration and conversion, cp. *Memorials from Journals and Letters of Samuel Clark*, ed. by his wife (1878), pp. 322–25.
[44]See *Kingdom of Christ* (1838), I, 176. Christ is "the Regenerator of Humanity": *Theological Essays*, pp. 231, 233 ff., 241; *Commandments*, p. 93.

was that of the race by the finished work of Christ, the regeneration of mankind which was the ground both of the regeneration claimed and asserted for each man in baptism and of justifying faith and final sanctification. Regeneration means "the renovation or restitution of that which has fallen into decay, the repair of an edifice according to the ground-plan and design of the original architect," not "the substitution in certain persons, at some given moment (say in the ordinance of Baptism, or at a crisis called conversion), of a nature specially bestowed on them, for the one which belongs to them as ordinary human beings."[45]

Maurice was quite prepared to say that a man "is made by Baptism a member of Christ, a child of God, an inheritor of the Kingdom of Heaven"[46] and to defend this language, pertinaciously if obscurely, to Kingsley, who had misgivings about it.[47] But it must be confessed that R. H. Hutton had some reason for complaining that he interpreted the language in a non-natural sense,[48] if by "non-natural" is meant a sense somewhat different from, or at any rate not explicit in, that in the minds of its framers and that generally understood. Maurice clung to the language because it asserted what he believed to be the true ground of regeneration against the teaching of the Evangelicals. It would have been better if he had allowed that it did not express altogether satisfactorily what he himself took it to mean. To express his meaning stronger, not weaker, more universal, not narrower, language, would be needed.

In his preaching and teaching Maurice usually avoided the expression "made a child of God in baptism," and preferred other expressions, such as the following.

Your baptism proclaims you to be the sons of God.[49]

[45]*Theological Essays*, pp. 224 f.
[46]*The Prayer-Book and the Lord's Prayer*, p. 151.
[47]See *Life of F. D. M.*, II, 271–75.
[48]*Criticisms on Contemporary Thought and Thinkers* (1894), p. 87.   [49]*Christmas Day*, p. 96.

This is the good news which your baptism preaches to you, and which we on the warrant of your baptism declare to you, that God has adopted you to be His children.[50]

The baptism by which we are admitted members of Christ.[51]

Baptism is the sign that men and women and children of all countries are adopted into one family, are sealed with the name of the Father, and the Son, and the Holy Ghost.[52]

Our baptism was in very deed the witness to us that we are one and all citizens of the New Jerusalem.[53]

'Christ has a kingdom upon earth . . . an *universal* kingdom . . . of which we may register our children citizens before they exhibit one sign of intelligence or grace, and . . . in doing so we render homage to the finished work of Christ.[54]

By your baptism God hath given you a portion in Him who was made flesh.[55]

Each of us is baptized as a sign that his life is not in himself but in Christ, and Christ gives us His Holy Spirit in baptism to testify that we are united to Him, and are the sons of God in Him, and have power to do the work He gives us to do.[56]

When we were baptized He who breaks asunder the bonds of the captive, chose us as His redeemed children . . . then and there we were sacrificed to Him and signed with the sign of sacrifice.[57]

This is the covenant into which we are born by

[50]*Ibid.*, p. 53. Cp. *Lincoln's Inn Sermons*, V, 76.

[51]*Christmas Day*, p. 292.

[52]*Epistle to the Hebrews*, p. 9. Cp. *The Prayer-Book and the Lord's Prayer*, p. 230.

[53]*Apocalypse*, p. 418. Cp. *Lincoln's Inn Sermons*, IV, 36.

[54]*Christmas Day*, p. 73.

[55]*Ibid.*, p. 15. Cp. *ibid.*, p. 287: "He to whom I was bound in infancy by the solemn sacrament of Baptism, who took me then to be a member of His body, who bestowed upon me His Spirit. . . ."

[56]*Ibid.*, p. 222.

[57]*Doctrine of Sacrifice*, p. 63. Cp. *ibid.*, pp. 223 f.

our baptism. . . . Do we believe that God has said to us, "I will put my laws in your hearts, etc."?[58]

By the simple outward rite of Baptism, God has claimed us all for His spiritual children.[59]

By Baptism we claim the position which Christ has claimed for all mankind.[60]

We do not set aside election; our Baptism is the witness for it. By it we refer all things to God. We testify that He chooses without reference to their previous wants or behaviour, and that all gifts and graces come from Him.[61]

Baptism . . . was the most beautiful and broad testimony of their adoption—of their being clean and pure by being grafted upon the true root—of the new and divine well of life within them.[62]

We want to have this name, "Child of God," marked upon each infant before he can speak or think or know what it means. We want to be told that the names by which we are called by our friends and schoolmates betoken God's adoption. We want it to be so wrought into our confessions that we shall feel our sin consists in forgetting it, that we are only delivered from our sin by remembering it.[63]

I am to assure those who hear me that their baptism means that they may be possessed by this civilizing, reconciling, uniting Spirit, that they need not be possessed by any other.[64]

It is evident that Maurice would have died in the last ditch, and would have us die in the last ditch, against the imposition of any doctrine which refuses to acknowledge

[58]*Prophets and Kings*, p. 429. Cp. *Christmas Day*, p. 285; *Sermons preached in Country Churches*, p. 270.

[59]*Lincoln's Inn Sermons*, II, 343.

[60]*Life of F. D. M.*, I, 182. Cp. *Christmas Day*, pp. 51, 70; *Sermons preached in Country Churches*, p. 281.

[61]*Life of F. D. M.*, I, 376.

[62]*Ecclesiastical History*, p. 323. Cp. *Acts of the Apostles*, p. 26.

[63]*Faith of the Liturgy*, p. 13.

[64]*Conflict of Good and Evil*, p. 203.

that baptized children receive and are indwelt by the Holy Spirit. He naturally attached great importance to the duty of all who have to do with baptized children to cooperate with the Holy Spirit in their education, and he was far from making light of confirmation. Baptism is the sacrament of constant union, and the Church is the society in which this union is realized and gradually comes to fruition. There would be danger in asserting men to be sons of God if the further message were suppressed "that He who claimed them as sons and accepted them as pure and righteous in the only-begotten Son, took them under His education and gave them His Spirit, to make them aware of their parentage and to destroy whatever in them was inconsistent with it."[65] Because baptized children are members of the Church they "have a right to be educated or admitted into an apprehension of this state, and of all that is implied in it."[66]

Confirmation is an act which carries out and fulfils the intention of baptism. It shows that baptism imports a spiritual relation, which so far from belonging to a single moment of our existence, "should stretch its power and mystery to cover the whole of it."[67] It is a distinct acknowledgment of the truth that there must be a conscious and voluntary recognition of our church-membership.[68] Confirmation does not make baptism more complete, but shows how complete it is.[69] In confirmation the great Father owns those whom He has regenerated, as His children, "taking them out of the hands of subordinate teachers into His own immediate service, enduing them with the powers necessary for that service."[70]

In baptism you treat the child as a spiritual crea-

[65] *Lincoln's Inn Sermons*, V, 76.
[66] *Lectures on National Education*, p. 262.
[67] *The Church a Family*, p. 76.
[68] See *Subscription No Bondage*, pp. 112 f.
[69] See *The Church a Family*, p. 77.
[70] *Ibid.*, p. 81.

8

ture, because you know that it is one. It has none of
the signs or energies of a spiritual creature, as it has
very few of the signs and energies of an animal creature. Nevertheless, you are certain of the fact, and
you put it into that position in God's covenant, which
is alone consistent with such a fact. You believe that
it is now under the government of God's Spirit; every
faculty and energy awakened in it, you believe is
awakened by His power and operation; every thing
that is not sin and death, you believe to be His gift.
But there comes a time, when the child becomes *conscious* of these spiritual powers, when it not only feels
and thinks, but begins to know that it feels and thinks.
This is a wonderful crisis in education—woe to your
child if you do not mark it, woe to him if you too
eagerly anticipate it. . . . Now the Church seizes this
time of consciousness—this awful moment, when the
mystery of our own personality first begins to scare
and confound us—when there is a dim perception of
responsibilities, and a struggling of the sinful nature
. . . —then, I say, does the Church meet us with her
service of confirmation, tells us that these responsibilities are really ours, that these struggles of the sinful
nature must be overcome, and that the duties may
be discharged, the victory may be won; because the
hope is no dream—because the Spirit who took the
charge of us in childhood, who has been Himself
educating us to behold the light which now seems to
rush in upon us with such blinding power, will be
with us—not as heretofore the watchful nurse over
thoughts yet unborn, hovering over the waters before
the firm earth had yet been parted from them, before
the period of form and distinction had arrived, but
henceforth the awful friend, and companion, and
fellow-worker, the witness with our spirits that we are
the sons of God.[71]

[71]*Kingdom of Christ* (1838), I, 120 f. Cp. *Lincoln's Inn Sermons,* I, 89:

"We are children of God; Christ, by taking our nature, has

If parents, parish priests and teachers want to know
what explanation of the meaning of baptism Maurice would
have them give, I know of no better or simpler example
than a sermon which Hort preached to his parishioners
at Hitchin in 1867. In this matter he had been directly
influenced by Maurice.[72] Here are some extracts from it.
Having considered baptism as the entrance into the Church,
the preacher continues:

> Now we have to consider how baptism is the act of
> God and God alone. . . . By baptism God declares
> us to be His children. Our first birth by which we
> come into the world is like that of other creatures.
> If we were to take our thoughts of ourselves from
> that, we should have to call ourselves only a higher
> kind of animal. God has taught us otherwise. By send-
> ing from heaven His blessed Son to take our nature,
> He has bidden us believe that we have more to do
> with Him than with any lower creature, He has taught
> us to say "Our Father," and to believe that we are
> indeed His children. This glorious message is declared
> to us all in the Bible, and repeated in different ways
> all through the Prayer Book. But He has further
> ordained a certain pledge by which each man may
> assure himself that he has a right to say, "I am a
> child of God"; and that pledge is baptism. Baptism
> is not a conjuring trick by which something starts
> into being within the child which was not there be-
> fore. . . . God by it formally acknowledges the child
> as His own, gives him by it a right and title to enter

assured that title to us. It depends on no accidents; it rests not
upon any condition of our feelings. And because we are children,
God has sent forth His Spirit that we may call Him Father, and
that we may do the acts of children. The Spirit is the last great
gift to our race; the gift to it, not in its unconscious infancy,
but in its full ripe manhood. That Spirit was given that we
might know the treasures which God has freely given us—the
treasures of His own Nature."

See also *Life of F. D. M.*, II, 353; *Faith of the Liturgy*, p. 19.
[72]See A. F. Hort, *Life and Letters of F. J. A. Hort* (1896), I, 67.

on all the benefits which belong to His children. . . .

This . . . is no empty benefit. Those who will not trust the assurance which God gave them in their baptism are obliged to think that they can make themselves His children by some efforts of their own. They dare not call themselves by that happy name till they find in themselves a certain measure of faith, or certain changes of feeling, about which it is most easy to be deceived. . . . To trust to the mere baptism itself, as if it had any power of its own, would be a dangerous folly. But to trust the promises of God, as brought home to ourselves by His holy baptism, is for most of us the highest wisdom.[73]

But let Maurice himself have the last word.

Infant Baptism . . . has been a witness for the Son of Man and the universality of His kingdom, like no other. It has taught parents that to bring children into the world is not a horrible crime. It has led them to see Christ and His redemption of humanity through all the mists of our teachings and our qualifications. It has explained the nature of His Kingdom to the hearts of the poorest. Christ has preached at the fonts, when we have been darkening counsel in pulpits.[74]

[73] F. J. A. Hort, *Cambridge and Other Sermons* (1898), pp. 89 ff.
[74] *Kingdom of Heaven*, p. 282.

5

OTHER SIGNS OF
THE KINGDOM OF CHRIST

If you ask us, "Where are the signs of this kingdom? what are the proofs of its establishment on the earth?" we answer you boldly, every church that you see around you—every baptism to which you bring your children—every sacrament by which you bind yourself, and by which you see others binding themselves, to the Head and Lord of the whole body, is a witness of its establishment.—CHRISTMAS DAY, p. 71.

A universal Church is found existing, acknowledging the Trinity, acknowledging the Atonement as the foundations of its being. These great truths are expressed in Sacraments; their relation to the constitution of the Church and of society gradually unveiled in the written word; their meaning interpreted to the people, by a ministry connecting one generation with another; their meaning expressed in various acts of allegiance, and offices of thanksgiving, intercession, communion.—KINGDOM OF CHRIST (1838), I, 58.

BAPTISM, according to Maurice, is "the sign of admission into a Spiritual and Universal Kingdom, grounded upon our Lord's incarnation, and ultimately resting upon the name of the Father, the Son, and the Holy Spirit."[1] In this chapter we are to consider his teaching about other signs of the kingdom of Christ—the creed, forms of worship, the eucharist, and the ministry, reserving the Scriptures for the next chapter. They are essential signs and necessary safeguards of the Church's existence, which have been preserved to men by the providence of God, and which each generation of her children is bound to watch over.[2] "The principle of the Catholic Church . . . is the principle of a direct, real, and practical union between men and their Lord,"[3] and these signs are witnesses to that union, instruments through which it is expressed and realized. By them God "intended the being and life of His Church to be sustained through all times."[4] "That which ordinances serve for is to take truths out of the world of abstractions and bring them in contact with human creatures; to make men understand the exceeding truthfulness of truth by seeing it brought to bear upon all their untruthfulness and inconsistencies."[5]

1. The Creeds

"There is actually found at this present day," Maurice says, "in every Christian country, a certain document called a Creed. It is not necessary to inquire minutely at what time it was formed. Let it be admitted that there is an obscurity over its origin. . . . It is substantially what it was, to say the very least, sixteen hundred years ago. Dur-

[1] *Kingdom of Christ* (Ev. ed.), II, 1.
[2] See *ibid.*, II, 14.
[3] *Ibid.*, II, 132.
[4] *Ibid.* (1838), I, 204.
[5] *Life of F. D. M.*, I, 261.

ing that time it has not been lying hid in the closet of some antiquarian. It has been repeated by peasants and children of the different lands into which it has come. It has been given to them as a record of facts with which they have as much to do as any noble. . . . The most earnest and thoughtful men in different countries, different periods, different stages of civilisation, have felt that it connected itself with the most permanent part of their being, that it had to do with each of them personally, and that it was the symbol of that humanity which they shared with their brethren."[6]

It is closely linked with baptism, and with good reason. By the act of baptism we are proclaimed to be spiritual creatures, united to a spiritual Being; by the act of saying the creed, "we claim our spiritual position, we assert our union with that being. The name into which we are adopted there, is the name we confess here."[7] Baptism is the sign to us that we are saved by grace, by "a cognizance taken of the creature by the Creator." The creed is the sign to us that we are saved by faith. The position of union and fellowship with one another is freely given, and the power is given wherewith to claim it; the creed is given to us in order to enable us to make that claim.

We are baptized into the Name of the Father, the Son, and the Holy Ghost. The creed is the confession of the same Name. It is not a digest of doctrines or a summary of religious opinions. It is an act of allegiance or affiance to a Person.

A man is speaking in it. The form of it is, I believe. That which is believed in is not a scheme of divinity, but a name—a Father, who has made the heaven and the earth: His Son, our Lord, who has been conceived, born, and died, and been buried, and gone down into hell, who has ascended, and is at the right hand of

[6]*Kingdom of Christ* (Ev. ed.), II, 3 f.
[7]*Ibid.,* II, 5.

God, who will come to judge the world: a Holy Spirit who has established a holy universal Church, who makes men a communion of saints, who is the witness and power whereby they receive forgiveness of sins, who shall quicken their mortal bodies, who enables them to receive everlasting life.[8]

We are not to think of the Divine Name as a doctrine which we hold, but as a reality which upholds us.[9] That is what we confess when we say the creed. "The *Name* denotes that which a Person is in Himself, His own character."[10] Whereas on the one hand "every gross and cruel superstition has this origin and definition: it springs from ignorance of the name of God,"[11] so on the other hand the Name of the Father, the Son, and the Holy Ghost is "the complete Revelation of the Lord of Peace, the fulfilment of that idea of God which prophets and lawgivers had been unfolding, the reconciliation of all those different, separate names by which heathens had striven to explain the divine operations in Nature, the perplexing testimonies of their own hearts."[12] The creed is thus our deliverance from partial ideas of God, and from dependence on particular systems of doctrine, whether religious or philosophical. "Starting from the most opposite points, engaged in the most dissimilar occupations, holding what seemed to be quite irreconcilable opinions," men may find "in that Name into which we are baptized, the reconciliation, the σύνδεσμος of their most inward and radical convictions, the deliverance from the intellectual dogmas which had kept them asunder."[13]

Can this be said of the Nicene, as well as of the Apostles', Creed? Yes, certainly, Maurice answers. "The *Nicene Creed*

[8]*Ibid.*, II, 4 f. Cp. *Sequel to the Inquiry*, pp. 231 f.
[9]See *Moral and Metaphysical Philosophy*, I, 522.
[10]*The Prayer-Book and the Lord's Prayer*, p. 319.
[11]*Ibid.*, p. 296.
[12]*Lincoln's Inn Sermons*, V, 284 f.
[13]*Ibid.*, II, 143. Cp. *What is Revelation?*, pp. 374 f.

agrees with the Apostles' altogether in its form and principle. It is still *I believe;* it is still belief in a name, and
not in notions. It differs in this, that it unites with a
declaration of the Divine relations to men, a declaration
of the relations in the Godhead."[14] The fact that every
churchman is taught to say this creed is a sign that the
very Being of God, and the mysterious relations within
the Holy Trinity, are of universal concern to all men, and
not merely a subject of inquiry for speculative theologians;
it is a sign that Divine relationship is the ground of human
relationship.

> To every peasant and child it (the Nicene Creed)
> speaks of this marvellous subject. Certainly a strange
> fact, doubly strange when one knows how much it has
> been the tendency of teachers and priests in all ages
> to believe that only a few initiated persons are fit to
> know anything which concerns the name and nature
> of God; and how much this tendency did actually
> mingle with the awe and reverence of those ages by
> which these creeds have been transmitted to us. That
> the doctors of the Church should have allowed the
> Apostles' Creed to be heard in every cottage is strange;
> that they should not have said that this deeper creed,
> though embodying the principles and data of the other,
> was only for theologians, is scarcely credible: yet so
> it was. Now if it were the purpose of God that His
> name should be revealed to men; if His name, which
> seems to most of us to be connected with the highest
> and most esoteric abstractions, be really the only
> ground of a universal society, we can interpret these
> facts.[15]

The creed, being a common and united form of utterance which the Church puts into the mouth of all her
members, is a safeguard against the identification of the
Gospel with any of the particular interpretations of it that

[14]*Kingdom of Christ* (Ev. ed.), II, 6.
[15]*Ibid.*, II, 6 f.

have been or are held by different individuals or schools of thought. It recalls all who repeat it from the divisive and mystifying controversies of speculative divinity to the plain confession of God Himself and His gracious and uniting acts for us men and for our salvation.

This is a suitable point at which to say something about Maurice's attitude to the Thirty-Nine Articles, although of course he did not describe them as one of the signs of the kingdom of Christ. He regarded the creed and the Articles as "generically different"[16] and "essentially distinct in their nature"[17]—the one being a personal confession of faith, the other a set of intellectual propositions affirming conditions of thought. Nevertheless, he held that the Articles, rightly understood, were in their character consonant with the creed and served a complementary purpose.

When in 1860 he was instituted to the incumbency of St. Peter's Church, Vere Street, he preached upon the Articles, and said: "I have declared my unfeigned assent and consent to the Articles this afternoon because I believe that they do not put themselves in the place of Christ; because I hold that they protect the faith of the simple Christian man from a number of theological subtleties and technicalities which have threatened it and threaten it still."[18] He said that he accepted them still, as he had done at his ordination, as the guides of his studies and his teaching, and that he was more than ever convinced that they were a protection "from the tyranny of different schools, and of our own private fancies."[19] He found that

[16]*Subscription No Bondage*, p. 2.
[17]*Ibid.*, p. 83.
[18]*Faith of the Liturgy*, p. 23. Cp. *Lincoln's Inn Sermons*, I, 25.
[19]*Faith of the Liturgy*, pp. 24 f. Cp. *The Prayer-Book and the Lord's Prayer*, p. 3: "The Divine . . . will, I believe, find them (the Articles) quite invaluable for the method into which they will guide him; for the deliverance from systems which they will enable him to work out for himself; for the tracks of thought which they will teach him to enter upon and to avoid." See also *Kingdom of Christ* (1838), I, 291.

they followed the method of the Bible and of the Gospel.

> I wish you to take notice of the method which the compilers of these Articles have followed. The first eight refer to God, as He has revealed Himself to us, and to the true state of man as united to God in Christ Jesus. The next division, from the Ninth to the Nineteenth, concerns men as sinful creatures, and the means which God has taken to raise them out of their sinful condition and restore them to their right condition. The third division, from the Nineteenth to the end, refers to men as members of a Christian society.[20]

He attached much significance to the fact that the redemption was asserted before the fall, and man's righteousness before his sin.

> The Second Article passes at once to "the Word or Son of God which was made very Man." Here . . . you have the straight line before you have the crooked one. We hear nothing of the first Adam till we are told of the second Adam, the Lord from Heaven. He is set forth first in His entire and perfect union with the Father, then in His entire and perfect union with our nature, then as the thorough reconciler and redeemer of that Nature from all that evil, original and actual, of which we are to learn more presently.[21]

> There is no assertion (he said elsewhere), in all our dogmatic formularies, of the Living Word, as the root of all life and good to men, so distinct as that which is contained in the second article. I have always turned to that Article, occurring where it does, as the great witness for a theology constructed not like that of Knox or the Westminster Assembly, on the basis of the Fall, but on the basis of Redemption; or rather on the original constitution of men in the Only-be-

[20]*Faith of the Liturgy,* pp. 25 f.
[21]*Ibid.,* p. 31. Cp. *Kingdom of Christ* (Ev. ed.), II, 289; *Sequel to the Inquiry,* p. 249; *Doctrine of Sacrifice,* pp. xxi f.

gotten Son by which the Redemption itself must be interpreted.[22]

It was on grounds like these, and not as though they were tests of orthodoxy to be legally enforced,[23] that Maurice defended clerical subscription to the Articles, and would have defended it to the last, had he not been reluctantly driven to the conclusion that, on account of the way in which they were generally treated in the Church, the continued imposition of clerical subscription might do more harm than good.[24]

But his first theological work, *Subscription No Bondage* (1835), had dealt with a different question, subscription to the Articles at the university. At the time, he had defended this also on the ground that the Articles were not terms of communion or a confession of faith, but conditions of thought, "primarily designed to assist education by warning students against superstitions, which have hindered, and are likely to hinder, the pursuit of knowledge, and the attainment of truth."[25] By conditions of thought he meant the assumptions or axioms on the basis of which education in a university is conducted. Every educational institution, every teacher, he pointed out, makes such assumptions whether or not they are professed. Subscription to the Articles at Oxford was an acknowledgment of what they were there, so that both teachers and students were not kept in the dark about them. Other universities might suppress their conditions of thought, but all the same they inevitably had some. Maurice worked the matter out

[22]*Life of F. D. M.*, II, 568. Cp. *Kingdom of Christ* (1838), I, 294 f.

[23]"If we use the Articles to find out the errors of other men, and not to help us out of our own, I do not think we shall ever know what they mean, or in any real sense believe them." —*The Prayer-Book and the Lord's Prayer*, p. 13.

[24]See *Life of F. D. M.*, II, 491, 506 f.; *Claims of the Bible*, p. 17.

[25]*Subscription No Bondage*, p. 13. Cp. *The New Statute and Mr. Ward*, p. 15.

in considerable detail, and his argument was worthy of a more promising cause. He never abandoned the principles which he asserted in this book, but he came to see that subscription to the Thirty-Nine Articles was not an appropriate way of applying them.[26]

Subscription No Bondage is one of his most seminal and also most readable books. In 1870 he said of it: "No book which I have written expresses more strongly what then were, and what still are, my deepest convictions."[27] It is well worth reading today; it deals with the fundamental postulates of university education—a subject the importance of which is at length being realized and discussed in Great Britain[28] and still more, I believe, in the U. S. A. *Subscription No Bondage* might with advantage be republished now; it much more deserves to be than Keble's sermon on National Apostasy which was republished some years ago.[29] It argues that in the end only theological principles can secure that all subjects are studied profoundly. If the need for such principles is not recognized, that is because academic studies are being pursued in a purely technical and narrow way. It is men "who are never launching into an open sea of discovery, but always coasting in creeks and shallows" who "do not feel that they need charts or compasses (such as the Articles used to provide), but rather are disposed to throw them overboard."[30] Theology, properly understood, does not hinder but promotes "freedom of enquiry, and even the toleration of dangerous opinions."[31] "We are likely to revolve in endless circles, not to advance at all, if we assume that nothing has been done or proved

[26]See *Life of F. D. M.*, II, 154 f.

[27]*Ibid.*, I, 174. Cp. *ibid.*, I, 181; *Claims of the Bible*, p. 17.

[28]*E.g.*, see A. S. Nash, *The University and the Modern World* (1945); *University Pamphlets*, ed. by R. H. Preston (1946), especially Nos. 1–4.

[29]At the time of the Oxford Movement Centenary by the Rev. R. J. E. Boggis, Vicar of St. John's, Torquay.

[30]*Subscription No Bondage*, p. 74.

[31]*Ibid.*, p. 97. Cp. *Kingdom of Christ* (1838), II, 39 f.

yet in the world concerning moral and spiritual principles."[32] "A university," Maurice wrote to Trench at this
time, "cannot be created by drawing together a troop of
Professors and appointing a set of studies uncemented by
any principle and tending to no object."[33]

But we must return to the signs of the kingdom of Christ.

2.   Forms of Worship

Maurice regarded forms of worship as "one of the clear
and indispensable signs of a spiritual and universal fellowship."[34] He meant liturgical forms in the broadest sense—
such, for example, as are contained in the Book of Common Prayer.[35] "If the meaning of Baptism be," he said,
"that we are brought into God's family, and that we become therefore capable, with one mind and one mouth,
of glorifying His name; if the creed be teaching us, as
children of that family, severally and unitedly to acknowledge that name, and how it is related to us; we must
feel that acts of worship should be, of all acts, those which
most belong to our position, and in which our fellowship
is most entirely realised."[36]

The fact that the simple folk of England are bidden to
use forms of prayer which they owe to Hebrews and Greeks
and Latins is a sign of the universality of God's family in
space and time. Moreover, "the prayers written in the first

[32]*Life of F. D. M.*, II, 228. On *Subscription No Bondage* see
also *Learning and Working*, pp. 199 ff.; *Life of F. D. M.*, I, 168,
524, II, 605.

[33]Letter (of 1835) from F. D. M. to R. C. Trench in *Letters
and Memorial of Richard Chevenix Trench* (1888), I, 191.

[34]*Kingdom of Christ* (Ev. ed.), II, 25.

[35]Though he seems himself to have been quite content with
the 1661 English Prayer-Book, he did not idealize it. "I hope,"
he said, "you will never hear from me any such phrases as our
'excellent or incomparable' Liturgy, or any of the compliments
to our forefathers or ourselves which are wont to accompany these
phrases."—*The Prayer-Book and the Lord's Prayer*, p. 6.

[36]*Kingdom of Christ* (Ev. ed.), II, 20 f.

ages of Christianity are in general more free, more reverent, more universal, than those which have been poured forth since,"[37] and are therefore providentially fitted for permanent use in the Church. Prayer can be a true and reasonable service only when it is "being presented by men, as members' of a body or family, which continues the same from generation to generation, and which converts the notion of a human race from a dream into a reality."[38]

> It is heart-cheering to feel that a Catholic Church is not circumscribed by space any more than by time; that national barriers have been overcome;[39] that we can feel with men of other climes, and kindreds, and tongues. Glorious fruit of the day of Pentecost! Blessed token that the kingdom of Christ is indeed in the world! Sure prophecy of the perfect fellowship which it shall one day establish.[40]

The public and permanent provision of forms of common prayer is a sign that worship and prayer are normal and regular human activities. In order to worship or to pray aright men do not have to wait for some peculiar or

[37]*Ibid.*, II, 30.

[38]*Ibid.*, II, 34.

[39]"Except the prayers for the Sovereign and the Royal Family our daily Service contains nothing which belongs to England more than to any other country in the world."—*The Prayer-Book and the Lord's Prayer*, p. 2.

[40]*Kingdom of Christ* (1838), II, 225. Lest this should be taken to imply the desirability of a single liturgical language throughout the world, he continues:
"We cannot, indeed, consent to sink the distinction of languages which we believe is essential to national life and freedom; we cannot, for the sake of the name of a one universal language, lose the thing, and exclude nine-tenths of our congregations from the privilege of joining with the understanding, as well as with the spirit, in our prayers; but we will preserve, to the best of our power, the idea of a universal language, and be reminding our people, that the words now expressed in their native language, and embodying their own wants, were conceived by men who worshipped the same God under a different sky, and in different words."

spasmodic influence or inspiration visiting certain persons at certain seasons. That is a pagan notion.[41] "The Prayers framed for all the motley body which frequents our Churches, assume that all may call upon God as a reconciled Father."[42] Forms of worship "assert that man is a spiritual being . . . you must claim for him a right and power to pray—you must give him a common prayer— *common prayer* in every sense of the word, not *special* prayers adapted to special temperaments and moods of character, but human."[43] For prayer "is the special prerogative and ordained utterance of that creature who is formed in the image of God, and is appointed to serve Him day and night in His temple."[44] It is "one of the healthy, necessary, and regular acts of the regenerate will."[45] Forms of worship are a sign that man is the priest of the whole creation who "should . . . compel every portion of it to bring gifts and offerings to his Lord and King."[46]

Again, forms of worship are a necessary safeguard against individualism and selfishness in prayer. They are a sign that we are "members of one body, and each man incapable of exercising his own spiritual functions excepting in connection with that body."[47] "Prayer is meant to be an expression of the wants of humanity, uttered through the one Head and Lord of man; individuals, if they would pray really and spiritually, must learn to take part in the speech and music of humanity, and not to isolate themselves in phrases and discords of their own."[48] Forms of worship "draw us out of that individuality which is our curse and ruin, and lead us, one and all, to take up our

[41]See *ibid.* (Ev. ed.), II, 24 f.
[42]*Doctrine of Sacrifice*, p. xxii.
[43]*The Prayer-Book and the Lord's Prayer*, pp. 11 f.
[44]*Kingdom of Christ* (1838), II, 201.
[45]*Ibid.*, II, 210 f.
[46]*Ibid.*, II, 212 f. For "priest of creation," see also *ibid.*. II, 235; *The Prayer-Book and the Lord's Prayer*, p. 13.
[47]*Kingdom of Christ* (1838), II, 218.
[48]*Ibid.*, II, 221.

position on the same ground of being justified and redeemed in Christ."[49]

Nevertheless, it is also true that the common prayers of the liturgy teach men how to pray when they are alone, how to attain in the closet the breadth and universality which belong to the temple. "When thou art most alone thou must still, if thou wouldest pray, be in the midst of a family; thou must call upon a Father; thou must not dare to say *my*, but *our*."[50]

Furthermore, the liturgy, based as it is upon the Christian year, brings the whole range of the Gospel regularly before men's minds, and does not leave them to be dependent on the notions or extemporaneous inspirations of individual ministers. Forms of worship "invite us on certain days to remember our Lord's acts, condescension, humiliation, triumph. They teach us that if we forget the days, we shall be in danger of forgetting that of which they speak. . . . These forms authorise certain days and seasons, during which the members of Christ's body may enter into His humiliation, and chasten themselves with His stripes, that so they may keep down the evil inclinations which separate them from their brethren, may sympathise in the sorrows of mankind, may realise the blessings which are given to the whole Church."[51]

These ancient forms have then a power similar to that of baptism and the creed, "a power before which all human systems . . . must at last shrink and quail."[52] Settled forms of worship are a sign to the world, and to all the kingdoms of the world, that a universal and spiritual kingdom has been set up on earth, grounded on the relation of mankind to a universal and invisible King, not on historical accidents or on the opinions of a transitory sect. A sect without permanent and universal forms of worship fails to challenge the

[49] *Ibid.*, II, 231.
[50] *Ibid.* (Ev. ed.), II, 26.
[51] *Ibid.*, II, 41 f. Cp. *ibid.*, II, 170.
[52] *Ibid.*, II, 42 f.

9

pride of liberal statesmen, who can contentedly tolerate it, if not entirely ignore it or complacently exploit it.

But this they complain of—that men by their *Te Deums* and *Gloria Patri's*, by their steeples going up towards heaven in every parish, by their outward sacraments, should proclaim that the Lord is the God of the whole earth, and should call upon us to fear Him and give glory to Him. This is very insolent; this affronts men whose feelings ought to be respected; of this, therefore, liberalism, by its creed of tolerance, is bound to be intolerant. And intolerant we know she will show herself; the wolf's hide will come forth out of the fleece of wool; people will be permitted to have as much religion as they please, only they must not speak of a living and true God, and declare that He and He only is to be worshipped.[53]

3. The Eucharist

We shall expect Maurice's teaching concerning the eucharist to draw out its social character and its universal witness. We shall not expect him to talk about "making my communion"—language in which even ardent professors of Catholicism betray their latent individualism. We shall not expect him to urge attendance at the holy eucharist as "a religious duty," failure to comply with which involves a man in mortal sin.[54] "We speak of the Eucharist as a religious duty which must be performed if we would escape perdition—not as the celebration of a wedding which the Son of God has made with our race."[55] By the sacrament of baptism God brings men into the regenerate *state*, which Christ vindicated for them when He took their nature and reconciled them to God; the sacrament of the Lord's Supper is the means whereby God communicates and preserves to

[53]*Ibid.* (1838), II, 258.
[54]See *Sermons on the Sabbath-Day*, pp. 61 f.
[55]*Kingdom of Heaven*, p. 227.

men that regenerate *life,* which Christ claimed for them when He ascended on high.[56] Baptism lays the foundation of all the services and acts of the Church; holy communion is their crown, without which all the rest are unintelligible.[57]

The eucharist, being thus the crown and centre of the Church's life, is a sign that

> communion with God in the largest and fullest sense of that word, is not an instrument of attaining some higher end, but is itself the end to which He is leading His creatures, and after which His creatures, in all kingdoms, and nations, and languages—by all their schemes of religion, by all their studies of philosophy, by art, by science, by politics, by watching, by weeping, by struggling, by submitting, by wisdom, by folly, in the camp and in the closet, in poverty and in riches, in honour and in shame, in health and in sickness, are secretly longing and crying, and without which they cannot be satisfied.[58]

The eucharist is a sign that the kingdom of Christ has been set up on earth, since it testifies that

> a living and perpetual communion has been established between God and man; between earth and heaven; between all spiritual creatures; that the bond of this communion is that body and blood which the Son of God and the Son of Man offered up to His Father, in fulfilment of His will, in manifestation of His love; that God is as careful to nourish their spirits as their bodies; that as He provides bread and wine for the strength and life of the one, so in this body and blood of His Son is the strength of the other; the Sacrament of His continual presence with His universal family; the witness to each man of his own place in that family, and of his share in all its blessings; the pledge

[56]See *Kingdom of Christ* (1838), I, 201 f.
[57]See *ibid.,* I, 258.
[58]*Ibid.,* I, 259.

and spring of a renewed life; the assurance that that life is His own eternal life.[59]

Each man in the sacrament eats the one bread which is to sustain all as well as himself. Though each receives for himself, the gift contains a promise and prophecy for the whole Church and for mankind.[60]

The setting forth of this sacrament, which links heaven and earth, as the supreme bond between men is a witness that man is not simply a creature of this world but has his home and his citizenship in another world.[61] It is a sign that there is an order of reality with which the senses cannot grapple, and which is most awful and necessary for men, and that the deepest principle of human society is mysterious.[62] But it is a sign that this eternal order is neither unknown nor inaccessible, for the sacrament proclaims that a perfect atonement has been made for the whole world, that men are invited to participate in the humanity which Christ has taken within the veil, and that in Him they are admitted to the knowledge of His Father and their Father.[63] The glorified body of Christ is the permanent bond between men and God.[64] It is the temple in which God meets man and man may meet God.[65]

Again, the sacrament is a sign that Christ is the redeemer of men's bodies as well as of their spirits.

The elder church believed that the outward and visible elements proclaimed, by their very outwardness and visibility, a most precious principle—that not only the soul, that which thinks and judges, but the body also, that which sees, and hears, and smells, and tastes, and handles, is the subject of Christ's redemption, was

[59]*The Prayer-Book and the Lord's Prayer*, pp. 230 f.
[60]See *ibid.*, p. 276.
[61]See *Kingdom of Christ* (Ev. ed.), II, 76.
[62]See *ibid.*, II, 69.
[63]See *Lincoln's Inn Sermons*, I, 48.
[64]See *Kingdom of Christ* (1838), I, 205.
[65]See *Lincoln's Inn Sermons*, I, 9.

raised up with Him when He left the grave, was
glorified by Him when He ascended, and shall in each
man be redeemed out of the bondage of corruption,
and enter into the liberty of the children of God.[66]

Maurice would not think of a descent of Christ into
the eucharistic elements, but he thought of them as being
taken up into, and identified with, the glorified body of
Christ, so that the worshippers are taken within the veil
and enabled to claim their privilege of union with the
ascended Lord.[67] The "real presence" means that there is
an actual communion between the Living Head and His
members.[68] Faith does not create the presence, but appre-
hends what is actually there. Christ is really present in the
eucharistic feast, and the words of institution are to be
taken literally.[69] But the body to which they refer is the
glorified body. It was not at the Last Supper, but after
the ascension that the Apostles realized what they meant.
"The words of the institution were to get their life from
events to which those who first heard them had not yet
been witnesses."[70] The words are "the pledge that we are
members . . . of the Church of the first-born, of the assembly of just men made perfect . . . that we have no
need for Christ to descend into earthly elements, because
our spirits may be with Him in those heavens where
He is."[71]

As regards the eucharistic sacrifice, Maurice teaches that
the eucharist is a feast celebrating the completed sacrifice
of Christ. "I have maintained," he says, "that because the
sacrifice had once for all accomplished the object of bringing our race, constituted and redeemed in Christ, into a

[66]*Kingdom of Christ* (1838), I, 309 f.
[67]See *ibid.* (Ev. ed.), II, 70 f. Cp. *The Church a Family*, p.
148.
[68]See *Kingdom of Christ* (1838), I, 266.
[69]See *ibid.* (Ev. ed.), II, 76.
[70]*Ibid.* (1838), I, 308.
[71]*Lincoln's Inn Sermons*, I, 73.

state of acceptance and union with God, *therefore* it was most fitting that there should be an act whereby we are admitted into the blessings thus claimed and secured to us."[72] "The Sacrament of the Lord's Supper witnesses that the sin-stricken man who has discerned that he never had, and never can have anything righteous in himself, may become altogether childlike and spotless when he turns from himself, and seeks for fellowship with Him in whom is no sin."[73]

In its regular celebration of the eucharist the Church bears a calm and steady witness that

without a sacrifice for sins there could be no communion between God and His creatures. His sacrifice removes those impediments to the communion, which the blood of bulls and goats, sacrifices of mere arbitrary appointment, though most precious as instruments of moral and spiritual education, could not possibly have removed. Until One appeared who said, "Lo! I come, in the volume of the book it is written, to do thy will, O God"—until He offered up Himself as a perfect and well-pleasing sacrifice to God, how could there be perfect contentment in the mind of a holy and loving Being, how could a perfect communion exist between Him and man? And thus the church . . . teaches that a sacrifice, a real and spiritual sacrifice, was necessary to the atonement of God and His creatures; that this sacrifice was offered up once for all, and was accepted for the sins of men; that the consciences of those are purified from sin, who by faith receive this sacrifice as their reconciliation to God; that this purification is itself only a means and preparation for our drawing nigh unto God with pure hearts and faith unfeigned, through Him who is the Priest, as well as the sacrifice, the ever-living Mediator of a covenant which is estab-

[72]*Kingdom of Christ* (Ev. ed.), II, 56.
[73]*Lincoln's Inn Sermons*, I, 84 f. Cp. *Doctrine of Sacrifice*, pp. 292 f.

lished, not in the law of a carnal commandment, but in the power of an endless life.[74]

The eucharist is the sign of what Christianity is, as the Passover was the sign of what Judaism was.[75] The Passover festival commemorated a complete deliverance, and the act was perpetually renewed so that the people of God was brought to understand that by sacrifice it subsisted and consisted. "By such a renewal its members realised the permanent and living character of the good that has been bestowed upon them, so it is here. The sacrifice of Christ is that with which alone God can be satisfied and in the sight of which alone He can contemplate our race; it is therefore the only meeting-point of communion with Him: but this communion being established, it must be by presenting the finished sacrifice before God that we both bear witness what our position is and realise the glory of it; otherwise we have a name without a reality."[76]

The sacrament itself, it seemed to Maurice, was a deliverance from the various perplexities in which different doctrinal systems became involved, and in the final version of *The Kingdom of Christ* he worked this idea out with reference to Quakerism, Zwinglianism, Calvinism, Lutheranism, and Romanism.[77] The eucharist itself—not a doctrine about it—is the centre of unity; it "keeps doctrines from perpetual clashing with each other, and men from being the slaves of doctrines."[78] The sacrament itself contains the whole truth, "embodying and concentrating those half-truths which the lagging intellect staying at the foot of the mountain, on which the spirit is gone up to worship, contrives to cage in its formal and logical propositions."[79]

[74]*Kingdom of Christ* (1838), I, 275 f.
[75]See *ibid.*, I, 308. Cp. *Doctrine of Sacrifice*, pp. 65 f.; *Life of F. D. M.*, II, 281.
[76]*Kingdom of Christ* (Ev. ed.), II, 56 f. Cp. *The Prayer-Book and the Lord's Prayer*, pp. 230 f.
[77]See *Kingdom of Christ* (Ev. ed.), II, 49–82.
[78]*Ibid.* (1838), I, 315.   [79]*Ibid.*, I, 272.

Christ has, of His love and mercy to mankind, provided us "with a simple and wonderful testimony against these narrow notions and dividing tendencies. . . . He has embodied in a living feast the complete idea of His kingdom, which we, looking at things partially, from different sides, through the prejudices and false colourings of particular times and places, are continually reducing under some name, notion, or formula of ours."[80]

The eucharist is the sign of an already existing communion between all redeemed creatures, on this side of the grave and the other; they have the same delights, the same occupations; there is one centre to which all eyes are turned, one food by which all are sustained. Conditions of space and time cannot affect their union, or hinder the blessings of it.[81] Finally, the eucharist is the sign of the promised consummation of the kingdom of Christ at the end of the world. It looks backward to the beginning, onward to the end of all things; it speaks of Him from whom all things have proceeded, and in whom all shall be gathered up, whether things in heaven or things in earth.[82] It is "the witness that we are not dreaming a dream, but expecting that which . . . must be, when we look for a coming of Christ in the glory of His Father and the Holy Angels, for a day of Redemption, when He shall claim the Universe which He has purchased. This is the voice coming to us all out of the depths of sorrow and anguish: 'Rejoice in the Lord always, and again I say, Rejoice.' "[83]

The principles of Christianity cannot be expounded fully or satisfactorily except in terms of this sacrament. It expresses them in a deep, practical, and universal way—in a way that dogmas cannot do, nor even the Bible.

> Ask yourself then solemnly and seriously—"Can I find Christianity—the Christianity I want—a Christianity of acts, not words, a Christianity of power and

[80]Ibid. (Ev. ed.), II, 54.　　[82]See Gospel of St. John, p. 195.
[81]See ibid. (1838), I, 281.　　[83]Lincoln's Inn Sermons, I, 73.

life, a divine, human, Catholic Christianity for men of all countries and periods, all tastes and endowments, all temperaments and necessities so exhibited as I find it in this Sacrament?"[84]

4. The Ministry

"The principle of the Catholic Church," says Maurice, "which I have endeavoured to develop in reference to Baptism, the Eucharist, the Creed, the Forms of Worship, is the principle of a direct, real, and practical union between men and their Lord."[85] We have now to see how he develops this principle in reference to the ministry, and why he regards the ordained ministry in the Church as a sign of the establishment of the kingdom of Christ on earth.

The fact that there is an ordained ministry in the Church is, to begin with, a sign that there is a constitution and an order for mankind. The Church is neither a crowd nor an anarchy, but has an enduring structure.

I believe that this spiritual and universal body was not made by Christ to depend upon the feelings, or faith of men, because these feelings and faith are nothing, unless they have something to rest on—because it is a monstrous contradiction and absurdity to suppose that they create that without which they would have no existence. I believe that He meant His Church to stand in certain permanent and universal institutions . . . in a permanent ministry through which He should declare His will, and dispense His blessings to the whole body, and the main office in which should be that apostolic office which belongs characteristically to the new dispensation, seeing that it expresses the general oversight of Him, who no longer confines Himself to any particular nation, but has ascended up on high that He might fill all things.[86]

[84]*Kingdom of Christ* (1838), I, 287.
[85]*Ibid.* (Ev. ed.), II, 132.
[86]*Three Letters to the Rev. W. Palmer,* p. 8.

The ministry is a permanent institution in the Church. Certain men are taken into a particular and settled relation to Christ, which depends upon His choice. "It is one of those fixed relations into which a man is brought, and which he cannot shake off."[87] The ministry is a sign to the whole body that its life depends upon such permanent relations. It is God's instrument for bringing to light the society that lies beneath all others.[88]

The relation of the ministry to the whole body is a sign of the principle upon which human society is constituted and in which it must abide if it is to be a human society.

> When our Lord laid down the principle that in His kingdom the chief of all is the servant of all, He proclaimed the great paradox on which all society rests, one which the rulers of states and the chief of hosts must act upon, if subjects and armies are not to be in slavery or in anarchy. But in the Church this law was to be embodied and carried out, that men might see it working there, and confess it to be indeed God's law, and the law of their lives.[89]

Church order bears this witness, provided that the true relation between the ministers and the members is rightly acknowledged and expressed. This relation is one of sacrificial service. When it is forgotten or contradicted, as it often has been and is always liable to be, the ministers come to be regarded as mere officials, a hierarchy is substituted for a polity, and the Church becomes a world. But the charter of the ministry is a sign that God has sent the Church "to remould the world, not to make a world for herself."[90] However this charter may have been neglected or perverted in practice, still "from the Bishop of Rome down to the founder of the last new sect in the United States, every one who deals with the Gospel at all, or pretends in any sense

[87]*The Church a Family*, p. 146.
[88]See *ibid.*, p. 165.
[89]*Ecclesiastical History*, p. 357.   [90]*Ibid.*, pp. 358 f.

to have a Divine commission, assumes this name (*minister* or *servant*) as the description of his office."[91]

The offices or functions of the ministry in the Church witness to the relation of the ascended and invisible Lord to the members of His body and to the work that He has done and is doing for mankind. As the state of the whole Church and of every member in it is the image of His state who has redeemed it, so every office in the Church is an image of some office performed by Christ in His own Person and is the means by which that office is presented to men, and made effectual for them through all time.[92] Thus the episcopacy, the priesthood and the ministry of Christ are not only talked about or proclaimed in word, but these offices are embodied in living and visible persons to the eyes of the wayfaring man, who is merely puzzled when he hears talk about Christ's offices and nothing more. "We show him what an Overseer, what a Presbyter, what a Deacon is—most imperfectly, but still livingly."[93]

The original and characteristic ministry in the kingdom of Christ was the apostolate. The four gospels might be described as "The Institution of a Christian Ministry."[94] They describe the call, the training and the preparation of the apostles, but it was on the day of Pentecost, when they met not as individuals but as a college, that they were endowed with the gifts which Christ had designed for them. "The Spirit of God, by a wonderful demonstration, declares that He is dwelling among men; that an organised body of men has been provided for His habitation; that through this body His blessings are to be transmitted to the world; that through a portion of this body, His blessings are to be transmitted to the rest."[95] "Then they became Apostles indeed; the founders of a kingdom, not merely the heralds of one; the witnesses for our Lord in His as-

[91]*Kingdom of Christ* (Ev. ed.), II, 83.
[92]See *ibid.*, II, 111.   [94]*Ibid.* (Ev. ed.), II, 90.
[93]*Ibid.* (1838), II, 178.   [95]*Ibid.*, II, 107 f.

cended glory; the princes reigning with Him, and setting Him forth as the Great King and Overseer of His Church."[96] "On the day of Pentecost they felt and knew that they were a society. . . . They had not formed themselves into one. They had not devised an organization for themselves; He had framed it. The united society did not choose the apostles into a certain position; they held that position already."[97]

This original apostolic office comprised, brought together and made universal the partial and provisional ministerial offices of the old covenant;[98] it contained in principle or in germ all the ministerial offices of the new covenant, which were enfolded in it and were to be apportioned out of it. The apostolic order is the root of all the orders of ministry in the Church; in it they all originally dwelt.[99] As the Church expanded and developed, and fresh circumstances and more extensive demands were made upon the ministry, its functions were differentiated. It is not that new functions were created. Christ had sufficiently provided for His Church. The apostles "could not add to what He had done; they could only apportion, or rather felt that He who was Lord of all circumstances, *was* apportioning, to different husbandmen in His vineyard, works which could not be performed by themselves alone."[100]

As the early Church was intended to provide a creed which should set forth the result of the Gospel, so far as it is a revelation of the *name* of God, so the early Church was commissioned to put church institutions into that posi-

[96]*Ibid.* (1838), II, 170.

[97]*The Church a Family*, pp. 155 f.

[98]See *Kingdom of Christ* (1838), II, 169. Cp. *The Church a Family*, pp. 177 f.: "The Apostolic office was one, which though closely connected with all that had been before, though bound by the most obvious links to the old tribes, yet had a comprehensiveness which could not attach to any office in the Hebrew commonwealth."

[99]See *Kingdom of Christ* (Ev. ed.), II, 125.

[100]*The Church a Family*, p. 156.

tive and consistent form, which is the result of the Gospel, so far as it is a revelation of the *kingdom* of God.[101] A considerable period elapsed before the functions of the ministry were clearly differentiated, as was the case with the settlement of the canon of Scripture. The course of development in the first and second centuries is obscure. We have no history of the choice and adoption of the titles, presbyter and bishop; nor can we tell when and by what process the offices were distinguished.[102]

> You will hear great discussions about the time when the Orders in the Church began to be clearly distinguished from each other, when the Overseer obtained the full recognition of his difference from the Presbyter, when the Presbyter learnt how he stood apart from the Deacon, when the broad line was drawn between the Clergy and the people or laity. You will find much learning on all sides; you will sometimes be quite bewildered by the evidence which shows that these differences were and were not clearly perceived in the second century.[103]

Maurice did not consider that anything essential hung on the outcome of these learned controversies. He did not regard the polity of the Church as made up of a set of three or more offices. The essential question is whether the ministry that was originally enfolded in the apostolate was intended to be permanent.

> The question . . . to be decided . . . is simply whether there was or was not to be continued in the Church, any office corresponding in its essential characteristics to that one which we judge from the New Testament to be the distinguishing one of the Church at its foundation. The common opinion is, that by the

[101]See *Kingdom of Christ* (1838), II, 28 f.
[102]See *The Church a Family*, p. 162; *Kingdom of Christ* (Ev. ed.), II, 113.
[103]*Ecclesiastical History*, p. 358.

perpetuation of this office the Church has been perpetuated; the connexion of different ages with each other realised; the wholeness and unity of the body declared. The changes which have taken place in the condition of this office we suppose to be changes as to name, as to the number of the persons filling it, as to the limits of their government; changes some of them presupposed in the very existence of a body which was to have an unlimited expansion; none of them affecting its nature or its object.[104]

The episcopate is "the main constituent" of the church polity;[105] it is the fundamental order, witnessing to the permanent and universal episcopacy of the invisible Head of the Church.

The existence of the Church depends upon the acknowledgement of the Son of God as the Universal Bishop of it . . . every step in the Jewish economy was leading up to the revelation of Him as the substitute for the earthly High Priest . . . in Him all orders are constituted . . . the Succession and Consecration of Bishops are the witnesses of His permanent and present Government.[106]

The word Overseer came gradually to be used as the especial designation of the chief minister in each church, because it denoted happily and conveniently the general care and government of Him who had the charge of the whole flock, and who directed the acts and movements of the particular shepherds.[107]

[104]*Kingdom of Christ* (Ev. ed.), II, 114 f.
[105]*Christmas Day*, p. 371.
[106]*Three Letters to the Rev. W. Palmer*, p. 78.
[107]*The Church a Family*, p. 180. Maurice continues:
"It superseded partly, though not wholly, the world Apostle—since that, according to its etymology, pointed rather to the Missionary than to the settled and limited Pastor, and because there was a reverence due to those who had witnessed the resurrection, and who had represented the passage from the old economy to the new. But no change in the name could affect the radical nature of the vocation."

The episcopate expresses the universal, diffusive, cosmopolitan element in the constitution of the Church.[108] It "presents Christianity in the character·of the great flying eagle—diffusing itself everywhere."[109] Bishops are especially responsible for expressing, upholding, and extending the universal mission of the kingdom of Christ.

Bishops being as we believe the witnesses and representatives of Christ's universal kingdom, are the very instruments of our communion with other nations. If there be no such institution—no apostleship—in the Church now, then the Church has lost its universal character; then the idea of the Church as existing for all space, and all time, perishes; then the commission, "Go ye into all nations," has no persons to whom it is directed. We cannot then recognize a Church without Bishops.[110]

The bishops are the true missionaries; they have a commission from heaven already, and do not need a fresh one from a committee upon earth.[111] The episcopal institution is "one of the appointed and indispensable signs of a spiritual and universal society."[112]

The fact that bishops are called "Fathers in God" is a sign that the Church is above all to be thought of as a family.[113] The apostles felt their office to be characteristically a fatherly office, and bishops should do so too, realizing that their calling, so far from interfering with, witnesses to, the universal Fatherhood of God.

Though no one might usurp this universal fatherhood—though it would have destroyed the very con-

[108]See *Kingdom of Christ* (1838), II, 179 f. Cp. *ibid.*, III, 177.
[109]*Ibid.*, II, 289.
[110]*Three Letters to the Rev. W. Palmer*, pp. 34 f. Cp. *Life of F. D. M.*, I, 524.
[111]See *Kingdom of Christ* (1838), III, 318. Cp. *Christmas Day*, pp. 368 f.
[112]*Kingdom of Christ* (Ev. ed.), II, 91.
[113]See *The Church a Family*, Sermon XI.

stitution of the Church to do so—each circle or society
was to be an image of the great family, each was to
have its own father. The Apostles loved and cherished
that name, and all that it implied, and all that illustrated it. They much preferred it to any title which
merely indicated an office. It was more spiritual; it
was more personal; it asserted better the divine order;
it did more to preserve the dignity and sacredness of
all domestic relations. It is a sad day for churches, yes,
and for nations, when men begin to regard themselves
as officials sent forth by some central government to
do its jobs, and not as men who are bound by sacred
affinities and actual relations to those whom they pre-
side over.[114]

The episcopal succession Maurice regarded as an important witness to the permanence of the Church's constitution. He could speak of "the necessity for Apostolic
Succession and Episcopal Ordination."[115] The act of consecration through the agency of three existing bishops sig-
nifies "that the person newly entering upon the function
receives the same kind of authority and the same kind of
gifts as those who were first endowed with it."[116] The idea
of ministerial succession is justified by the analogy of God's
dealings with His people under the old covenant, and the
new dispensation has not introduced anything that makes
it obsolete. The idea is manifested or presented now in a
different mode because of the difference between a national
and a universal kingdom. The hereditary tradition was the
appropriate mode in the one case,[117] as consecration without any national or family limitation is in the other.[118] "The
divine scheme of the Jewish dispensation has passed into
something higher and nobler, but higher and nobler *of its
own kind*."[119]

[114]*Epistles of St. John*, p. 54.
[115]*Kingdom of Christ* (1838), II, 112. Cp. *ibid.*, III, 223.
[116]*Ibid.* (Ev. ed.), II, 87.
[117]See *Doctrine of Sacrifice*, p. 80.
[118]See *Kingdom of Christ* (Ev. ed.), II, 121.
[119]*Ibid.* (1838), II, 153.

The Christians believe that their ministers who live centuries after the Son of Man has left the earth as much receive their commission from Him as those on whom He first breathed. Those who first received the power ordained others and committed it to them. This is the law of Christ's kingdom. It testifies that He abides the same from generation to generation, that all who exercise powers are exercising them under Him, and that whatever blessings are communicated through men are really communicated by the Lord of men.[120]

While on these grounds episcopacy and the episcopal succession must be asserted as an essential sign in the Church, we are not required or entitled to say that those Christian bodies which are without episcopal succession are put out of the Church. We have not to draw this negative conclusion, though we cannot recognize them as parts of the Church as long as they reject the institutions which make universal communion possible. But if some of the links which bind them to the universal Church have been cut, it does not follow that all have been.[121] Maurice of course rejected the notion that the grace of ordination is transmitted like a contagion; it is Christ present in the Church who comunicates actual powers to His ministers.[122] He did not adopt the Tractarian view that Presbyterians were not churchmen.[123] He recognized that the Churches of Sweden and Denmark had preserved the institution of episcopacy, and that other Protestant Churches had preserved "some witness of its existence."[124] He approved of the scheme for the Jerusalem Bishopric,[125] and it can hardly be doubted that in our own day he would have welcomed the Scheme of Church Union in South India, which has

[120]See *Christmas Day*, pp. 366 ff. Cp. *Acts of the Apostles*, p. 227.
[121]See *Three Letters to the Rev. W. Palmer*, pp. 32 ff.
[122]See *Kingdom of Christ* (Ev. ed.), II, 125.
[123]See *Life of F. D. M.*, I, 236.
[124]*Kingdom of Christ* (Ev. ed.), II, 86.
[125]See *Three Letters to the Rev. W. Palmer*.

been the occasion of a similar, though less responsible, controversy in the Church of England. He did not set up the Apostolic Succession against the principles to which other forms of church order bore witness, but maintained that it was consistent with them, and that they would make a much stronger witness when it was restored to them.[126] Meanwhile he held that in nine cases out of ten it is "a very solemn duty for us to remain in the church wherein we are born, though we dislike many of the conditions under which she exists."[127]

The episcopal office witnesses to the invisible God and Father of all; the presbyteral office witnesses to the Elder-Brotherhood and the Priesthood of Christ. Christ is the Elder-Brother who represents the human family in its Father's house.[128] But Maurice will not admit that "the presbyter does not include the ἱερεύς."[129]

As the Priest of the old dispensation witnesses that men have separated themselves from God, and that they must be reunited by sacrifice; the Priest of the new dispensation witnesses that Christ, through the Eternal Spirit, hath offered Himself up to God, and that with that sacrifice God is well pleased; the one declares the need for purification, the other that the Spirit is given to purify; the one tastes of the sacrifice as the pledge of a communion hereafter to be established with man, the other feeds the people with it as the pledge of a communion already consummated.[130]

The priestly office testifies to "the fact that the utmost

[126]See *Kingdom of Christ* (1838), II, 159 f., 181 f.
[127]*Three Letters to the Rev. W. Palmer*, p. 19. The context refers to Anglicans and Romanists, but that Maurice would say the same to, *e.g.*, Presbyterians is clear from *Life of F. D. M.*, I, 247 f.
[128]See *The Church a Family*, p. 162.
[129]*Ibid.*, p. 166.
[130]*Kingdom of Christ* (1838), II, 151. Cp. *Lincoln's Inn Sermons*, VI, 208 f.

which a Christian minister can do is to assert the reconciliation of God with men in Christ, and on the strength
of that accomplished fact to beseech them to be reconciled
to God."[181] So far from obscuring or interfering with the
High Priesthood of Christ and the priestly character of the
whole Church the ordained priesthood is an effectual sign
of both the one and the other.

> If the priestly idea dropped out of the circle of Chris-
> tian ideas, the sense of what mankind had gained by
> the ascension of Christ would disappear also . . . if it
> were limited to Him who had fully realized, and can
> alone fully realize it, the belief of His union with the
> creatures whom He has called His brethren, would
> grow feeble . . . if it were claimed merely by the
> Christian body, the belief of the unity of that body
> in its distinct portions, and as a whole would evaporate,
> and merely a vague blessing be asserted for each per-
> son.[132]

The priest's characteristic acts are celebrating the eucharist and absolving. "These two duties never have been separated, and it is most needful that they should be contemplated in their relation to each other."[133] The eucharist is
the act in which the worshiper is brought into direct communion with his Lord, in which the mere human and visible
agent is most entirely lost and forgotten; he simply bears
witness that He whom he serves is a living and actual person.[134] In celebrating the eucharist, the very highest act he
can perform, he utters nothing of his own, he is merely a
servant, and so is humbled and taught how he should do
all his work.[135]

[181]*Lincoln's Inn Sermons*, I, 48.
[132]*Epistle to the Hebrews*, p. 86. Cp. *Doctrine of Sacrifice*,
p. 290.
[133]*Kingdom of Christ* (Ev. ed.), II, 117.
[134]*Ibid.*, II, 117 f.
[135]See *Lincoln's Inn Sermons*, I, 49. Cp. *Kingdom of Christ*
(1838), III, 227.

His whole object is to present Christ to men and men to Christ really and practically. . . . He is a witness of Christ's continual intercession for every member of His flock. But still this can be but half his duty. The incarnation means very little, the kingdom of God is a mere delusion, if there be not a voice speaking from heaven as well as one crying from earth: if the one be not an answer to the other: if the minister may not say to the congregation, "God has heard your petitions, rise up as pardoned men, with strength to offer praises and prayers, with strength to do your work." . . . If he may not say in like manner to the sick and solitary penitent, God accepts thy tears and pardons thy sin, I do not see what he means by saying that he has authority to *preach* forgiveness.[136]

It is of supreme importance to remember that the Christian ministry is *representative* and not *vicarial*. The vicarial conception is that the priest is doing the work of one who is absent and who only at certain times and under certain conditions presents himself to men. The priest comes to be looked upon as a machine, possessing certain invisible properties, of which he can move the springs or wires.[137] "By the word representative, I mean to express the truth that the minister sets forth Christ to men as present in His Church at all times, as exercising those functions Himself upon which He entered when He ascended on high."[138]

[136]*Ibid.* (Ev. ed.), II, 118. Cp. *Lincoln's Inn Sermons*, IV, 153: "The Christian Priest may do for a sinner and sufferer what a mere kind friend, who receives his confidence, cannot do equally well. For by his office he testifies of the Universal Sacrifice, of the Universal fellowship. By his office, therefore, he declares his own personal inefficiency, he directs the individual man to the One Centre, the One Deliverer, the One Mediator. By his office he warns each man that to seek his life anywhere but in the common Lord and Head of Mankind, is to lose it."

See also *The Prayer-Book and the Lord's Prayer*, p. 248. On the evil consequences of regarding the priest as "the depository of the grace" which he transmits, see *Lincoln's Inn Sermons*, I, 50 f.

[137]See *Three Letters to the Rev. W. Palmer*, p. 12.

[138]*Kingdom of Christ* (Ev. ed.), II, 131 f. *Cp.* T. O. Wedel, *The Coming Great Church* (1947), chap. IV.

"According to the representative doctrine all ministers exhibit Christ in that office to which they are called."[139]

It seemed to Maurice that the cardinal error of Romanism was that it treated the ministry as vicarial instead of representative, so that in this respect the Romish system and the Catholic Church, instead of being identical, were deadly opposites.[140] Romanism regards the Pope as the Vicar of Christ and substitute for Him. It not only treats belief in God as though it were dependent on belief in the Church, thus inverting the order of the creed,[141] but it substitutes for the ascended Christ, who is the ever-present and invisible Head and centre of unity of the Church, to whom the whole body of bishops and each bishop in his own diocese bear witness, a visible Head and a centre of unity on earth. Whereas the sight of a bishop ought to carry up men's thoughts to an eternal, universal bishop, from whom immediately he receives his authority, whose image he is to reflect, and to whom he is responsible, under the Romish system it carries men's thoughts "no higher than to a bishop dwelling in the city of the Caesars, whose death we see recorded every few years in the newspapers."[142]

I do not think Maurice had anything of particular value to say about the office of deacon. Anglican theologians seldom have. This is an office about which we have much to learn from, and little to impart to, others.

We may conclude by observing that Maurice regarded the calling and commission of the ordained ministry in the Church as a sign to all men that they are to look upon their work in the world as a vocation to which they are ordained; it is the office of the ordained ministry to interpret

[139]Ibid., II, 134.

[140]See ibid., II, 134–37. Cp. ibid. (1838), II, 47 ff., 162 f., III, 172 f.; Three Letters to the Rev. W. Palmer, pp. 9 f.; Theological Essays, p. 399; art. on "A Few Words on the Pope's Encyclical Letter" in Macmillan's Magazine (1865), xi, 276 ff.; Letter on "Church and State" in The Daily News, September 25, 1868.

[141]See Doctrine of Sacrifice, p. xxiv.

[142]Kingdom of Christ (1838), III, 361.

to each man his own calling and ordination.[143] Ordained
ministers are "signs and instances to all men of the meaning
and derivation of all power."[144]

The Christian Church claims to be a body of twice-
born men; claims to be a witness of that mighty
privilege which men have of conversing with the Unseen
and Infinite, as well as a witness of the tendency which
there is in man to be merely animal and sensual. The
Christian Church claims a set of ministers, who shall
represent the spiritual glory and privileges of the
whole body, shall be instruments in overcoming the
low and grovelling propensities of its members.[145]

[143]See *ibid.* (Ev. ed.), II, 96 f., 128 ff.; *The Church a Family,*
pp. 146 f., 152; *Life of F. D. M.,* II, 497.
[144]*Kingdom of Christ* (Ev. ed.), II, 130.
[145]*Religions of the World,* p. 168.

6

THE BOOK OF THE WAYS OF GOD[1]

*In easy days the words of all books, and of
the Bible especially, furnish famous topics for
criticism and debate! Such eloquent comments
are written upon them; they can be tortured
to such different senses; they can be proved to
mean everything, anything, or nothing. In times
of stress and anguish they are devoured. They are
taken not to soothe the reader, nor to condemn
those whom he dislikes. They nourish him by
their bitter qualities as much as by their
pleasant; he needs both and he accepts both.—*
APOCALYPSE, p. 185.

*I use the Scriptures because I conceive they
set forth Christ as the Son of God and the Lord
of every man. I do not use them because I think
they set forth some standard which is good for
a set of men called Christians, who are different
from other men, and who have not the same
God with other men. I use the Scriptures to
show us what I believe is the law and the life
for all of us, that law and life of which men in
the old world had only a partial glimpse. I
should not use them if I thought them less universal and more partial than the books of*

[1]See *Subscription No Bondage,* pp. 86 f.: "The Bible . . . in
its true and real character as the record of the ways of God to
man."

155

heathens or of later moralists.—EPISTLES OF ST. JOHN, p. 14.

I go to the Bible—I would bid you go to it—because I feel how much darkness surrounds you and me; because I believe that He, in whom all light dwells, is ready to meet us there; to reveal Himself to us; to guide us onward to the perfect day.—PATRIARCHS AND LAWGIVERS, p. 49.

A CCORDING to Maurice, the Bible is itself one of the signs of the kingdom of Christ, and it also enables us to interpret the other signs. It reveals the divine constitution for man.[2] I propose in this chapter to consider various aspects of Maurice's teaching about the Bible and his method of using it. Doctor H. D. A. Major has said that Maurice "interpreted Scripture in the mystical and allegorical method of the Catechetical School of Alexandria."[3] If that were true he would not have a message for us today that we could not learn better from other and more ancient sources. But we shall see how far from the truth Doctor Major's statement is, and how averse, perhaps too averse, Maurice was to the mystical and allegorical method of interpreting Scripture. At all events, *pace* Doctor Major, Maurice himself said that he "disapproved very strongly . . . of the allegorical method of treating Scripture, into which Origen and others have fallen."[4]

[2]See *Kingdom of Christ* (Ev. ed.), II, 137 f.
[3]*English Modernism* (William Belden Noble Lectures) (1927), pp. 27 f.
[4]*Moral and Metaphysical Philosophy*, I, 469. Cp. *Kingdom of Christ* (Ev. ed.), I, 311 f.

The period of his theological activity, *i.e., circa* 1830–1870, was a period of revolution in Biblical studies and exegesis. It was the time when the work of German Biblical critics was becoming known in England, and when George Eliot translated Strauss's *Life of Jesus*. It was the time when the clash between scientific discoveries and the Biblical history as it had been traditionally interpreted was beginning to be realized.[5] The two forces finally produced a storm in the Church of England about 1860, occasioned by the publication of Darwin's *Origin of Species* and still more of *Essays and Reviews*. Of the latter volume Disraeli said that it "convulses Christendom, and seems to have shaken down the spire of Chichester Cathedral."[6] "Christendom" was a characteristic exaggeration, but the storm was not confined to England. It raged with a special ferocity in South Africa, where Bishop Colenso of Natal, though he seems to have spent much of his time in England, was busily occupied in exposing the incredibility of the pentateuchal narrative.

Maurice remained calm amid the storm. He had taken his bearings long ago, and his faith was anchored to something deeper than the letter of Scripture. He could align himself with neither side in the controversy. Not with Bishop Lee of Manchester, who in the course of a denunciation of Bishop Colenso, declared that "the very foundation of our faith, the very basis of our hopes, the very nearest and dearest of our consolations are taken from us when one line in that Sacred Volume on which we base everything is declared to be unfaithful or untrustworthy."[7]

[5] For the effects of Biblical criticism and scientific discovery in Anglican theology, I may refer to the opening chapters of *The Development of Modern Catholicism* by W. L. Knox and A. R. Vidler (1933).

[6] G. E. Buckle, *Life of Disraeli* (1916), IV, 326.

[7] *The Guardian* (1863), pp. 302, 323. *Cp.* Christopher Wordsworth in *Replies to Essays and Reviews* (1862), p. 456: "*If* Holy Scripture is inspired, then its author is God; and then the Bible must be interpreted as a book written by a Being to whom all

Not with Bishop Colenso who in reply diverted attention
from theological principles by labouring the point that the
hare does not chew the cud (Leviticus, XI, 6).[8] Not with
the unholy alliance between the High Church and Evangelical parties which was got up in order to suppress the
authors of *Essays and Reviews*.[9] Not with the negative and
destructive criticism of *Essays and Reviews*, with which he
could not be satisfied, though he would stand out against
any attempt to suppress the essayists, or any one else who
happened to be unpopular with the factions in the Church
that were powerful at the moment.[10]

This is an old story; is there anything to be gained by
reviving the memory of it? Can any message for today be
extracted from this dark age of the controversy about the
Bible? In the first quarter of the present century the war
between the traditionalists and the critics seemed to be
drawing to a close. What may be called the critical interpretation of the Bible was firmly establishing itself
throughout Western Christendom. The reluctance of Romanism and Protestant Fundamentalism to admit its co-
gency partook of the nature of a rearguard action. But
this has been followed by a period, if not of confessed reaction, yet of evident misgiving and discontent. Some, indeed,
who may not profess to want to go right back on the whole
critical movement, nevertheless give the appearance of
wanting to do so. They minimize its achievements and
importance, and speak slightingly of its adepts. A more
common condition, however, is one that acknowledges the
duty of continuing to use critical methods in studying the
Bible, but has become aware that this is not the final task
of the Biblical theologian.

Critical preoccupation with literary and historical ques-

things are present, and who contemplates all things at once in
the panoramic view of His own Omniscience."

[8]See *The Guardian, loc. cit.* Cp. *Claims of the Bible,* Letter XIII.
[9]See *Life of F. D. M.,* II, 465 ff.
[10]See *ibid.,* II, 388 ff.

tions resulted in a neglect of the essentially theological question: What is the Biblical revelation, and what is its authority? How does the Bible witness to Christ? The more fascinating and engrossing a man found the critical inquiries to be, the easier did he find it to stop short of what for the Church must at last be the main question. Probably the analytic movement had to go a long way before the need for a fresh synthetic movement became apparent. Preachers of the Gospel had meanwhile to make shift as best they could. It was common to distinguish between the use of the Bible in the study, which must be rigorously critical, and its use in the pulpit or in prayer, which was called "devotional." Few theologians would now be satisfied with this double-mindedness. Most are anxious to find the right way of overcoming it. It must be a way that preserves loyalty to critical methods and achievements, and at the same time enables men to use the Bible in the Church. When we accept the most rigorous and radical critical standards, can we see the Bible, the Old Testament as well as the New, as a witness to God's self-revelation in Christ and as the meeting-place of God with man?

It looks as though this question will be the dominant one in Biblical theology in the coming period. Many essays have already been forthcoming that reflect this interest, but the best so far are those that endeavor to exhibit the obligation of facing the question and to show what is involved in it, and that do not attempt to anticipate too confidently what will be the outcome of work that is likely to occupy more than one generation. I am certainly not going to claim that we have only to unearth Maurice's teaching about the Bible in order to discover the way ahead. Nevertheless, we may find that he has some valuable hints and clues to propose to us.

First, we must consider Maurice's attitude to the criticism of the Bible. C. F. G. Masterman said that Maurice "disliked and distrusted the new movement of Biblical

Criticism."[11] But the criticism which he disliked and distrusted was the analytic criticism that exhausted itself in cutting up a book into its component parts and into separate items, that disregarded the fact that the Bible constituted a whole, and that did not attempt to discover the purpose which actuated and informed it.[12] It was because the critical movement, as he knew it, seemed to have this negative character that he disliked and distrusted it, and was not really interested in it.[13] In any case he felt that he had no special aptitude for this kind of work. He cared more for the contents of the Bible than for "proofs about it."[14] "I leave critics to discourse about documents," he said, "what their value is, or whence they come. I merely take what I find."[15] He always thought of the Bible as a whole; he saw it as the revelation of a divine kingdom, the record of its gradual manifestation.

He studied the Bible as one who already believed in this kingdom. He went to the Bible to receive light upon its constitution. He expected to find, and he did find, that through the Bible God was ever teaching men about their place in His kingdom. He went to it as a learner, not as one who had got a ready-made dogmatic system which he was determined that the Bible should prove. It was very wrong to go to the Bible with the intention of making it give out the answers you wanted.[16] He would have no forced construction of particular passages, or special pleading for traditional ascriptions of authorship. "The mere sentimental feeling which attaches a particular passage to a particular name will be readily sacrificed by a lover of truth. The more firmly we believe the Bible to be from God the less serious will that sacrifice seem to us. We shall

[11]*Frederick Denison Maurice*, p. 5.
[12]See *Kingdom of Christ* (Ev. ed.), II, 145.
[13]See *ibid.* (1838), III, 232 f.
[14]See *What is Revelation?*, p. 453.
[15]*Social Morality*, p. 68.
[16]See *Claims of the Bible*, p. 87; *Gospel of St. John*, p. 485.

hear God's voice speaking to us by whatever appellation we denote him who is the instrument of the communication."[17] "The more I read the Bible and believe it," he said, "the deeper is my sense of the fearful sin of sacrificing truth in the slightest degree, for the sake of making out a case in favour of it."[18]

The inconsistencies and incredibilities with which Bishop Colenso and others laboured do not seem to have worried Maurice. This was partly because he instinctively perceived some of the critical conclusions, which have since been reached, and which render otiose the ingenious and far-fetched theories of harmonizers. For example, concerning the order and chronology of the synoptic gospels Maurice wrote in 1854:

> With respect to the times, it seems quite clear that each Evangelist is always ready to sacrifice mere chronology to that order or succession of events which most revealed his purpose. In the short period of our Lord's ministry there are certain great land-marks, such as the Temptation, the Transfiguration, the Entry into Jerusalem, which all observe. Within those land-marks they follow the bent and course of thought which the Spirit has given to each; they group events according to another than a time order.[19]

A further reason for Maurice's lack of concern about many of the questions with which the critics were occupied was his habit of dwelling on those facts in a book or passage of the Bible which were significant of some permanent principle and disregarding what was adventitious to that. Thus on occasion he could treat even light-heartedly matters which others took very seriously. For instance, in 1841 he wrote to a friend about the age of the patriarchs:

[17]*Prophets and Kings*, p. 274.
[18]*Unity of the N. T.*, p. 197. Cp. *Theological Essays*, pp. 344 f.
[19]*Unity of the N. T.*, p. 244. Cp. *Kingdom of Christ* (1838), II, 75 f.

Now as the ages of the antediluvians, being myself in great ignorance, I can offer very inadequate explanations. I have always heard that they came to be rather old gentlemen, and not having any reason to disbelieve it, I supposed they were. If you like to write a tract on the juvenility of Methuselah, I shall read it with great pleasure, and I dare say shall be the wiser for it. I do not see my way on the subject, but, as it is not part of the creed, "I believe that so-and-so was nine hundred and sixty," I can tolerate dissent on the subject, provided it be supported by sound, unmistakable evidence.[20]

These words are revealing. Maurice himself was quite satisfied with conservative positions, but he was willing for them to be called in question. They were not foundations of the faith. Theories about the authorship or construction of particular books do not affect the truths which they assert.[21] "If the Gospel is a Divine message to mankind, it *cannot* depend for the proof of its veracity, for its influence over men, upon any theories about the composition of the books which contain it, upon any arguments about their authenticity or inspiration, upon any definitions which we can give of the words 'Authenticity' and 'Inspiration.' "[22] "The dispute about authorship (of the Epistle to the Hebrews) may entertain those who have leisure for it; the meaning of the Epistle is a question of business for us and for our children."[23] Mistakes or inconsistencies that do not affect the meaning of the facts or the integrity of the writers may be admitted.[24] "God . . . *has* given us an assurance that we shall have His Spirit to guide us into truth. He has not given us a promise that

[20]*Life of F. D. M.*, I, 311 f.
[21]See *Kingdom of Christ* (Ev. ed.), II, 162; *Claims of the Bible*, pp. 82 f.
[22]*Kingdom of Heaven*, p. xxxii.
[23]*Conflict of Good and Evil*, p. 161.
[24]See *Kingdom of Christ* (Ev. ed.), II, 152. Cp. *ibid.*, II, 61.

there shall be no errors in the letter of the Scriptures."[25] Further, there can be no theological interest in maintaining theories which natural science has disproved. "Whatever is true must be satisfactory. . . . The most beautiful dreams and the most exquisite reasonings are good for nothing, if they are at war with that which is. . . . Moralists and theologians never can have an interest in maintaining any proposition that is physically unsound."[26] This is really in principle to grant to critical aims and methods all that they require in order to proceed.

Let us now try to see what Maurice's positive teaching was about the Bible as a whole. Regarding it as one of the signs of the kingdom of Christ, he held that it must always be contemplated as a guide to the constitution of that kingdom and in relation to its other signs. It can never be understood if it is looked upon as a solitary fact placed in the hands of the individual man.[27] The Bible and the Church interpret one another. "The Church exists as a fact, the Bible shows what that fact means. The Bible is a fact, the Church shows what that fact means."[28] Again, "a creed needs a Bible, to show that it has something to rest upon; a Bible needs a creed, to show that it has done what it proposed to do."[29] Baptism and the ministry are signs that every man is not left to interpret the Bible as best he can by himself. The presence of the Spirit in the whole body of the Church and in each of its members means that each member has a capacity for understanding the high privileges which have been obtained for him, and

[25]*Claims of the Bible*, p. 112.

[26]*Doctrine of Sacrifice*, p. 116. Cp. *Theological Essays*, p. 277.

[27]See *Kingdom of Christ* (Ev. ed.), II, 140.

[28]*Ibid.*, II, 164. Cp. *ibid.* (1838), II, 68: "It seems to me, that the loss of the doctrine that the Church is the great schoolmistress of mankind, to educate us into the highest knowledge and happiness of which we are capable, has confused all the thoughts and language as well of the Biblicists as of the Rationalists."

[29]*Ibid.* (1838), II, 27.

that the ministers of the Church can educate their flocks into an apprenhension of them.[30] Thus the Bible is bound up with a living society; it is not a dead book nor an isolated book. It is an instrument which the Holy Spirit is always using in order to address and educate mankind.[31]

Subject to the Holy Spirit, the Church too is the appointed instrument for educating mankind. Its power is parental, not dictatorial. Its office is not to keep us from thinking, but to give us the power of thinking and to give our thoughts a right direction.[32] The Church should use the Bible in this way. It should show us that in the Bible God tells us what we are, and reveals to us our true position in His kingdom.

> "The Bible," we are told sometimes, "gives us such a beautiful picture of what we should be." Nonsense! It gives us no picture at all. It reveals to us a fact; it tells us what we actually are; it says, This is the form in which God created you, to which He has restored you, this is the work which the Eternal Son, the God of truth and love, is continually carrying on within you.[33]

The Bible is the history of the establishment of God's universal kingdom.[34] It is the history of the gradual development and manifestation of this kingdom and of the permanent principles upon which it is constituted.[35] It is a history that not merely records events, but is constructed for the express purpose of expounding principles, of setting forth the relations between the superintending providence of God and the will of man.[36]

[30]See *ibid.* (Ev. ed.), II, 165 f.
[31]See *Claims of the Bible*, pp. 94 f. Cp. *ibid.*, p. 142.
[32]See *Kingdom of Christ* (1838), II, 46.
[33]*The Prayer-Book and the Lord's Prayer*, p. 221.
[34]See *Kingdom of Christ* (Ev. ed.), I, 254. Cp. *Sequel to the Inquiry*, pp. 273–78.
[35]See *Kingdom of Christ* (Ev. ed.), II, 139. Cp. *Sermons on the Sabbath-Day*, p. 6.
[36]See *Kingdom of Christ* (1838), II, 237.

The Theology of the Bible . . . is the unveiling of
the Righteous Being to the heart and conscience of
the only creature that is capable of being righteous,
because of the only creature that is capable of departing from Righteousness. It is an invitation, first to
a man, then to a family, then to a nation, to trust
in this Righteous Being who has shown that He cares
for them, and will not forsake them. It is at last the
manifestation to all nations of that original Righteousness which had been the root of all Righteousness in
them; the Manifestation of the Divine Righteousness
in a Man, who came into the world to reconcile men
to His Father, that they might receive His Spirit, and
be able to be just, as He is—to do justly, as He does.[37]

These principles are not revealed in general or abstract
terms, but are always exhibited in reference to some present
or approaching contingency, and thereby the interpretation
of similar contingencies or circumstances is made possible
till the end of time.[38] The Bible is the great lesson-book
out of which the Church is to teach the world. "Here the
circumstances and relations of ordinary life are exhibited
as the ladder through which God is guiding man up to a
knowledge of Himself."[39] The object of the Bible is to
show us what a father, legislator, prophet, king is—to set
before us the idea of the office. It is part of the nature of
the book "that the idea of the office should be gradually
brought out through the acts of imperfect men, and partly
by means of their imperfections; and that the full realization of each character should be in the God-Man."[40]

What is the subject-matter with which the Bible is
conversant? You would say, perhaps, that it is the

[37]*Lincoln's Inn Sermons*, V, 250 f. Cp. *Kingdom of Christ* (Ev.
ed.), II, 137; *Subscription No Bondage*, p. 85.
[38]See *Kingdom of Christ* (Ev. ed.), II, 139. Cp. *What is Revelation?*, pp. 455, 461; *Social Morality*, p. 52.
[39]*Kingdom of Christ* (1838), II, 50 f.
[40]*Ibid.*, II, 64. Cp. *What is Revelation?*, p. 280.

11

supernatural, the transcendent. But see! There is no
book which speaks so much of shepherds and their
flocks, of the most ordinary doings of families, of nations and laws, and wars; of all that we are wont to
call vulgar and secular things. You might call the
subject-matter of the greater part of the Book of
Genesis, the disputes between brothers, and the
famines which afflicted Palestine and Egypt; the subject-matter of the Book of Exodus, the escape of certain tribes from captivity, and their wanderings
through a desert; the subject-matter of Leviticus, the
management of sacrifices, and the treatment of dis-
eases; the subject-matter of all the books of the Old
Testament, the various fortunes of an Eastern people.
And only by the most violent and tortuous processes
can you separate what may be called the transcendent
or supernatural part of the narrative from these affairs of common life.

Must we not then say that the Revelation or unveiling of the divine or supernatural, if it is made at
all, is made *through* these relations of ordinary daily
life? Is not this the great characteristic of the Book,
the one which, if we take it to be the record of a
continuous Revelation, prepares us for the full manifestation in the Son of Man?[41]

This indicates what was Maurice's method of interpreting Scripture. It can be distinguished from the dogmatic
and the allegorical methods. By the dogmatic method is
meant the use of the Bible as a storehouse of texts which
can be employed to underwrite a dogmatic system. Its
popular formula is: "The Church (= the party or the
sect?) to teach: the Bible to prove." The Bible is treated
as a provision of material to confirm a set of definitions.
The interpreter already knows the truth; his task is to show
that the Bible supports a particular system of doctrine. He
does not go to the Bible to get his system of doctrine and

[41]*Claims of the Bible,* pp. 27 f.

its leading terms interpreted, corrected, pulled about or upset; he interprets the Bible in terms of the system that he brings with him. This was the reverse of Maurice's method. With regard to "the dry and artificial rules and arrangements of divines," he said:

> I am far from wishing you to forget the names and titles by which, both in popular and learned treatises, what we call the doctrines of the Gospel are denoted. They may be of great value to us, if instead of translating the New Testament into them, we ask the New Testament to tell us what they signify, to show us the bonds of living connexion between them, to remove the confusions which torment us when we think of them.[42]

He speaks of the attempt to convert the Bible into a framework of notions and propositions as a great fiction and a monstrous insult to the Divine word.[43] He denounces "the notion that the Bible is a collection of articles of faith, or logical propositions, and that the way of determining religious controversies is by balancing sentence against sentence, under pretence of doing homage to the word of God."[44]

He was no less severe in his comments on the use of the allegorical or mystical or typical method of interpreting Scripture. The desire to find forced analogies in the divine history interferes with the acknowledgment of it as history and is as much to be avoided as "that inhuman (*i.e.*, merely critical) method which takes the juice and meaning out of all events."[45] "There is room for all possible ingenuity and subtlety in detecting resemblances between that which we read in the Old Testament and in the New. But there

[42]*Doctrine of Sacrifice*, pp. 202 f.
[43]See *Subscription No Bondage*, pp. 84 f. Cp. *Claims of the Bible*, p. 21.
[44]*Subscription No Bondage*, pp. 85 f.
[45]*Lincoln's Inn Sermons*, I, 23.

is infinite danger that the reality of the first as well as of the second may disappear through that very ingenuity."[46] "I cannot say how much mischief seems to me to be done, when instead of striving to follow strictly the actual statements of the Old Testament writers, we insist upon wringing out of texts or symbols, which we have moulded according to our fancy, the proof of some New Testament revelation. It is not the law and the prophets only which suffer from such violence. The gospel and the apostles suffer much more."[47]

Maurice's rejection of the allegorical method of interpreting Scripture was too sweeping. As Professor C. H. Dodd has said,[48] there is a sound basis for the use of this method, although it very easily gets out of hand. It is difficult to see how any one can succeed in interpreting some parts of the Bible, for example, the Song of Songs and many passages in the Psalms, as parts of the Christian (or indeed the Jewish) Scriptures without employing this method, though it is necessary to distinguish between legitimate and illegitimate modes of applying it.[49] Moreover, it is a method that is to some extent employed in the New Testament itself in interpreting the Old Testament. Maurice managed to disguise this fact by drawing an unconvincing distinction between it and the method employed on occasion by St. Paul;[50] or by passing over passages where allegory is involved, pleading that he could not understand them.[51]

[46]*Ibid.*, III, 246. Cp. *ibid.*, V, 194.

[47]*Prophets and Kings*, p. 441. Cp. *Kingdom of Christ* (Ev. ed), II, 236 ff.; *Commandments*, p. 12; *The Prayer-Book and the Lord's Prayer*, p. 97; *Social Morality*, p. 247.

[48]*The Bible To-day* (1946), p. 18. Cp. *ibid.*, p. 16.

[49]See an art. on "The Use of the Psalms To-day" in *Theology* (May and June, 1947), by H. de Candole, who proposes a distinction between the "allegorical" and the "spiritual" interpretation of the Psalter.

[50]See *Lincoln's Inn Sermons*, I, 26 ff. (on I Corinthians, X).

[51]See *Unity of the N. T.*, p. 197 (on Matthew, XII, 40).

At the same time, he draws a pertinent and important distinction when he writes with regard to the senses in which a prophecy may be said to be fulfilled:

> It is a very different thing to maintain that a prophecy may have a double or treble sense, where by double or treble you mean that what is true of one time may be even more clearly and emphatically true of another, just as ordinary historians have remarked that the same principles swayed the conduct of Charlemagne and of Napoleon, that even the facts of the history repeat themselves, and that the laws which govern those facts are brought out more completely in the latest facts than in the earlier; and to use words in a double sense, where by "double" we mean that the signification of them in the very same narrative or discourse is changed, so that it is at the pleasure of the interpreter to make them signify one thing in reference to one part of the subject and another in reference to another. To say that a prophet not only does, but that he must transgress the limits of a single event when he lays down a great law of the Divine mind, is to claim for him that very insight and foresight which his name implies; to say that he palters with words in a double sense, is nothing less than to call him a false prophet, to identify him with a heathen oracle.[52]

The Bible may play upon the double sense of words in ways that Maurice was unwilling to perceive, but he saw clearly that the meaning of the most distant future emerges out of the prophets' discourses not when we divorce them from local and immediate occurrences, but when we observe how they brought eternal truths to bear upon them.[53]

We shall already have discerned the method of interpretation which Maurice himself sought to follow. In in-

[52]*Ibid.*, p. 133.
[53]See *Prophets and Kings*, p. 352.

terpreting a book or a passage in the Bible he aimed at discovering what its original and simplest meaning was, and then he asked how the facts so disclosed asserted or illustrated the eternal principles of the divine kingdom, the constitution of mankind in Christ, and the manner of God's dealings with His people. He went to work with the assumptions that the Bible contains an inexhaustible wealth of truth which God would impart to His people, and that the Holy Spirit is alive and active in all who come to it as willing learners. He described his own method of expounding Scripture as follows:

> Those of you who have attended my Bible class on Sunday evening will know that I have taken some pains to show you that the Bible may be read as a continuous history, and that it is the history of the unveiling of God to the creature whom He has made in His image. I have tried to show you this by taking separate books in the New Testament, and examining them chapter by chapter, verse by verse. I have tried to show it you by beginning at the beginning of the Old Testament, and tracing the course of its narratives. I have tried to show it you by comparing the Old Testament with the New. I have not used any arguments to prove that the book was divine or was worthy of our attention. If it was divine and worthy of our attention, I thought it would make good its claims for itself, though I could not make them good. All I wanted was that we should find out what it is that it is saying to us. . . . What I chiefly desired was, that I might put myself as little as possible between you and the revelation which I was sure the book contained.[54]

The greater part of Maurice's published work consists of sermons and expositions of Scripture, in which he follows this method with singular faithfulness. He regularly

[54]*Epistles of St. John*, p. 9.

tries to find out what is the actual meaning of the passage which he is expounding, to discern what permanent principle it illuminates, and finally to show how that principle bears upon contemporary affairs and upon the decisions which he and his hearers have to take and the work they have to do.[55] The rightness of the method does not stand or fall with his own applications of it. His sermons and expositions are of value chiefly because they show the possibility and the rewards of adhering to the method and to the assumptions on which it rests.

It goes without saying that now his exegesis will often seem archaic. He used the best resources that he knew in order to discover the original meaning of each book and passage, but the resources that have since been made available as a result of the labours of the literary and historical critics were not available then. In following the method today we should of course be bound to make full use of our present resources. It is likewise an obstacle to the modern reader that Maurice persists in treating mythological or legendary narratives as though they were strictly historical. It does not seem to have occurred to him[56] that, just because the Bible is a revelation through the history of a real people, it must like all other histories of real peoples be bound up with illuminating myths, especially around its beginnings, and that God can use these as well as the rest in His education of mankind.

All commentators who seek to bring out the full meaning of Scripture and its message to their contemporaries are exposed to the temptation of reading their favourite ideas into the passages they are expounding. Although Maurice was aware and fearful of this danger, he often unintentionally succumbed to it. There is justice in Principal Tulloch's judgment on Maurice's exegesis, though he overstates the case:

[55]For an excellent example of this method, see *Sermons on the Sabbath-Day*, pp. 1–77.
[56]See *Kingdom of Christ* (1838), II, 65 f.

> Scholar and thinker as he was, no man was ever less of a purely historical critic. He saw everywhere a reflection of his favourite ideas. . . . His vivid faith in the Divine—the strength of his root-convictions, mounting to a species of infallibility—made him see from Genesis to Revelation the same substance of Divine dogma.[57]

Much the same was said, and with even more justice, by Principal Shairp about Thomas Erskine's interpretations of difficult texts: "They were exceedingly ingenious, and such as could only have occurred to a meditative and highly spiritual mind. But it often seemed as if the interpretation was born from within his own thought, rather than gathered from impartial exegesis. So strong was the heat of his cherished convictions, that before them the toughest, most obdurate text gave way, melted and fused into the mould which his bias had framed for it."[58] It must be confessed that Maurice's exegesis often leaves an impression of this sort upon the mind, and sometimes makes it seem that he was trying to evade the force of a passage whose *prima facie* meaning told against his own treasured teaching.[59] These, however, were faults in the application of the method, not in the method itself. Maurice would have been the first to own that they were faults, if he had realized what he was doing.

A great deal will obviously depend on whether a reader of Maurice's sermons and expositions considers that "his favourite ideas" were true or not. If Maurice's belief was true that the unveiling of God in Christ was the full

---

[57]*Movements of Religious Thought*, p. 278. *Cp.* J. Martineau, *Essays, Reviews, and Addresses*, I, 265; and John Sterling in *Letters and Memorials of Richard Chevenix Trench*, I, 239, 247 f.

[58]See William Hanna, *Letters of Thomas Erskine of Linlathen*[2] (1878), p. 525.

[5.]*E.g., Gospel of St. John*, pp. 279 f. (on John X, 7–10) ; *Conflict of Good and Evil*, pp. 193 f. (on Matthew, VII, 14). *Cp.* Hort's *Life and Letters*, II, 158.

manifestation of what had been His relation to mankind from the first, and of what was being gradually revealed under the old covenant, then he was justified in interpreting the Old Testament in the light of the New, and the earlier strata in the New Testament in the light of the later. The trouble is that while Maurice sometimes recognized that various levels of insight were represented in the Bible, and even in the New Testament,[60] his general tendency was to discover the highest level of insight at any and every point and to make the Biblical testimony consistent from beginning to end.[61] Thus there is a certain monotony in his exposition of Scripture in spite of the range and variety of the ground he covers and of his desire to let the Bible always speak for itself. He makes the authors of Scripture speak too much a common language. Yet he knew very well that Scripture is not consistent in this sense, and he said so.

> The inspired writers are never afraid of seeming to contradict themselves. They give the captious, disputatious heart of the natural man, all advantages—they let him amuse himself with their apparent inconsistencies, as much as he will; for they know well that if they left out either of two apparently opposite assertions, the other would be false, and that only by meditating upon both, can the spiritual man rise to a vital apprehension of the truth.[62]

Maurice did not look upon the Bible as a holy island

[60]*E.g.*, he allows that it was "perhaps" reserved for St. Paul to see more perfectly than St. Peter what the gift of the Spirit implied respecting man's creation and redemption. See *Religions of the World*, p. 192.

[61]*E.g.*, of the miracle of the coin in the fish's mouth, he says: "Those who value it because it seems to them an act of a more startling kind than others which they read of, must consider with themselves whether they will explain all miracles by this, or this by them."—*Unity of the N. T.*, p. 205.

[62]*Christmas Day*, p. 77. Cp. *Apocalypse*, pp. 176 f.

in an ocean of secular or profane literature.[63] He did not
suppose that the divine inspiration which was bestowed
upon the writers and the words of Scripture was confined
to them or that it was to be rigidly separated from the
inspiration that might be bestowed on other writers and
other words. "Inspiration is not a strange anomalous fact;
it is the proper law and order of the world. . . . According to the law of a spiritual kingdom, every man who is
doing the work he is set to do, may believe that he is
inspired with a power to do that work. . . . The question
therefore, is not really, Were these men who wrote the
Scriptures inspired by God? but, Were they in a certain
position and appointed to a certain work? . . . Was there
such a society as that which this book speaks of?"[64] When
we say that the Bible is inspired, we mean that it is inspired
for a certain purpose, to be a permanent record of, and
witness to, the constitution of the kingdom of Christ. We
do not restrict the work of the Holy Spirit.

> If we pray, we must confess that Inspiration for
> which our Collects continually entreat. We must sup-
> pose that we cannot think, believe, act without it;
> we must acknowledge that all wisdom, illumination,
> power to will and to do, proceed from the Divine
> Spirit. We dare not define or limit His operations. . . .
>   That holy men . . . of old spoke by the inspira-
> tion of God, that the same inspiration enables us to
> know what they said, to have any clear understanding
> of any kind: this has been the faith of the Church
> at all times. . . . To say that inspiration is confined
> to the writers of the Bible, is formally and directly
> to contradict those writers; to determine in what
> measures they or any other man have possessed in-
> spiration, is to tell Him who breathes where He

[63]"It has been a miserable part of our apologetic system to
set up Sacred History as a kind of rival to Profane; to treat one
as if it concerned God, and the other as if it was merely of the
earth."—*What is Revelation?*, pp. 462 f.
[64]*Kingdom of Christ* (Ev. ed.), II, 148.

listeth how *we* suppose He must breathe or ought to breathe.[65]

The Bible unfolds the scheme and purpose of this universe and its Creator. It shows men their own connexion with this universe, with those who have lived in it, and with Him who is the author of it. Men may learn from this book how to read every other book.[66] "We declare that there is a book which directly and formally connects letters with the life of man, with the order of God; a book, which so far as it fulfils its idea, becomes the key by which all books may be interpreted, that which translates them into significance and determines the value and position of each."[67] The Bible serves as a key book which enables us "to understand the histories and legends of various nations, to justify the true beliefs which were in them, to show what false beliefs or unbeliefs had mingled with these, to explain how they had become confounded."[68] If we will always aim at the highest truth and good, we shall learn to appreciate all the lower forms of truth and good and to eschew and detest the counterfeit and the evil.[69] The manifestation of perfect manhood in Christ enables us to evaluate the signs of moral sensibility and the aspirations after glory, in all nations and ages, to declare their origin and end, and "to vindicate every brave and true effort of men for the extirpation of sickness, sorrow, and misery, as prompted and inspired by Him."[70]

The Bible is a book not about religion but about God, His manifestation of Himself and of the divine constitution for man. Maurice doubly eschews the conventional distinction between natural and revealed religion. In the

[65]*Claims of the Bible*, pp. 120 f. Cp. *Sequel to the Inquiry*, pp. 51 f.
[66]See *Kingdom of Christ* (Ev. ed.), II, 153.
[67]*Ibid.*
[68]*Life of F. D. M.*, II, 229.
[69]See *Sequel to the Inquiry*, p. 295.
[70]*Ibid.*, pp. 257 f.

first place, he came to regard "religion" as a heathenish word.[71] He would not speak of the Gospel of the kingdom of God as "a religion." In the New Testament "we read nothing of a religion."[72]

> The struggle which occupied the first centuries of the modern world . . . was not a struggle between a Christian religion and another religion, or a multitude of other religions. It was the struggle between a kingdom which was grounded on the dominion of a man raised to be a God, with the announcement that the true King of men is one who, being in the form of God, took upon Him the nature of His subjects, that He might deliver them from all their oppressors bodily and spiritual.[73]

The word religion "is a peculiarly ambiguous one, and one that is likely to continue ambiguous, because we connect it habitually with the study and treatment of the Bible, though the Bible itself gives us no help in ascertaining the force of the word, apparently sets no great store by it or any similar one. So far as I am able to make out, it is best used to denote certain processes or habits or conditions of our own minds."[74] The "word 'godly,' " he said, "is an old Puritan word which I prefer very much . . . to the vague word 'religious.' "[75] "Religion against God. This is the heresy of our age," Maurice once exclaimed.[76] "We have been dosing our people with religion

[71]See *Life of 1. D. M.,* I, 86; *What is Revelation?,* p. 181.

[72]*Social Morality,* p. 229. Cp. *Kingdom of Heaven,* pp. xiv f.; *The Prayer-Book and the Lord's Prayer,* p. 109; *Doctrine of Sacrifice,* p. xvi. On the use of the expression "religious duties," see *Sermons on the Sabbath-Day,* pp. 58–61.

[73]*Kingdom of Heaven,* p. xix.

[74]*What is Revelation?,* pp. 239 f.

[75]*Cf. Few Words on Secular and Denominational Education,* p. 7. Cp. *Doctrine of Sacrifice,* pp. xiii, 19.

[76]*Life of F. D. M.,* I, 518. *Cp.* Thomas Erskine, *The Brazen Serpent* (1831), p. 200.

when what they want is not this but the living God."[77]
It seemed to him that the religions of the world were
various human schemes for ascending to God or for find-
ing a meeting-point with Him; they are significant of the
fact that there is such a meeting-point, although they cannot produce it. The Bible is the "proclamation of the One
Person in whom God is at one with His creatures, in whom
He can meet them and they can meet Him."[78]

This was the question in dispute between Maurice and
Mansel in their great controversy. It seemed to Maurice
that Mansel set forth Christianity as a revealed religion.
God Himself was not revealed to man, for the human
mind is, by the inevitable limits of its powers, incapable of
knowing God. What had been revealed were certain regu-
lative truths from which men might learn how best to
think of the unknowable God. Maurice, on the other hand,
believed that according to the New Testament "Revelation is . . . the unveiling of a Person—and that Person
the ground and Archetype of men, the source of all life
and goodness in men—not to the eye, but to the very man
himself, to the Conscience, Heart, Will, Reason, which
God has created to know Him, and be like Him."[79] The
Bible is a revelation of God,[80] but this does not mean that
it makes God comprehensible to men.

> We hesitate to say that the awful name of God
> can ever be thoroughly made known to man; and if
> we meant that He was less incomprehensible at the
> end of the book than at the beginning of it, we should
> indeed be uttering a great and terrible profaneness.
> No, the revelation is a progress from the comprehen-
> sible to the incomprehensible, a gradual, orderly, scien-
> tific progress from those manifestations of God which

[77]*Life of F. D. M.,* I, 369.
[78]*Ibid.,* II, 230.
[79]*What is Revelation?,* p. 54. Cp. *ibid.,* p. 107; *Lincoln's Inn
Sermons,* V, 113 f.; *Life of F. D. M.,* II, 511, 597.
[80]See *Kingdom of Christ* (1838), II, 18.

are apprehensible to the affections, and in some measure to the understandings of men, to those which we require for the satisfaction of the deepest and most awful longings of our spirits.[81]

Maurice was certainly right about the main question, despite the applause that Mansel received from contemporary orthodoxy. Nevertheless, Mansel was dealing with epistemological problems that cannot be met simply by an assertion of the Biblical testimony to the meaning of revelation. For the Biblical writers these problems did not exist, or at any rate had not been formulated; once they have been raised and formulated they can be dealt with only by a doctrine of analogy,[82] which neither of the protagonists in this controversy had at his disposal.

In the second place, Maurice eschewed the conventional distinction between natural and revealed religion[83] because he did not acknowledge natural reason and revelation as two different ways of acquiring knowledge. He deeply distrusted that manner of speaking according to which man is held to be able by the independent exercise of his reasoning faculties to acquire a certain knowledge of God, which may then be supplemented, completed or crowned by revelation. "I hold," he said, "that *all* our knowledge may be traced ultimately to Revelation from God."[84] "The Scripture . . . assumes it to be the normal condition of man, that he should receive communications from God."[85] "The postulate of the Bible is, that man could not be what he is, if God did not hold converse with him; that this is his distinction from other creatures; that this is the

[81]*Ibid.*, II, 22.

[82]*E.g.*, see M. T.-L. Penido, *Le Rôle de l'Analogie en théologie dogmatique* (1931).

[83]See *Moral and Metaphysical Philosophy*, I, xx f.; *The New Statute and Mr. Ward*, p. 23; *Social Morality*, p. 225.

[84]*Sequel to the Inquiry*, p. 97.

[85]*Patriarchs and Lawgivers*, p. 77.

root of all that he knows, the ground of what is right and reasonable in him."[86]

St. Paul does not say, as some of us might say, that the Jews received a revelation, and that the Gentiles were without one. He could not say that without contradicting the doctrine which he had been asserting in the two first (*sic*) chapters of this same Epistle (Romans), and of which the whole of it is a development. He there maintains that God *did* reveal His own righteousness in the conscience of the Gentile, and that the sin of those who worshipped the creature more than the Creator consisted in their not *"liking* to retain God in their knowledge."[87]

This is not, however, to say that there are no distinctions to be drawn as regards the modes of revelation. God reveals Himself through nature, through man, and finally through the Incarnate Son.

We often say that Revelation is progressive, and the writer of this Epistle (Hebrews) abundantly justifies the language. But by *progress,* some seem to mean a continual journeying away from the inmost centre; a movement towards the circumference. Here we seem to be taught that each step of it is bringing us nearer to the ground of things—nearer to the throne of God. The revelation of God in this sense is truly the unveiling of Himself. First, He speaks in that which is most distant from Him, the mere things He has formed; then in men whom He created to rule over these things; lastly, in Him who by the eternal law is the inheritor of all things, in whom and for whom they were created. The order of the world, the succession of ages, spoke of the permanence of God. Here He speaks in Him by whom He framed the order of the world, the succession of times. . . . Things,

[86]*Doctrine of Sacrifice,* p. 4. Cp. *ibid.,* p. 33.
[87]*Lincoln's Inn Sermons,* I, 125. Cp. *Moral and Metaphysical Philosophy,* II, 347.

in themselves cold and inanimate, are found to have a personal centre; the course of time, in itself dead and abstract, to have a living Mover. It is the Son of God, *"the brightness of his Father's glory, the express image of his substance."* Glimpses of His glory we have seen in His creation, brighter glimpses in the love and tenderness of human creatures. Here is He from whom they have both proceeded; here is the mystery which the prophets perceived in different portions, and expressed in divers manners; here is the whole WORD, of which they uttered different syllables . . . in Him creation has subsisted, in spite of all the elements of confusion and discord within it.[88]

When we read the Scriptures of the Old and New Testaments in a continuous order, as a series of Divine Lessons, we feel that one veil after another is in them withdrawn from our eyes, and that the last step in the process must be that which discloses the full Atonement of God and Man, of Earth and Heaven, and the full Name of God, just because this is that true Original Foundation which sin has been concealing, and denying, and seeking to destroy.[89]

Finally, Maurice did not regard miracles as prodigies which attested revelation. This seemed to him to be the view of Mansel and of the conventional orthodoxy of the time. Maurice believed in the miracles of the Bible, indeed with insufficient discrimination, but he regarded them as manifestations, not as violations, of order. The Bible itself commands us to reject the notion of miracles as prodigies which prove the divine commission of the person who enacts them.[90] The miracles are demonstrations "that spiritual power is superior to mechanical; that the world is subject to God, and not to chance or nature; that there

---

[88]*Epistle to the Hebrews*, pp. 28 f. Cp. *Lincoln's Inn Sermons*, I, 181 f.; *Life of F. D. M.*, II, 563.

[89]*The Prayer-Book and the Lord's Prayer*, p. 119.

[90]See *Kingdom of Christ* (Ev. ed.), II, 156.

is an order."[91] They teach man that he is not the victim of a set of blind natural agents. "Apparent breaches in the regular course of events, surprising visitations, prove at times what the evenness and persistency of nature proves habitually—that the just God, of whom man is the image, against whose laws he is so continually striving, is the Author and Ruler of all things."[92] Every miracle recorded in the Old Testament

> is recorded expressly as a witness, that the Jehovah, the I AM, the personal God, the Lord of the spirits of all flesh, is the King of the world. . . . Every miracle recorded in the New Testament is recorded expressly and professedly for the purpose of showing that the Son of man is the Ruler of the winds and waves; the sustainer and restorer of animal life; the healer and tamer of the human spirit; and that those who are the adopted children of God in Him, while they are doing His work, are not the servants of visible things, but their rulers.[93]
>
> We confess, and rejoice to confess, that there is an habitual appointed course of things; that each agent, voluntary or involuntary, has his proper place in the scheme; that no one link of this agency will be ever needlessly broken or dispensed with. But we say that no dishonour is put upon any of these agents, when He, who has assigned them their place, keeps them in their own relation to each other, imparts to them their powers, withdraws the veil which conceals Himself the prime worker, and so explains the meaning of His ordinances, the secret of their efficiency, the reason of their abuse.[94]

The question of the occurrence of such miracles in sub-

[91]*Ibid.*, II, 158. Cp. *Commandments*, p. 70; *What is Revelation?*, pp. 56–68; *Social Morality*, p. 259.

[92]*Doctrine of Sacrifice*, p. 28.

[93]*Kingdom of Christ* (Ev. ed.), II, 157 f. Cp. *Acts of the Apostles*, p. 39.

[94]*Ibid.*, II, 150.

12

sequent ages must be determined by a careful study of historical evidence. But "those who believe that miracles are for the assertion of order, and not for the violation of it, for the sake of showing the constant presence of a spiritual power, and not for the sake of showing that it interferes occasionally with the affairs of the world," will not be inclined to expect the frequent repetition of such signs.[95]

In the first edition of *The Kingdom of Christ* Maurice summed up his teaching about the Bible in this concluding paragraph:

> He who dwells with us and governs us, the Ever-blessed Word, has formed us to be one in Him; He seeks to make us one by bringing us to a knowledge of Himself; for this end He has revealed Himself to us, and has preserved the revelation in a book; this revelation He has entrusted to His Church, that she may impart it to men, and train men to apprehend its contents; the Church, in the exercise of her functions, has from Scripture formed a creed which is the first step in her scheme of education; when men were awakened by this creed, it became her duty to use the Bible, that they might know the certainty of those things wherein they have been catechised; with this Bible, she is able to cultivate the reason, which is the organ wherewith we apprehend spiritual matters; the Church tried what she could do without the Bible, and she became weak; the Bible has been set up against the Church, and has been dishonoured; the Reason has been set up against both Church and Bible, and has become partial, inconsistent, self-contradictory. Finally, bitter experience must lead us at last to a conviction, that God's ways are higher than our ways; that a universal Church, constituted in His Son, and endowed with His Spirit, is the proper instrument for using His universal book; and this book the instrument for educating the universal reason.[96]

[95]*Ibid.*, II, 166 f.   [96]*Ibid.* (1838), II, 87 f.

7

A LIVING POLITICS

Whether there shall be a living Politics, grounded on the acknowledgement of a permanent Order, adapting itself to the changing wants of man, or only endless altercations between one political dogma and another, ending in a Tyranny in which men acquiesce, because they have tried all plans and notions and have found them barren.—SEQUEL TO THE INQUIRY, p. 193.

MAURICE, we have seen, was continually underlining the universality of the kingdom of Christ and its all-embracing unity. But he did not conceive this universality and unity to be opposed to the distinctness of individual persons and families or to the diversity of nations. "I am more and more convinced," he wrote to R. C. Trench in 1835, "that we must not use *personal* and *individual* as synonymous words; but that, in fact, we shall have most sense and lively realization of our distinct personality when we cease to be individuals, and most delight to contemplate ourselves as members of one body in one Head."[1] He believed that within God's constitution for mankind persons, families, and nations all had a secured position and only within that constitution could they come to their

[1] *Letters and Memorials of R. C. Trench* (1888), I, 190. Cp. *Conscience*, p. 174.

completion. Sects, parties, associations, grounded in the opinion and choice of men, are one thing; the societies that have been created and ordained by God and that are grounded in His will are another. These have a permanent place in His kingdom and are necessary to its full unfolding. "The Father of all does not regard special nations less, because by the birth and death of His Son, He has redeemed mankind."[2] "The State is as much God's creation as the Church."[3] The families which God has established are witnesses of His Fatherhood, and the nations which God has established, each under its own proper ruler, are witnesses of an unseen and righteous kingdom.[4]

It was first through a family, then through a nation, and finally through a universal society, that God had made Himself manifest, and the earlier manifestations were intended to be continued within the last. The smaller societies are training grounds where lessons are learned that are to be lived out in the wider and universal sphere.

> The family order and constitution is the first great bulwark which God has provided against the dominion of the senses and of the outward world,— . . . the feeling, "I am a member of a family, I am the son and brother of such a person," is the great balancing power against the feeling, that there are certain pleasant objects which my eye sees, and my ear hears, and my palate tastes,— . . . it is the great influence which redeems the affections from things, and gives them a direction towards persons,— . . . it is the commencement of all society,— . . . it is the first step towards the acknowledgment of God.[5]

No doubt there is a great risk in leaving children to the chance prudence of particular parents, but it is a far

[2]*Lincoln's Inn Sermons,* I, 103.
[3]*Kingdom of Christ* (1838), III, 76.
[4]See *Lincoln's Inn Sermons,* I, 250.
[5]*Kingdom of Christ* (1838), III, 11.

greater and more terrible risk not to recognize the family principle, not to assert the parental responsibility.[6] The meaning of authority and obedience is learned in the relationship of fathers and sons, the meaning of trust in the relationship of husbands and wives, the meaning of fraternity and equality in the relationship of brothers and sisters.[7] These relations are not the creation of formal law; they are implied in it, they lie beneath it, they must be recognized and accepted by it so soon as it comes into existence.[8] They express and actualize the necessary dependence of human beings, one upon another. They are the core of human society; they are implied not only in its well-being but in its very being. "If we do not take account of those societies in which we must exist, we shall attach a very disproportionate value to those in which we *may* exist. The Class and the Club will be superlatively precious and dear as the Family is lost out of sight."[9]

The characteristics of a nation are that it has a law, a language and a government.[10] Membership of a nation teaches a man that he is under law and that he is personally responsible. "We find a Law; it claims us as its subjects; we learn by degrees that we *are* subject to it. That is a very great discovery. . . . Just so far as it is brought home to me I know that I am a distinct person; that I must answer for myself."[11] "Each man is taken apart from every other. Each one is met with a 'Thou.' The Law is over families, but it is addressed to every one who hears it separately, without reference to his ancestors or his descendants."[12] Through his inheritance of a language a man acquires the power of communicating with his neighbours, of distinguishing between truth and false-

[6]See *Lectures on National Education*, p. 51.
[7]See *Social Morality*, Lectures II, III, and IV.
[8]See *ibid.*, pp. 43 f.
[9]*Ibid.*, p. 59.
[10]See *ibid.*, Lectures VIII, IX, and X.
[11]*Ibid.*, p. 119.   [12]*Ibid.*, pp. 124 f.

hood, of being educated. "The faculties which are given
to man never have had their proper development and
expansion, except in a *national* community."[13] By being
placed under a government a man learns the meaning of
loyalty, learns that Law is not a mere abstraction, but is
grounded in the will of a Person.

> What binds me to the other members of this nation?
> What holds the limbs of this nation together? . . .
> That *What* must pass into a *Who,* or you will be dis-
> honest citizens. Whether you are hands or feet in the
> body politic, whether you make laws, or administer
> them, whether you bring them to bear upon others,
> or only submit to them yourselves; you will be tempted
> to deny your relationship to your fellow-citizens, you
> will be tempted to act unfaithfully by them, and
> therefore to lower and degrade yourselves, unless you
> feel that it is not an abstraction, but a Person, who
> unites you to them, who admonishes you of your
> transgressions against them, who makes you under-
> stand and fulfil your obligations.[14]

We shall understand now why Maurice refused to think
or speak of national life as "secular."

> There are many Christians who would persuade us
> that the life of a Nation is what they call a secular
> thing; that it may be very well on mere earthly
> grounds to care for the land in which we have been
> born and nurtured, in which our affections have
> grown, in which alas! they may have withered; but
> that if we would turn our minds to heavenly con-
> templations and be in the true sense servants of God,
> we must be looking to a time when all that belongs
> to us as citizens shall have passed away. . . . I sol-
> emnly deny that a Nation is a secular thing. . . . If
> by "secular" is meant that which belongs to the fashion

[13]*Kingdom of Christ* (Ev. ed.), I, 233. Cp. *Conscience,* pp.
129 ff.
[14]*Lincoln's Inn Sermons,* V, 239 f.

of a particular age—that which shuts out the acknowledgement of the permanent and the eternal,—that, I grant, is hostile to Christian faith, that is the "evil world" against which we are to fight. But one of the greatest weapons which God has given us in our conflict with this enemy—whether it invites us to worship the conceits of our own age, or of some departed age, —is the assurance that the Nation has lived, lives now, and will live in Him, who was, and is, and is to come.[15]

The teaching about national life in the Old Testament is not abrogated by the New Testament but carried forward into the new dispensation. "I do not expect to find the principles of the universal society developed in the Old Testament, nor the principles of the national society in the New. I do expect to find each illustrating and sustaining the other."[16] The Jewish history contains the divine specimen of a national life.[17] The key to the history of all nations is furnished in the history of that one nation; God's methods with that are a guide to His methods with all.[18]

The Church of Christ, so far from dissolving national bonds as the Roman Empire had done, gave nations a new vitality and distinctness, and created within them a national organization altogether different from the ecclesiastical organization.[19] It was the will of God that nations should come into being, and this was necessary not for the chastisement of the Church, but for its development.[20] The universal society, as it put itself forth substantially in the world, did not extinguish, but justified, all family

[15]*Hope for Mankind*, pp. 45 f.
[16]*Kingdom of Christ* (Ev. ed.), II, 181.
[17]See *ibid.*, II, 179; *Sermons on the Sabbath-Day*, p. 7; *Commandments*, pp. 12, 78; *What is Revelation?*, p. 39; *Doctrine of Sacrifice*, p. 63.
[18]See *Sermons on the Sabbath-Day*, pp. 107 f.
[19]See *Kingdom of Christ* (Ev. ed.), II, 186.
[20]See *ibid.*, II, 243.

and national life.[21] The nations were brought into their distinct life by the Church, and cannot retain their distinct life without the Church.[22] It had been the great misery and sin of the Jews, at the time when our Lord appeared among them in the flesh, that they had lost the sense of national unity, and had become covetous individuals, herding together in sects, knit to each other by opinions and antipathies, not by the sense of a common origin, a common country, a common Lord.[23]

It seemed to Maurice that life in a national community, as distinguished from the preoccupations of a sect on the one hand, and from absorption in a world-empire on the other, was a necessary condition for the preservation of a living faith in God.

> Destroy national characteristics, reduce us merely into one great society, and whether the bond of that society is a pope, or an emperor, or a customs-union, the result is the same. A living God is not feared or believed in; He is not the centre of that combination; His name or the name of a number of Gods may be invoked in it, but His presence is not that which holds its different elements together. Therefore let us be sure that if we would ever see a real family of nations, such as the prophets believed would one day emerge out of the chaos they saw around them, a family of nations which shall own God as their Father and Christ as their elder Brother, this must come from each nation maintaining its own integrity and unity.[24]

The Biblical testimony that the nation of Israel had a calling from God is a witness to every nation that it has a holy calling. "I believe that we have as much right to call England a holy nation as the prophets had to call

[21]See *The Church a Family*, p. 96.
[22]See *Three Letters to the Rev. W. Palmer*, p. 19.
[23]See *Gospel of St. John*, p. 188.
[24]*Sermons on the Sabbath-Day*, pp. 93 f.

Judaea a holy nation. I believe that it is holy in virtue of God's calling; that the members of it are unholy when they deny their calling and their unity."[25]

> We cannot reverence heaven or know what it is, if we do not reverence the earth on which Christ walked and which He redeemed. We cannot attain Christ's likeness, if we do not learn to care for England as He cared for Palestine, when it was in its lowest condition. We cannot hope in Christ for ourselves if we suppose that He is indifferent about the righteousness and the freedom of our nation.[26]

The citizens of each nation ought to regard their own nation in this light, recognizing that the same holds good for every other nation. "If we believe that our nation has a holy calling, we shall believe every nation to have a holy calling."[27] "If I count it an unspeakable blessing for myself to be the citizen of a nation, I must count it an unspeakable blessing for every man. If I, being an Englishman, desire to be thoroughly an Englishman, I must respect every Frenchman who strives to be thoroughly a Frenchman, every German who strives to be thoroughly a German. I must learn more of the worth and grandeur of his position, the more I estimate the worth and grandeur of my own."[28]

> If I were a German, I would hate and denounce all Anglo-maniacs,—I would tell them, that they had no business to talk about the excellence and the blessedness of another land; that they ought to be seeking out all the capacities of good which lie in their own; I would tell them that, if they cannot feel the rich blessings which God has given them, in being born where they are born, they never can be able to value (however they may fancy it) the good which is pro-

[25]*Ibid.*, pp. 71 f.
[26]*Hope for Mankind*, p. 49.
[27]*Lincoln's Inn Sermons*, II, 59. [28]*Social Morality*, pp. 106 f.

duced on different soil. For, assuredly, no man hath ever done good to mankind who was not a patriot.[29]

Maurice commonly used the terms "nation" and "state" interchangeably, as is frequently done, but in the first edition of *The Kingdom of Christ* he defined a State as follows:

> A body connected together in a particular locality, united in the acknowledgment of a certain law, which each member of this body must obey, or suffer for its violation; a body recognizing a supreme and invisible Being as the author and sanction of this law; a body recognizing a relationship between its members, grounded originally upon actual kinsmanship, but now expressed simply in the term neighbourhood,—this is what I call a *State,* and in such a *State,* I say every man must dwell not only for purposes of safety and protection, but in order that his moral and spiritual being may be properly developed. Such a State, I say, is as much implied in the constitution of man as a Church is implied in that constitution; such a State is as much a witness for God in one way as a Church is a witness for Him in another way.[30]

This leads us to a consideration of the relation between Church and State, and between National Churches and the Church Universal. Maurice did not regard Church and State as contraries; the State is the vestibule to the Church; each is the support of the other.[31] The Church is not degraded by working together with a body that has functions distinct from its own, but like itself is established by God to accomplish the ends of His providence.[32] "The State, though it deals with the outward life of man, is not . . . a secular body, but appeals to, and acts upon the conscience of man in a way in which the Church

[29]*Kingdom of Christ* (1838), III, 377.
[30]*Ibid.,* III, 13 f.
[31]See *Lincoln's Inn Sermons,* II, 72.
[32]See *Kingdom of Christ* (1838), III, 103 f.

cannot appeal to that conscience or act upon it, bears a witness for God which the Church cannot bear. . . . The Church is necessarily a maimed and imperfect thing without the State, not because it wants its revenues or its sword, but because God hath ordained an eternal connection between the law, which is embodied in the State, and the religious, life-giving principle which is embodied in the Church, so that one shall always sigh and cry till it has found the other to be its mate."[33] The State bears "a witness for law and justice, for a God of Law and Justice, which the Church, under no conditions, has borne, or could bear."[34] It is impossible for evangelization and civilization to exist apart.[35]

> We hold the State and the Church do live to promote the same end; that both alike are religious societies instituted and ordained by God, that both alike are to accomplish His will towards His creature man, that both alike are to preserve that creature from the mischiefs to which an evil nature exposes him. But seeing that this man is a twofold creature, seeing that there are certain outward acts which he may do to the detriment of himself and his fellows; and seeing that there are certain inward principles, governing those outward acts, imparting to them their essential goodness or evil, and themselves more sacred and important than the effects which flow from them, we believe that God has appointed one body, the State, as His minister for dealing with the outward formal, visible conduct of men, and another minister, the Church, for dealing with the inward spiritual invisible origin of that conduct. Abolish the distinction, confound acts with principles, and of necessity you merge the one in the other.[36]

[33]*Ibid.*, III, 106.
[34]Letter in *The Daily News*, September 2, 1868.
[35]See *Kingdom of Christ* (1838), III, 319.
[36]*Lectures on National Education*, pp. 293 f. Cp. *Moral and Metaphysical Philosophy*, II, 197 f.

We distinguish most carefully between that which is spiritual and that which is legal, that which is ecclesiastical and that which is national, that which concerns the knowledge and cultivation of good, and that which concerns the suppression of evil. But we say that one of these, as much as the other, is to be referred to God . . . that each has the Divine impress upon it, that they can only exist in harmony.[37]

The offices of State and Church correspond to the offices of the Law and the Gospel. "What I mean by the union of Church and State is the co-operation of spirit with law; the abandonment of the attempt to put one for the other, or to dispense with either."[38] The Law protests against the selfish, individual principle, and raises a standard against it; the Gospel comes to exterminate that same selfish principle out of the mind and heart of man.[39] The revelation of God as universal love is not inconsistent with the prior revelation of Him as the Being who is carrying on continual strife with whatever in the world resists law and order.[40] The establishment of outward law, the formation of national societies, are parts of God's great scheme for developing more fully the nature and character of Christ's kingdom.[41] Thus it may be said that "the union between Church and State . . . stands upon no decrees or acts of parliament, but exists in the laws of society, in the nature of things."[42]

These two powers are meant continually to act and react upon one another, and to learn better, by each new error they commit, their distinct functions and their per-

[37]*Kingdom of Christ* (1838), III, 389 f.

[38]Letter in *The Daily News*, August 27, 1868.

[39]See *Kingdom of Christ* (Ev. ed.), II, 210. Cp. *Kingdom of Heaven,* p. 121.

[40]See *Kingdom of Christ* (Ev. ed.), II, 215.

[41]See *ibid.,* II, 239.

[42]*Macmillan's Magazine* (April, 1860), p. 424. Cp. *Lincoln's Inn Sermons,* II, 319.

fect harmony.[43] There could be no example of the true relation between Church and State in the first ages of the Church, when nations had not been brought forth into distinct existence, nor in the period when the Church was artificially linked to a falling empire, nor again in the Dark and Middle Ages, when it was struggling to assert its title to be a rival empire to that which had its seat in Germany.[44] The true pattern of the relation between Church and State is not then to be looked for in the arrangements made by Constantine and his successors. That was an alliance between the Church and an empire —and a decaying empire at that, not between the Church and a nation. "No inference as to the intention of God respecting the connexion of His Church with the kingdoms of the earth, can be drawn from the accidents of its connexion with a superannuated military empire, carrying about within it the seeds of predestined destruction, and only kept alive till the new nations of the West were ready to inherit the blessings, which it was the appointed means of transmitting to them."[45]

The Christian Church came into life when there were no States. There had been great and glorious States in Palestine, in Greece, in Italy. They had all been lost in a huge Empire. The Caesar was the king of kings—he was, in the strictest sense, hailed as the god of this earth, to whatever gods in some other region it might become him to pay homage. The Christian preachers assumed a universality greater than that of the Roman Empire for their society. They declared it was for all kindreds, and tongues, and peoples. The question was, *what* kings reign over these kindreds, and tongues, and peoples? The preachers of the Cross said, "Not the Caesar, not any one like the Caesar; one who took upon Him the form of

[43]See *Kingdom of Christ* (Ev. ed.), II, 189.
[44]See Letter in *The Daily News,* August 17, 1868.
[45]*Kingdom of Christ* (1838), I, 216.

a servant, one who was put to death as a malefactor."
That was the issue between the two societies. The
Christians might profess loyalty to the Emperor, might
mean to obey him. But the wisest, the most tolerant,
Emperors felt that the Christians were proclaiming a
rival kingdom—that two such societies could not dwell
together—one must be crushed. When Constantine
had discovered that the Christian Church could not
be crushed, he made the plausible experiment of an
alliance with it. The policy was skilful, but hopeless,
hastening the downfall of that which it was intended
to preserve.

This alliance has been called a union of Church
and State. How could it be that? The Roman Empire
was what it had always been—the absorber, the destroyer of States. None could live within it, none could
grow out of it. Was that assertion equally true of the
other universal society? Time would show.[46]

Like Mr. Gladstone, Maurice maintained that the State
has a conscience,[47] and that a nation is a moral person.
"The time is come . . . when the Bible must be thrown
either into the fire as an old worn-out document, or when
a nation must be felt to be *not* a formal corporation but
a spiritual reality, a society of which we *can* predicate
spiritual conditions and spiritual emotions, which can repent and be reformed as an individual can."[48]

Maurice consistently repudiated contemporary notions
about popular sovereignty and the utilitarian maxim concerning the greatest happiness of the greatest number. A
people or a majority has no more right than a monarch
or an oligarchy to do what it wills or what it likes.

Whatever involves the worship of Demus as of a
divine monarch who may decree what he likes, may

[46]Letter in *The Daily News*, August 17, 1868.
[47]See *Kingdom of Christ* (1838), III, xv; *Conscience*, p. 140.
Cp. my book, *The Orb and the Cross*, chap. IV.
[48]*Prophets and Kings*, pp. 403 f.

put down one and set up another, dealing with all as
his tools to execute his commands, I repudiate . . .
Whoever flatters a mob . . . does not reverence a
people, does not love them, but hates or despises them.
With this flattery I would join the boast of conform-
ing to the will of a majority. So help me God, I do
not mean to follow the will of a majority, I hope
never to follow it, always to set it at nought. And for
that expression about "the greatest happiness of the
greatest number" I do not understand it. I have no
measure of it. I cannot tell what happiness is, or how
it is to be distributed among the greatest number, or
how the greatest number is to be ascertained. If it
could be put to the vote of the greatest number what
they would have for happiness, I have no security that
they would not decide for something profoundly low
and swinish.[49]

Democracy, thus understood, was an object of dread
to Maurice. It set opinion above law, and was hostile to
individual freedom.[50] He held to the "old forms which
denote a belief the most opposite of this, forms which indicate that the highest ruler of the land, and every subordinate magistrate, derives his authority from an Invisible
Person, to whom he is under a fearful responsibility for
the fulfilment of his duties."[51]

A king given, an aristocracy given, and I can see
my way clearly to call upon them (the English people)
to do the work which God has laid upon them; to
repent of their sins, to labour that the whole manhood of the country may have a voice, that every
member of Christ's body may be indeed a free man.

[49]*The Workman and the Franchise*, pp. 201 f. Cp. *Life of
F. D. M.*, I, 485: "The sovereignty of the people, in any sense
or form, I . . . repudiate as at once the silliest and most blas-
phemous of all contradictions."
[50]See *ibid.*, II, 440.
[51]*The Prayer-Book and the Lord's Prayer*, p. 388. See the
whole passage.

But reconstitute society upon the democratic basis—treat the sovereign and the aristocracy as not intended to rule and guide the land, as only holding their commissions from us—and I anticipate nothing but a most accursed sacerdotal rule or a military despotism, with the great body of the population in either case morally, politically, physically serfs, more than they are at present or ever have been.[52]

If this doctrine of rulers reigning by the Grace of God is cast aside as an obsolete doctrine; if we do not look into the force of it, and claim it for our children and our children's children, then I can see no hope of growth, nothing but endless vicissitude: a continual return to the point from which we started; republics succeeding monarchies; empires swallowing up republics, theories trying to do justice for facts; facts overwhelming theories; men crying for liberty of thought, then crying as loudly for an iron despotism which shall crush all thought.[53]

Nor did he limit this doctrine to England, or to monarchies in the strict sense. "If our princes rule by the Grace of God, they rule as witnesses that all kings, presidents, kaliphs, *quocunque gaudent nomine,* rule by the same grace."[54] So far as England was concerned, he held that each of the political schools of his time stood for a truth, and that their positive principles needed to be reconciled and united. "The Tory brings his belief that God does

[52]*Life of F. D. M.,* II, 129.
[53]*Tracts for Priests and People,* No. X, "Do Kings Reign by the Grace of God?", p. 41.
[54]*Tracts for Priests and People,* No. X, p. 56. Cp. *Social Morality,* p. 170:
"Our business is not to set England above other countries; to foster any national conceit. We are not to maintain that Nations are only good and true when they have a Sovereign and a House of Peers, and a House of Commons. But since this is the form of Government under which we have been nurtured, which has moulded the thoughts of us and our fathers, our loyalty to it will be the best security that we honour the institutions and desire the growth of every other Nation."

uphold the sovereign; the Whig brings his belief that there is an order or constitution, without which the sovereign's power is nothing; the Radical brings his belief that the well-being of the whole people is the end for which sovereigns reign and constitutions exist."[55]

It is the office of a National Church to witness to the monarch, to the aristocracy, and to the democracy that they are all under the Law of God and responsible to Him. The Law of God is expressed in the Ten Commandments, which the Church should be continually addressing and interpreting to the nation. "If we do not receive them as Commandments of the Lord God spoken to Israel, and spoken to every people under heaven now, we lose the greatest witnesses we possess for the national morality and the civil freedom."[56] In his book, *The Commandments considered as Instruments of National Reformation*, Maurice drew out their meaning for nineteenth-century England, and it is a fine example of the method that a National Church ought always to be following.

A National Church should mean a Church which exists to purify and elevate the mind of a nation; to give those who make and administer and obey its laws, a sense of the grandeur of law and of the source whence it proceeds, to tell the rulers of the nation, and all the members of the nation, that all false ways are ruinous ways, that truth is the only stability of our time or of any time. It should exist to make men tremble at the voice of God speaking to them in their consciences, to tell them that what He is telling them will be proclaimed before the universe, that every deed which men wish to hide shall be brought forth into the clear and open day. This should be the meaning of a National Church; a nation wants a Church

[55]*Tracts for Priests and People*, No. X, p. 53. Cp. *Friendship of Books*, p. 152.
[56]*Commandments*, p. xi. Cp. *Conscience*, pp. 134 f.

13

for these purposes mainly; a Church is abusing its
trust if it aims at any other or lower purposes.[57]

In this exalted sense it is the office of the Church to
educate the nation, as it is the office of the State to govern.
As a corollary of this distinction, Maurice sought to maintain that the education of the people ought to be in the
hands of the Church. The State requires an educated
people, but is not itself qualified to educate; it ought therefore to provide freedom for the Church to do this work.
This was the theme of Maurice's book, *Has the Church,
or the State, the power to educate the Nation?* Education
by the Church would bind the people into unity, whereas
education by sects divides them. "The man who shall bring
a set of youths together, and shall form them into a body,
without teaching them, whether they like it or no, what
the bond of their fellowship is, and in what way they
are to feel that they are a fellowship, is little better than
a madman."[58] It is the Church that is qualified to proclaim, and by its universal ordinances to make effective,
the bond of the fellowship that exists not only between the
members of the nation but between all the members of
the race.[59]

But as time went on, Maurice had to acknowledge, as
Gladstone had to do also with regard to his Church and
State doctrine, that this was not a practicable policy
under existing conditions in England. Owing to the sectarianism of Christians,[60] the National Church was not
in a position to do its proper work, and therefore the State

[57]*Lincoln's Inn Sermons*, II, 93 f.
[58]*Lectures on National Education*, p. 73.
[59]See *ibid.*, p. 159.
[60]"In our pulpits we exhort our hearers to believe in a Person
who is the Head of the human race. In our creeds we all join
in the confession of Him. And then in the face of these traditions, exhortations, obligations, we wrap ourselves in our sect-
mantle, and say that unless we wear it we shall not retain any
'distinctive' religious belief."—Letter in *The Daily News*, September 25, 1868.

had to provide for the education of the people as best it could. At the time of the 1870 Education Bill Maurice wrote that the statesman

> ought to get all the force which he can get, all the force which there is in the land, to struggle against its ignorance and the crimes of which ignorance is the parent. He ought to acknowledge facts, and to hope that if he does acknowledge them, the next generation will have better facts to deal with than he has. He ought therefore to claim all the belief of the land—the belief of English Churchmen, the belief of Protestant Dissenters, the belief of Romanists, the belief of Secularists—to conquer the enemies which are destroying us. He cannot conquer them by Act of Parliament. He cannot stamp with his foot and raise up a body of teachers armed to encounter them. He must take those which are in the land already. He must take them impartially, subject to all the contradictions which are impairing their efficiency.[61]

Yet although as things are a National Church in England, and of course in many other countries too, cannot do all that it ought, it must do all that it can "to uphold the national life . . . by its prayers, its confessions, its sacraments."[62] Its ministry expresses to the nation the idea that the national existence has a divine ground and keeps up the feeling of a communion between the visible and the invisible world.[63] The highest honour of the Church "is to be the life-giving energy to every body in the midst of which she dwells."[64] In each nation the Church stands for the principle that the bond which unites its members to the men in other nations and lands is their common

[61]*A Few Words on Secular and Denominational Education*, p. 16. Cp. Letter in *The Daily News*, September 16, 1868; *The Workman and the Franchise*, p. 186; *Life of F. D. M.*, II, 611 ff.
[62]*Lincoln's Inn Sermons*, III, 230.
[63]See *The Church a Family*, p. 158.
[64]*Kingdom of Christ* (Ev. ed.), II, 240.

relation to an invisible and not to a visible person.[65] Each Church which puts forth the claim to be a National Church is asserting that there can be but one universal Church, "limited by no condition of time or of locality, the same in all countries and all ages,"[66] but adapted to the characteristics and needs of each nation within which it dwells.

> The greatest and deepest desire that I am conscious of, is that of bringing all men to the feeling that there can be but one Church—though that Church may exist in a number of different nations—though it may be quite right that in some subordinate particulars it should be modified by the character of those nations —though it is, I believe, actually demanded by its constitution, that it should recognise and sustain the distinct government of each of those nations.[67]

The principle of Catholicism is that of the universality of the Church; the principle of Protestantism is the assertion of the responsibility of every nation and person to God. Protestantism is predicable of a nation, not of the Church. It was the good pleasure of God, that at the time of the Reformation the evil to the existence of nations, and the evil to the individual soul of man, which resulted from the headship of a visible ruler over the Church, should be perceived, understood, and protested against.[68] The positive principle of Protestantism is that a nation stands in the acknowledging of a Righteous God to whom it is directly responsible. So far as the State is concerned, it is neither more nor less than a declaration that the Lord Paramount over the king is an invisible, and not a visible, monarch.[69] Every nation, when converted to Christianity, became in effect a Protestant nation. Protestantism has

---

[65]See *Lectures on National Education*, p. 46.
[66]*Kingdom of Christ* (1838), III, 7.
[67]*Three Letters to the Rev. W. Palmer*, p. 51.
[68]See *ibid.*, p. 12.
[69]See *Kingdom of Christ* (1838), III, 97.

assumed a negative form since the Reformation because of the papal contradiction of this principle. "The Papacy was a more distinct deposing of the God of righteousness from His throne over each nation than paganism was, because all responsibility to an invisible power on the part of each particular sovereign was set at nought by the doctrine of his responsibility to a visible Head of the Church."[70]

Maurice was equally concerned to assert that the Church of England was Catholic and that the English nation was Protestant. "Our nation of England acknowledges God for its King, just as much as the nation of the Jews did. We call Him, in our prayer for Queen Victoria, 'King of kings and Lord of lords.' Just as He was the King over King David, so He is the King over our Queen. And our laws which say, 'Thou shalt not kill, thou shalt not commit adultery,' are God's laws; they are not the Queen's laws; she did not make them, nor any king or queen that was before her. She and her servants execute them, and she and they are answerable to God how they execute them."[71] Calvinists stand for a polity directly ordained by God, Romanists for a polity organized under the Vicar of Christ, Englishmen for a polity directed by a national sovereign.[72] But England does not assert this principle for itself alone. "For whom do we protest? For all the nations of Europe; for those who most differ from us in custom, language, opinion; for those whose customs, languages, opinions, will all present some aspect of the divine humanity which ours would fail to present."[73]

Protestantism stands for the direct responsibility to God of each individual man as well as of each nation. The truths which constitute Protestantism concern man as a personal being, "assert his individual responsibility and re-

[70]*Life of F. D. M.*, I, 141 f. Cp. *ibid.*, I, 329.
[71]*Kingdom of Christ* (1838), III, 41.
[72]See *Moral and Metaphysical Philosophy*, II, 140.
[73]Letter in *The Daily News*, September 25, 1868.

lation to God, and provide that this responsibility and relation shall be realities and not dreams."[74] Thus it "has a
standing-point of its own . . . it is not merely condemna-
tory, merely negative . . . so far as it keeps within its own
proper and appointed province, it denounces and condemns
only that which is itself negative, and which sets at naught
something that is needful for the life and being of man."[75]

Catholic and Protestant principles sustain and balance
each other.[76] "There is a Catholic side of the Gospel as
well as a Protestant; a side that has reference to Society
as well as one that concerns each of us. We . . . are bound
to recognise both. . . . We shall not do justice to one truth
if we let go the other. We shall not make that stronger by
weakening this. We want each in its fullest strength."[77]
"We shall have to learn Protestantism again as well as
Catholicism."[78] We shall have to learn both if we are to
have a living and a Christian politics.

All his life Maurice was seeking to act upon the principles which he asserted. He was not one of those clergy-
men who lay down lofty, abstract principles in the pulpit,
and leave the laity without any definite guidance about
how they can be applied to actual conditions. He was not
an absentee from the politics of day to day. In his sermons
he was constantly bringing permanent principles to bear
on current affairs. But he was not content with doing that.
Not only by word but by example he illustrated his precepts
that "a Churchman must be a politician,"[79] and that the
office of reproving the actions of Governors and Magis-

---

[74]*Methods of Supporting Protestantism*, p. 4. Cp. *Kingdom of
Christ* (Ev. ed.), II, 57; *Moral and Metaphysical Philosophy*,
II, 422.

[75]*Kingdom of Christ* (Ev. ed.), I, 82.

[76]See *Methods of Supporting Protestantism*, p. 18. Cp. *Three
Letters to the Rev. W. Palmer*, p. 7.

[77]*Lincoln's Inn Sermons*, II, 15. Cp. *Kingdom of Christ* (1838),
III, 175.

[78]*Life of F. D. M.*, I, 357.

[79]*Kingdom of Christ* (1838), III, 387.

trates is one with which the representatives of the Church have been entrusted.[80] "Christ came to establish a kingdom, not to proclaim a set of opinions. Every man entering this kingdom becomes interested in all its relations, members, circumstances; he cannot separate himself in anywise from them; he cannot establish a life or interest apart from theirs."[81]

Maurice's participation in the Christian Socialist movement, in Cooperative Associations, his manifold educational enterprises, sprang directly out of this concern. He was more successful as an educationalist than as an active politician. For he was a man of thought rather than a man of action, made more for uttering prophecies than for framing policies. His determination to look for and cleave to principles—to principles of which his collaborators seldom had so firm a grasp as he had—made him a difficult man to work with.[82] Yet he was personally so humble and his insights were so profound that his fellow-workers were never happy unless they could carry him with them. Moreover, he himself was always eager to move out into action, since he admitted that "the test of all principles affecting to be moral and human must be their application to the circumstances in which we are placed."[83]

The circumstances in which we are placed (whether in England or in other countries today) are naturally different from those in which he was placed. We could not, even if we would, copy his practical experiments. It is not in them that we shall discover that he has a message for today. His message for us lies in his assertion that politics have a theological foundation, that there are permanent principles to which power ought to be subordinated and to which in the end it will be subordinated. A relativistic politics, which leads to a nihilistic tyranny, is a deadly

[80]See *Subscription No Bondage*, p. 11.
[81]*Kingdom of Christ* (1838), III, 387.
[82]Cp. C. F. G. Masterman, *Frederick Denison Maurice*, pp. 67 f.
[83]*Social Morality*, pp. 371 f. Cp. *Conscience*, p. 175.

politics, and this menace is more real now than it was then. Theology is not so well-equipped to meet this menace that it can afford to neglect Maurice's hints.

He bids us ask whether the Bible does not bear witness to the divine constitution for mankind, in which the life of the person, the life of nations, and the life of the universal Church, all have their ordained place. Does the Church affirm and sustain the bond of neighbourhood (the nation) as well as the bond of blood (the family)? Are nations subject to the law that God has revealed, and is freedom to be secured only by obedience to that law? Are not monarchy and aristocracy as well as democracy necessary constituents of a healthy national· life? Is not imperialism, whether political or ecclesiastical, a contradiction of the principle of national existence and national responsibility to God? Is not the Catholic Church meant to consist of National Churches, instead of either a federation of sects or a world Church under a centralized government with a visible head? Are not civil governors as well as the ministers of the Church ordained by God? Are not their appointed tasks complementary and interdependent?

These are all living questions, even if they are not all yet being livingly asked. We have to answer them in the light of the manifestation of the kingdom of Christ. At the same time, we have to act with reference to the facts of today. Maurice, as we have seen, expressed the hope that a succeeding generation would have better facts to deal with than he had. Perhaps if his teaching had been heeded, we might have had better facts to deal with. As it is, if we are led to assert the principles to which he bore witness, we are likely to find it even more difficult than he did to apply them. But if these principles are indeed permanent, if they are grounded in the constitution of the universe, we shall know that the realization of a truly human life for men and nations depends upon their acknowledgment, and we shall be confident that in striving to be faithful to them we shall be doing what is right, however unpopular it may be and, what will be vindicated at last, however ineffective it may appear to be now.

Even beneath a world tyranny, the true State and the true Church would be found in the holes and corners where the principles of the kingdom of Christ were being asserted. "If in the midst of . . . Anarchy some two or three should proclaim the dignity of Law, and should say, 'We at least will obey it,' those two or three would constitute a State, and till the Majority joined with them, the Majority would be no State at all."[84] We should not have the resolution to resist seemingly omnipotent dictators or majorities, unless we really believed that they were usurpers, and that there is a King of kings who does bring down the mighty from their seats. Again, "the universal Church, we say, stands, the great representative of mankind—redeemed and restored mankind—and this it would do, though it had but a dozen members, and though but one of those members really understood his position."[85] It is because Maurice understood his position, that he can help us to understand ours.

In a note about "assurance in principles" that is buried in one of his earliest and least-known writings there is an apostrophe which was fulfilled in his own life and which is no less apposite to our time than to his.

Never do we more require a set of men to arise who shall teach us the worth of authority, and prescription, and antiquity, as vestibules to the temple of truth, not as barriers to keep us from venturing into it. The science of theology, above all others, has need of such men. May God in His mercy raise them up for us, and endow them with all gifts and graces, and mostly that chief grace of humility, to sustain them in their noble, but hazardous adventure! It will

[84]*Social Morality*, p. 123.
[85]*Kingdom of Christ* (1838), I, 46.

be one in which few will cheer them on; in which they will have much obloquy to bear from evil men; much misunderstanding from the good. No sect will, probably, gather itself round them; the public will be indifferent to their labours; their own generation will, perhaps, scarcely know them; but they will not therefore be useless even to it. They will send many thoughts abroad which will not die; they will save many truths from perishing, through the ignorance of those who assert them.[86]

[86]*Lectures on National Education,* pp. 307 f.

8

A UNITED CONFESSION OF THE NAME

A united Confession of the Name, a united
Worship of the Father, the Son, and the Spirit
—such a Confession—such a Worship as the past
contains only a dim shadow of—we have a right
to look for. It may come when we least expect
it; it will probably come after a period of dark-
ness, fierce contention, utter unbelief. But the
confession will only be united when we cease to
confound our feeble expressions of trust and
affiance, our praises and adorations, with Him
to whom they rise, from whom they proceed;
when we are brought to nothingness, that He
*may be shown to be all in all.—*LINCOLN'S INN
SERMONS, II, 144.

SINCE the Reformation men both within and beyond
the borders of the Church of England have asked,
and given various and indeed contradictory answers to, the question: What is the Church of
England? But not until comparatively recent times
has another question, which *prima facie* may appear to be
the same, been formulated, namely: What is Anglicanism?
The word "Anglicanism" in fact was not used before the
nineteenth century. The very useful volume of extracts
from seventeenth-century divines, edited by Paul Elmer
More and F. L. Cross, which bears this word as its title

and includes an essay on "Anglicanism in the Seventeenth Century," contains no contemporary instance of its use. According to the *Oxford English Dictionary* it was first used in 1846 (by Charles Kingsley). It was used by Maurice a few years earlier,[1] but that is of no consequence.

It is however significant that some other well-known terms date from the sixteenth or seventeenth century: Lutheranism (1560), Calvinism (1570), Puritanism (1573), Anabaptism (1577), Presbyterianism (1644).[2] These words ending in "ism" commonly denote systems of divinity; and it is significant, I say, that in the seventeenth century, which was the *grand siècle* of Church of England divines, neither its friends nor its foes thought of attributing to the Church of England a system of divinity. There is no such word as "Hookerism" to this day, and "Laudianism" or "Laudism" was not used until the nineteenth century. Paul Elmer More, who in the volume to which I have referred writes retrospectively of Anglicanism in the seventeenth century, is at pains to explain that he does not find there a system of divinity, but a direction.

How then has it come about that the question "What is Anglicanism?" is nowadays being canvassed with considerable zest and some anxiety?[3] It is undoubtedly a question that is calculated to perplex any who ask it, for the question itself implies that there is, or ought to be, an Anglican system of divinity to be set alongside those that have been named. The fundamental reason why the question is now asked—whether hopefully or despairingly—would seem to be that during the last hundred years Anglicans have become increasingly unconscious of the

[1] See *Three Letters to the Rev. W. Palmer*, pp. 7, 23.
[2] The dates given are those of the earliest citations in the *O. E. D.* To these may be added: Congregationalism (1716), Evangelicalism (1831), Anglo-Catholicism (1842), and Episcopalianism (1846).
[3] *E.g.*, see an article by J. H. Jacques on "Confessional Theology and the Anglican Church" in *Theology* (March, 1944), and a correspondence to which it gave rise in that periodical.

fact that it is characteristic of Anglican divinity to refuse
to confound allegiance to the Church with allegiance to
any system of divinity. Or where they have been conscious
of the fact, they have become doubtful whether it is
creditable.

There is by now an accumulation of factors that move
inquiring minds to desire a definition of Anglicanism, and
the following may be particularly noted.

First, whereas after the Reformation the Church of
England stood forth as a National Church, it can now
be represented as part of a world denomination. It claimed
then to be no more, though no less, than the true Church
of Christ in England,[4] and as such to be a true part of
the Church Universal. It never purported to be the expression or agent of a system of divinity with universal
ambitions like Romanism or Calvinism. It is the expansion
of the Church of England into the United States of America, into the British Colonies, and indeed into all parts
of the world, that has made plausible the idea that the
Anglican Communion, also a phrase first used in the nineteenth century,[5] is a world denomination alongside other
world denominations. Hence arises the supposition that
the Anglican Communion must stand for an "ism" com-
parable with Presbyterianism, Romanism or Methodism.
The old English divines never affected to erect an Anglican system, for which universal validity could be claimed.
They were content to defend the constitution of the Church
of England against the aggressive denials of Rome and
Geneva, each of which did make a universal claim for
itself. But can so modest a divinity be sufficient to warrant
the universal expansion of the Anglican Communion? In
order to justify this expansion must we not be more am-

[4]As regards the Anglican Church in Ireland and Scotland, see
Encyclopaedia Britannica (11th edition), II, 19.

[5]The earliest use of the phrase that I have noticed is in the
Report of the 1867 Lambeth Conference, but I do not suppose
that it was coined then.

bitious than our fathers were? This is the first circumstance that has given force to the inquiry: What is Anglicanism?

Secondly, during this period of expansion, especially in
the present century, and not least in England itself, there
has been a sad, though probably inevitable, decline in
acquaintance with the older English divinity on the part
of the clergy and the educated laity. Whereas Coleridge
could say, without seeming to be fantastic, "A Clergyman
in full orders who has never read the works of Bull and
Waterland, has a duty yet to perform,"[6] scarcely one
clergyman in a thousand will have read those works now
or indeed any substantial portion of pre-Victorian divinity.
Even Hooker disappeared from the syllabus of reading
required from candidates for ordination in most English
dioceses after the 1914–18 war, and probably it is at present
the case that only a minority of our clergy has read any
theology that was published even before 1900. This state
of affairs has had as one of its results a weakening throughout the Anglican Communion of the sense of inheriting
and sharing a common and long-standing theological tradition or orientation. Without roots of that kind, men become uncertain of their position, and are at a loss to know
what to say when they are asked, or when they ask themselves: What is Anglicanism?

Thirdly, the question derives some of its force and perplexing effect from the development during the last hundred years within the Anglican Communion, most con-
spicuously in England itself, of at least three organized
parties, each of which has seemed to stand for a different
system of doctrine. It is true that previously there were
different schools in the Church, but up till the nineteenth
century High Churchmen, Latitudinarians, etc., regarded
their primary allegiance as being due to the Church of

[6]*Aids to Reflection,* "Aphorisms on Spiritual Religion," No.
CXVII.

England itself, and not to a party. What distinguished them from one another was a particular emphasis in their interpretation of the teaching of the Church, or divergent pastoral methods, or a particular political affiliation. In any case there was no question of party *organizations* such as those with which we have since become familiar. But by the end of the nineteenth century it had come about that the typical party man (though not the men of larger and wiser spirit who often lent their names to a party) tended to ·regard himself primarily as an adherent of Evangelicalism, or Anglo-Catholicism, or Broad Church-manship, who was almost accidentally, or at least sec-ondarily, a member of the Church of England. It appeared that the parties stood for different systems, and incom-patible systems, and therefore the question arose: What does *the Church of England* stand for? Is it anything but a device for keeping in uneasy juxtaposition a number of sects, parties or systems that do not really belong together? Is there such a thing as Anglicanism? If not, ought not the Anglican Communion to be separated into its com-ponent elements?

Fourthly, the need that other Churches have discovered to take a "confessional" stand when confronted by the demands of totalitarian States is leading many Anglicans to wonder whether or on what grounds their Church could take such a stand, if confronted by similar demands. Lutherans, Calvinists and Romanists appear to have found in their respective systems resources which enabled them to make declarations of principle on the basis of which their resistance to totalitarianism could be founded. It is natural to inquire whether Anglicanism has any correspond-ing resources.

Fifthly, the intellectual confusion, not to say chaos, of the present age easily has the effect of inclining those who become aware of it to crave for some dogmatic system in·which they may feel secure. Romanists seem to have such a system in Thomism, neo-Protestants in what is called Barthianism. Can Anglicanism be propounded as an alternative to these, or may Anglicans seek to appropriate, and identify their Church with, one or other of those systems?

All these circumstances, and the inquiries they elicit, have conspired to underline for many thoughtful minds the question: What is Anglicanism? This book will have missed its mark if it has failed to suggest that Maurice, though he had not occasion to address himself directly to this question, nevertheless said very much that is pertinent to it. I need hardly say that I do not mean that there can be extracted from Maurice's writings a system of divinity which might be recommended as authentic Anglicanism. He maintained that the English Church, so far from being a competitor in the provision of religious systems, was a witness to man's deliverance from them. Similarly, the last thing that should be claimed for Maurice is that he is qualified to perform for Anglican divinity the function that St. Thomas performs for Romanist divinity, Luther for Lutheran divinity, Calvin for Calvinist divinity, etc. It would also be a contradiction in terms to desire the formation of a Maurician party or school of thought in the Church. It is not by these means that Maurice's teaching can illuminate the special calling of the Anglican Communion. If he is qualified to assist and stimulate Anglicans, and not only Anglicans, in their theological quest and in their ecclesiastical predicaments, it is because his teaching points us away from the rivalry of human systems to the principles which underlie them and to the divine society in which they are reconciled, away from past masters in divinity to the light that lightened them and that lightens every man, away from parties with their peculiar opinions to the all-embracing Church and its ground in the universal Name of the Father and the Son and the Holy Ghost.

In this concluding chapter I want to direct attention to Maurice's teaching about the calling of the English Church and, by implication, of the Anglican Communion. It will be evident that I have England mainly in view, as he had. I realize that what is said needs to be translated with regard to the conditions that hold in different countries and parts of the Church, but I am deliberately refraining from that work of translation which can be done only by those who in each case are familiar with local history and present circumstances.

Maurice certainly believed that the English Reformation —not so much because of the intention of our Reformers as under the overruling providence of God—had followed a course that enabled the English Church, and the Churches stemming from it, to bear a singular and direct witness to the kingdom of Christ. But Otto Pfleiderer entirely misconceived Maurice's meaning when he accused him of identifying the kingdom of Christ with the Church of England.

> While he (Maurice) teaches on the one hand that the entire human race is created and has its essential nature in Christ as its ideal Head, he seems to maintain on the other hand that it is only in the Church of England that the Kingdom of Christ has attained actual existence! This is a contradiction that a German intellect finds it hard to comprehend, or can only explain by supposing that the strong national feeling of the Englishman had got the better of the intellect of the theologian.[7]

Maurice of course believed that the kingdom of Christ is in actual existence everywhere. He *is* King of kings and Lord of lords, whether He is owned as such or not. The universal Church is the universal witness to this kingdom. In the universal Church, and in each National Church,

[7] O. Pfleiderer, *The Development of Theology* (1890), p. 378.

14

the kingdom of Christ is actualized—is articulated, realized, embodied, becomes explicit. But particular Churches bear this witness with varying degrees of clarity and with manifold distortions. To the English Church, despite all its faults and weaknesses, it had been given to assert more plainly than other Churches in divided Christendom that the bond both of universal and of national unity lies not in any system or combination of systems, but in the confession and worship of the Father, the Son and the Holy Ghost. The English Church had providentially been prevented from confounding the signs of the kingdom of Christ with theories about them or with dogmas which obscured or narrowed their universal efficacy.

> Our Church has no right to call herself better than other Churches in any respect, in many she must acknowledge herself to be worse. But our *position,* we may fairly affirm, for it is not a boast but a confession, is one of singular advantage. . . . Our faith is not formed by a union of the Protestant systems with the Romish system, nor of certain elements taken from the one and of certain elements taken from the other. So far as it is represented in our liturgy and our articles, it is the faith of a Church, and has nothing to do with any system at all. That peculiar character which God has given us, enables us, if we do not slight the mercy, to understand the difference between a Church and a System, better perhaps than any of our neighbours can, and, therefore, our position, rightly used, gives us a power of assisting them in realising the blessings of their own. By refusing to unite with them on the ground of any one of their systems, by seeking to unite with them on the grounds of the universal Church, we teach them wherein lies their strength and their weakness.[8]

No one will be able to understand Maurice nor, what

[8]*Kingdom of Christ* (Ev. ed.), II, 329.

is more important, the English Church and the Anglican Communion, who supposes that the Catholic Church and National Churches are incompatible, or that as a Church becomes more Catholic it becomes less national, or who doubts that the kingdom of Christ consecrates the life of nations. The Anglican Communion is confessedly a fellowship of national or regional Churches which "are independent in their self-government as integral parts of the Church Universal."[9] Its existence is a living protest on behalf of the principle of nationality and of the direct responsibility of bishops and rulers to Christ, and against the notion of a visible head of the Church and a centralized government.

National Churches are national not only in the sense of protesting against the super-nationalism of Romanism, but also in the sense of witnessing to the idea of a spiritual polity for each nation. A national Church stands thus in contrast to any sect whose members are separated from other people by the profession of certain opinions. At the Reformation the tendency to look upon Christianity as a system of doctrine, whether in the form of Popery or Protestantism, was resisted in England.

> Here the idea of the Church as a Spiritual Polity ruled over by Christ, and consisting of all baptized persons, did, owing to various providential circumstances, supersede the notion of the Church, as a sect, maintaining certain opinions; or to speak more correctly, the dogmatical side of Christianity was here felt to be its accessory and subordinate side, and the ordinances, which were the manifestation of it as the law of our social and practical life, were considered its principal side. . . .
>
> The Church is a body united in the acknowledgment of a living *Person;* every sect is a body united in the acknowledgment of a certain *Notion.*[10]

[9]*Lambeth Conference Report* (1930), p. 153.
[10]*Kingdom of Christ* (1838), II, 338.

Maurice did not claim that the English Reformers were aware of all that they were doing when they refused to follow the German and Swiss Protestants in substituting for the papal system a new dogmatic system or confession and in making that the bond of their union.

> In England we were not permitted to form systems of divinity and confessions, to supplant what had been accumulating by means of the writings of schoolmen, the decrees of councils, the bulls of Popes. By a series of acts, some violent, some accidental (where by accidental, I mean to describe those events unsought for, and unprovided by man, which are the effect, however, of previous determinations of his will, and mark how God, through that will, or in despite of it, is overlooking and arranging every step), we were brought into direct opposition to the rest of Christendom.[11]

It was due then to the providential action of God and not to any peculiar glory or excellence in the members or teachers of the Anglican Church that worship and sacraments, and the signs of the kingdom of Christ, were put in its polity before doctrinal definitions as the acts which directly connect man with God.[12] The same principle was asserted at the Restoration, even if again its implications were not fully perceived at the time. Whereas the Westminster Assembly had done its best to establish a uniformity of opinions, leaving the ministers free in their modes of worship, the opposite principle that the bond of national fellowship is the bond of worship was reaffirmed and efforts at a dogmatic uniformity were left to the genius of Presbyterianism, where they belonged.[13]

As Maurice contemplated the English Church in his own day, it seemed to him that the principles, to which

[11]*Ibid.*, I, 249.
[12]See *ibid.*, I, 255.
[13]See *ibid.* (Ev. ed.), II, 296 f.

it was called to witness, were being denied by the Liberal,
Evangelical and Catholic parties with their respective systems. Each had hold of a truth which was implicit in the
constitution of the kingdom of Christ, but which when
isolated, systematized apart from other truths, and turned
into a negation of them, became a destructive force.

The Liberal had hold of the truth that the Church is
indeed a living body; it is not tied down by the system
of any past age. "It must have an expansive power; it
must breathe and move; it must be able to throw off the
results of partial experiences; it must be able to profit by
all new experiences! With what sympathy do we listen to
him, when he says that the Church is meant to comprehend and not to exclude."[14] But the Liberal System aimed
at recasting the traditional forms of the Church so as to
bring them into unison with the spirit of the present age,
and to build a Church upon the comprehension of all current varieties of theological opinion. The Liberal

> proposes to us that we should abandon the Prayers
> which we have derived from ages gone by, and the
> Articles which have come down to us from the Ref-
> ormation; or he would have us adapt these to the
> maxims of our own time. But what if those Prayers
> should be the very means by which we have been
> preserved from the bondage to particular modes and
> habits of feeling, when they have been threatening
> to hold us fast? What if those Articles have kept us
> from sinking into a particular theological system, and
> have compelled us to feel that there were two sides
> of truth, neither of which could be asserted to the ex-
> clusion of the other? What if the abandonment either
> of the Prayers or the Articles, or the reduction of
> them to our present standards of thought, should bring
> the Church into the most flat and hopeless monotony,
> should so level her to the superstitions of the nine-
> teenth century, so divorce her from the past and the

[14]*Ibid.*, II, 308.

future that all expansion would for ever be impossible?
. . . If these suppositions be true, we must look some-
where else than to a liberal system, to produce the
effects which Liberals have dreamed of.[15]

Thus Maurice wrote in *The Kingdom of Christ,* and
towards the end of his life in a review of the past he said:

What sympathy . . . could I have with the Liberal
party which was emphatically anti-theological, which
was ready to tolerate all opinions in theology, only
because people could know nothing about it, and because other studies were much better pursued without
reference to it? . . . The Liberals . . . feel and I
feel that we are not a step nearer to each other in
1870 than we were in 1835. They have acquired a
new name. They are called Broad Churchmen now, and
delight to be called so. But their breadth seems to me
to be narrowness. They include all kinds of opinions.
But what message have they for the people who do
not live upon opinions or care for opinions?[16]

There is another ground of inclusion than that of Liberalism. "A Broad Church party . . . if it were possible
. . . would be unnecessary, seeing that a body has existed
here for about a thousand years, which is considerably
more inclusive than the new creation could ever become."[17]
The Evangelical had hold of the truth that it is the
mission of the Church to proclaim a Gospel and to evoke
conscious faith in a personal Saviour.[18] He was convinced
"that God had interfered on behalf of His creatures, and
was interfering on behalf of them still; that there is a real
relation between the creature and the Creator; that there
is a real power coming forth from the Creator to succour

[15]*Ibid.,* II, 308 f.
[16]*Life of F. D. M.,* I, 183 f.
[17]Introduction by F. D. M. to J. C. Hare's *Charges to the
Clergy of the Archdeaconry of Lewes* (1856), I, iv.
[18]See *What is Revelation?*, p. 296.

His creatures, and to enable them to do His will."[19] But what in effect was the message of the Evangelical party? Behold the negations of the system!

> Go forth and tell men that their baptism is *not* an admission into the privileges of God's spiritual Church; that they are *not* to take this sign as a warrant of their right to call themselves members of Christ, and to pray to God as their Father in Him. Go and tell them that they are not in a real relation with God, but only in a nominal one; go and tell them that if they are ever to enter into that relation they must bring themselves into it by an act of faith, or else wait till an angel comes down and troubles the waters; go and tell them that the Eucharist is not a real bond between Christ and His members, but only a picture or likeness, which, by a violent act of our will, we may turn into a reality; go and make these comfortable declarations to men, and mix them well with denunciations of other men for not preaching the Gospel; thus you will fulfil God's commission; thus you will reform a corrupt and sinful land.[20]

The Catholic had hold of the truth "that there is indeed a Church in the world, which God Himself has established; that He has not left it to the faith and feelings and notions of men; that He has given us permanent signs of its existence; that He has not left us to find our way into it, but has Himself taken us into it; that being in it we are under His own guidance and discipline; that we are not bound to prove ourselves members of it, by tests which exclude others who share the same privileges with us; that we are not bound to form ourselves into circles and parties and coteries; that we belong to the Communion of Saints, and need not seek for another."[21] But see how the Catholic system deprives these principles of their fertility.

[19] *Kingdom of Christ* (Ev. ed), II, 309.
[20] *Ibid.*, II, 310.   [21] *Ibid.*

The Church is a body which may combine with a State, or rather, submit to it, but which has no natural connexion with it. It has divine sacraments, an apostolic order, a power of binding and loosing; the practice and rules of the age of the Fathers are her model; to these she must be ever seeking to adapt herself. She must reject communion with the Dissenters in this country, not because they want the privileges of the State, but because they have cut themselves off from the universal Church; renouncing her orders, counterfeiting her sacraments. She must, in like manner, repudiate those Protestants abroad who have separated from and abandoned their succession; she must aspire after union with the orthodox Greeks and Latins, but must be content to wait till we or they are prepared for this union. At home we must labour to assert the worth of sacraments, to introduce discipline for the purpose of preserving baptismal purity in our children, and giving repentance to those who have lost it; of cutting off those who hold schismatical or heretical notions under the garb of Churchmen. We must stir men up to do good works, and to expect heavenly rewards for them. We must urge our disciples to retirement from the world, to penances and mortifications; we must preach repentance as the only way of recovering the privileges of Churchmen, which were given once, but which most men lose through sin; we must discountenance every exercise of private judgment, except in the matter of choosing teachers.[22]

With the contrast between these systems and the English Church itself in mind, Maurice, at the time when he was engaged in revising his book, *The Kingdom of Christ*, from which these extracts have been taken, wrote to Erskine of Linlathen as follows:

The English Church I look upon as merely one branch of the true Church; and every *system*, whether

[22]*Ibid.*, II, 307.

called Evangelical, Liberal, Catholic, or purely Anglican, which has been invented by the members of that Church in former times and in our own day to express their notion of the Church, I look upon as "of the earth earthy," and as much carrying in it the seeds of destruction as the systems of the different sects which have revolted from her. The Church—it seems to me—is a part, the highest part, of that spiritual constitution of which the nation and the family are lower and subordinate parts; implied in the acts we do and the words we speak, established before all worlds, manifested as the true and everlasting kingdom when the Son of God died, rose, and ascended on high, testified as the common property and inheritance of men by certain forms and ordinances which convert it from an idea for the mind into an actual reality for all who will enter into it and enjoy it, and which prove God to be true though all men be liars.[23]

Such was Maurice's message to the Anglicans of his own day. He was convinced that "there is a way out of party opinions; a principle which is not a compromise between them, but which is implied in both, and of which each is bearing witness."[24] I need hardly observe that *mutatis mutandis* this message is apt to our day too. Not least does it provide wholesome matter for self-examination for those of us who have been enmeshed in the toils of religious parties, and encouragement for those who have looked for a positive way out of them. At the same time recourse should be had to Maurice's warning about the temptation to form a "no-party" party, which I have quoted in a previous chapter.[25]

Maurice was not advocating the *via media*, at least as that is often understood. The English Church does not

[23]*Life of F. D. M.*, I, 306 f.
[24]Introduction by F. D. M. to J. C. Hare's *Charges to the Clergy of the Archdeaconry of Lewes* (1856), I, x.
[25]See pp. 90 f., *supra*.

stand on "an invisible equatorial line between Romanism and Protestantism."[26] She is not half Catholic and half Protestant, but "most Catholic when she is most Protestant."[27] It is a union of opposites, not a mere balance of opinions, that we find in the Anglican formularies, and that is remarkably represented by Hooker.[28] Their language is studied and accurate, and a tone of decision prevails throughout. The Anglican who understands his position is quite different from the man of the *juste milieu*. The latter

> delights in generalities, he escapes into vagueness, he dares not denounce anything, he dare not affirm anything. He thinks A has a great deal to say for himself, and so has B; but *what* A has to say for himself, and *what* B has, he prudentially shrinks from declaring; and he is most pleased when, having deprived A's thoughts of all their life, and B's thoughts of all their life, he has succeeded in producing a dead residuum or deposit, to which all men lay equal claim, and to which the wise man willingly abdicates his claim altogether. It is not to such divisions and apportionments of truth as these, that men such as our Reformers will submit.[29]

> Most of all is that tone of speaking dangerous and disgraceful to us, which appears to indicate that our condition is most safe when we can keep the elements of which our body politic consists, the Protestant and the Catholic, feeble, each balancing and counteracting the other; whereas in very deed we need them both in their fullest vitality, in their utmost concentration, that we may accomplish the tasks which have been committed to us, that we may not utterly lose what we have inherited, that we may not cease at once to be a Nation and a Church.[30]

[26]*Kingdom of Christ* (Ev. ed.), II, 311.
[27]*Three Letters to the Rev. W. Palmer*, p. 16.
[28]See *Moral and Metaphysical Philosophy*, II, 192.
[29]*Subscription No Bondage*, pp. 103 f. See the whole passage.
[30]*Lincoln's Inn Sermons*, II, 36. Cp. *The Church a Family*, p. 185; *What is Revelation?*, pp. 368 f.; *The Prayer-Book and the Lord's Prayer*, pp. xiii f.

"Compromise," said Maurice, "must always tend to the impairing of moral vigour, and to the perplexing of conscience, *if it is anything else than a confession of the completeness of Truth, and of the incompleteness of our apprehension of it.*"[81] But he knew very well how easily the so-called Anglican genius for compromise, which at its best is a homage to truth, and at which we should always be aiming, can become a blight—"that quality of being neither hot nor cold,—of being not much in earnest for any principle, yet of preserving a decent respect for principles; that habit of congratulating ourselves on this temperance, as if it were a high virtue."[82]

The Anglican Church does not say then to other Churches and sects: See how easy and pleasant a thing it is to maintain a union by combining heterogeneous opinions or by striking a balance between them! The witness she is called to bear, despite the contradictions of her members, is that there is in the constitution of the kingdom of Christ a Divine Order, a God-given bond of unity, for which our conflicting systems are miserable, partial and human substitutes.[83] The way to unity does not lie in the universal adoption of "Anglicanism" any more than of Romanism or Presbyterianism, but in the painful discovery that the positive principles underlying our several systems are held together and reconciled, and so rescued from their negations and their exclusiveness, in the divine society which already exists beneath all human associations, and is awaiting its full manifestation, as the signs of the kingdom of Christ everywhere testify.[84]

I think the Church of England is the witness in our land against the sect principle of "forming churches" which is destroying us and the Americans too. . . .

[81]*Life of F. D. M.*, II, 392 (Italics mine). Cp. *Prophets and Kings*, p. 265.
[82]*Lincoln's Inn Sermons*, IV, 164.
[83]See *Kingdom of Christ* (Ev. ed.), II, 314.
[84]See *ibid.*, II, 290 f.

As long as we think we can form churches we cannot be witnesses for a Humanity and for a Son of man. We cannot believe that we do not choose Him, but that He chooses us and sends us to bear witness of His Father and of Him. Everything seems to me involved in this difference. I admit that the English Church is in a very corrupt, very evil condition. I am not afraid to own that, because I believe it is a Church and not a sect. The sect feeling, the sect habit is undermining it. The business of us who belong to it is to repent of our sectarianism and to call our brothers to repent, to show that we have a ground on which all may stand with us.[35]

Maurice had himself been brought into the Church from a sect. "I came to the Prayer-Book out of a dissenting school, and it was the largeness of its declarations which struck me as the great escape from their narrowness and sectarianism, from the narrowness and sectarianism of those who, like the Unitarians, utterly severed God from His creatures, as much as from the pseudo-Calvinism which made Him the Saviour of the elect, the destroyer of mankind."[36] He thought that it was "the express vocation of the English Church—to bring together feelings which were never meant to be separate, though the evil nature of man is always trying to separate them; to do justice to Romanism, and justice to Protestant dissent, not by yielding a jot to either, but by satisfying the real cravings of the earnest spirits who are entangled in both."[37] "We shall no further assert the superiority of the Anglican Church, than as we prove it to have a wider platform of truth, and to be less arrogant and intolerant than others."[38]

English Churchmen will prize their own history

not because it separates us from men to the left and

[35]*Life of F. D. M.*, II, 299 f.
[36]*Ibid.*, II, 571. *Cp.* p. 11, *supra.*
[37]*Methods of Supporting Protestantism*, p. 20.
[38]*Kingdom of Christ* (1838), I, 290.

to the right, but because it enables us to do each justice; not because it gives us the right to despise either, but the privilege of learning from both; not because it tempts us to copy portions of the systems of the one or the other, but because we can see from it that each has something better than a system; not because it cherishes in us a love of theoretical wavering, but because it provides us with a basis of practical certainty; not because it makes us satisfied with our exclusive nationality, but because by not abandoning that nationality, we become witnesses of a bond and centre for all.[39]

The Anglican Church does not desire other Churches to renounce either their past traditions or their present principles.

Let us make the members of the sects understand that we are setting up no opinions of ours against theirs, no leaders of ours against their leaders; that we desire to justify all that they find and their fathers have clung to in their darkest and bravest hours, all that their leaders taught them when they were inspired with most indignation against our indifference to Christ and His Gospel; that what we preach is Christ the One Head of a body which time and space cannot bound, Christ the source and object of their faith and ours, Christ the destroyer of all sects, inasmuch as He unites men to God. Let us make Spaniards, Frenchmen, Italians, understand that we do not ask them to leave their churches for ours, to accept any single English tradition which is not also theirs, or to travel through the path by which God led the Teutonic nations in the sixteenth century.[40]

All through his life Maurice's overriding quest was for

[39]*Epistle to the Hebrews*, p. cxxvi. Cp. *The Prayer-Book and the Lord's Prayer*, p. 159.
[40]*Lincoln's Inn Sermons*, II, 86. Cp. *Patriarchs and Lawgivers*, p. xxv; *Theological Essays*, pp. 315, 408.

the realization of the unity of mankind which he knew
to have its ground in the unity of God, Father, Son and
Holy Ghost.

> The idea of the unity of the Father and the Son
> in the Holy Spirit, as the basis of all unity among men,
> as the groundwork of all human society and of all
> thought, as belonging to little children, and as the
> highest fruition of the saints in glory, has been haunt-
> ing me for a longer time than I can easily look
> back to.[41]

> The pursuit of unity being the end which God has
> set before me from my cradle upwards. . . . I do
> perceive that if I have any work in the world it is
> to bear witness of this Name, not as expressing certain
> relations, however profound, in the Divine nature, but
> as the underground of all fellowship among men and
> angels, as that which will at' last bind all into one,
> satisfying all the craving of the reason as well as of
> the heart, meeting the desires and intuitions that are
> scattered through all the religions of the world.[42]

It was said then, as it is now, that we must not give up
truth for the sake of unity. And indeed, as Maurice said,
"no one shall persuade us, for the sake of Unity, to part
with this Name (of the Father, the Son and the Holy
Ghost) or explain it away, or substitute some other bond
of union in the place of it."[43] But the question is whether
we must not allow God to bring us into unity in order that
He may teach us that this Name is a name of inclusion,
not of exclusion, in order that we may learn from one another and together apprehend truth in its fullness.

> I believe that the language of some excellent per-
> sons, who say, we must not give up truth for the sake

---

[41]*Life of F. D. M.,* I, 414. *Cp.* Letter from Maurice to Trench
in *Letters and Memorials of R. C. Trench* (1888), I, 158.

[42]*Life of F. D. M.,* II, 388. Cp. *ibid.,* I, 41, 240; II, 168, 518,
632; *Religions of the World,* p. 237.

[43]*Lincoln's Inn Sermons,* II, 145.

of unity, though it contains a valuable meaning, is yet far less sound than it appears to be; for I see that truth is suffering every day and hour from the absence of unity.[44]

It is certainly the will of God that we should come to the knowledge of the truth. But does He not call us into unity in order that we may come to that knowledge?

> Unless we look upon ourselves as *called* to Unity, we shall never be united. If God does not will that we should be united, what can our devices for producing it avail? Whereas, if we believe that it is His Will, and that we are fighting against His Will by our divisions, we have a right confidently to hope that He will at last bring us to repentance, or if we do not repent, will accomplish His purposes in spite of us.[45]

Nevertheless, confident as Maurice was that it is the will of God to bring men into unity, confident as he was that underneath humanity are the everlasting arms preserving and sustaining us even amid our infinite discords and attempts to destroy one another, confident as he was that the unity of mankind would at last be manifested at the coming of Christ in glory, yet the warnings of Scripture, the study of history, and his own experience told him that it is through many tribulations that men must enter into the kingdom of God. He entertained no easy-going hopes concerning the future. He was altogether free from that secular optimism which nowadays is too indiscriminately attributed to the Victorians. "Are we to live in an age," he asked, "in which every mechanical facility for communication between man and man is multiplied ten-thousandfold, only that the inward isolation, the separation of those who meet continually, may be increased in a far greater measure?"[46]

[44]*Subscription No Bondage*, p. 101.
[45]*Hope for Mankind*, p. 71.   [46]*Lincoln's Inn Sermons*, V, 24.

Moreover, he detected in his contemporaries, and had in himself[47] to fight against, that torpor or fatalism, which is more evident and widespread now than it was then.

> We feel sometimes as if we were born into a busy, and excited, and yet into an exhausted age; when men, even boys, have become prematurely wise about the vanity of human wishes. . . . There is a decay of hope, and all the moral strength which hope awakens. Men are not content with what they see about them, far less content with themselves, yet they do not look for anything higher or better. . . . They expect changes, they assume them to be inevitable. But they expect no good from them, more than from the continuance of that which they find so wearisome. There is a sleepy, dreary fatalism into which we are settling down. The sleep is disturbed from without by the noisy clatter of disputing sects, and by the groans of suffering multitudes. It is disturbed from within by dreams of what we ought to do, of what we might be. We need something more than an earthly or human voice to break that slumber, and prevent it from passing into death.[48]

Perhaps things would have to become much worse before the divine voice would be heard. "When all schemes of human policy crack and crumble; when we discover the utter weakness of the leaders and teachers we have trusted most; when we begin to suspect that the world is given over to the spirit of murder and lies; He says to us, 'The foundations of the universe are not built on rottenness; whatever fades and perishes, I AM.' "[49]

> It may be given to these later ages, when kingdoms are falling down, and ecclesiastical systems are wearing out, and scholars are finding nothing solid remain-

[47]See *ibid.*, I, 291.
[48]*Doctrine of Sacrifice*, pp. 296 f.
[49]*Gospel of St. John*, p. 258.

ing in heaven and earth except their own criticisms and their own conceptions, to see the Word of God coming forth in His living power and majesty as the King of kings and Lord of lords, the foundation of that heaven and earth wherein dwelleth righteousness.[50]

Maurice reckoned, as we have to, with the possibility of barbarian anarchy and universal despotism and atheism, but his faith was not shaken that, whatever befell, Christ the true King and Head of the race would be manifested.[51] He anticipated that the way to a new Christendom might lie across greater upheavals than those of the sixteenth century. "I foresee a terrible breaking down of notions, opinions, even of most precious beliefs, an overthrow of what we call our religion—a convulsion far greater than that of the sixteenth century—in our way to reformation and unity."[52] And at the end of his life he wrote: "I do not despair of the sunrise when the night is most chilly, and I would cheer my neighbours to hope for it. About the different expedients for keeping ourselves warm and kindling lights while we are waiting for it, I am growing painfully sceptical."[53]

But his last word to us shall be the conclusion of a sermon which he preached in 1852 on "The Valley of Dry Bones," and through which, being dead, he yet speaks to our age and to every age like ours.

The hand of the Lord was upon me, and carried me out in the spirit of the Lord, and set me down in the midst of the valley which is full of bones, and caused me to pass by them round about. And behold there were very many in the open valley, and lo, they were very dry. And

[50]*Ibid.*, p. 473.
[51]See *Life of F. D. M.*, I, 487. Cp. *Doctrine of Sacrifice*, pp. 310 ff.
[52]*Life of F. D. M.*, II, 354.   [53]*Ibid.*, II, 635.

15

He said unto me, "Son of Man, can these bones live?"
And I answered, "O Lord God, Thou knowest" (Ezekiel
xxxvii, 1–3).

The vision and the interpretation are of this day. Do
you not hear men on all sides of you crying, "The Church
which we read of in books exists only in them. Christendom consists of Romanists, Greeks, Protestants, divided
from each other, disputing about questions to which nineteen twentieths of those who belong to their communions
are indifferent. And meantime what is becoming of the
countries in which these different confessions are established? What populations are growing up in them? Does
the present generation believe that which its fathers believed? Will the next generation believe anything?" . . .
Christians in general are far too eager to urge special
exceptions when they hear these charges preferred; far too
ready to make out a case for themselves while they admit
their application to others; far too ready to think that the
cause of God is interested in the suppression of facts. The
prophets should have taught us a different lesson. They
should have led us to feel that it was a solemn duty, not
to conceal, but to bring forward all the evidence which
proves, not that one country is better than another, or
one portion of the church better than another, but that
there is a principle of decay, a tendency to apostasy in
all, and that no comfort can come from merely balancing
symptoms of good here against symptoms of evil there,
no comfort from considering whether we are a little less
contentious, a little less idolatrous than our neighbours.
Alas, for this Church or for any Church, if its existence
now, if its prospects for the future, are to be determined
by such calculations as these! No, brethren, our hope has
a deeper foundation. It is this; that when the bones have
become most dry, when they are lying most scattered and
separate from each other, there is still a word going forth,

if not through the lips of any prophet on this earth, then through the lips of those who have left it—yet not proceeding from them, but from Him who liveth for ever and ever—the voice which says, "These bones shall rise." It is this; that every shaking among the bones, everything which seems at first a sign of terror—men leaving the Churches in which they have been born, forsaking all the affections and sympathies and traditions of their childhood—infidel questionings, doubts whether the world is left to itself or whether it is governed by an evil spirit—are themselves not indeed signs of life, but at least movements in the midst of death which are better than the silence of the charnel-house, which foretell the approach of that which they cannot produce. It is this; that all struggles after union, though they may be of the most abortive kind, though they may produce fresh sects and fresh divisions, though they must do so as long as they rest on the notion that unity is something visible and material, yet indicate a deep and divine necessity which men could not be conscious of in their dreams if they were not beginning to wake. It is this; that there are other visions true for us, as they were for Ezekiel, besides the vision of dry bones. The name of a Father has not ceased to be a true name because baptized men do not own themselves as His children. The name of a Son has not ceased to be a true name because men are setting up some earthly ruler in place of Him, or are thinking that they can realize a human fellowship without confessing a Man on the throne above the firmament. The name of the Spirit has not ceased to be a true name because we are thinking that we can form combinations and sects and Churches without His quickening presence, because we deny that He is really in the midst of us. It is this; that when all earthly priests have been banished or have lost their faith, though there should be none to mourn over the ruins of Jerusalem, or to feel its sins as his own, yet that there is a

High Priest, the great Sin-Bearer, ever presenting His perfect and accepted sacrifice within the veil, a High Priest not of a nation, but of humanity. It is this; that though all earthly temples, in which God has been pleased to dwell, should become desecrated and abominable, though all foul worship should go on in the midst of them, and though what is portrayed on their walls should too faithfully represent what is passing in the more secret chambers of imagery, though at last the shrines that have been supposed to contain the mystery which they set forth should be utterly destroyed, and a voice should be heard out of the midst of them, saying, "Let us depart"—yet that this will not be the sign that the Church of God has perished, only the sign that the temple of God has been opened in Heaven, and that from thence must come forth the glory that is to fill the whole earth.[54]

Just over a hundred years ago[55] five Cambridge men, not bound to Maurice by any special tie, were discussing a recent execution, previous to which the chaplain of the jail had spent the whole day with the condemned man. They all agreed that there were very few persons whose presence at such a time and for such an interval would not add a new horror to death. The conversation then turned on the choice which each man would make, in the last hours of his life, of a companion to accompany him to its utmost verge, and it was agreed by all five that each should write down the name of the person he would choose. The five papers, when opened, were found to contain a single name—that of Frederick Denison Maurice. Almost

[54]*Prophets and Kings,* pp. 460–63. Cp. *Christmas Day,* pp. 71 f. And yet H. P. Liddon could speak of "Maurice's singular egotism, assuming the form of a quasi-prophetic claim, and his irrepressible tendency to paradox on the most serious subjects!" See *Letters and Memorials of R. C. Trench,* I, 316 f.

[55]This episode was recorded, on the authority of Lord Houghton, by Julia Wedgwood; see her *Nineteenth Century Teachers and other Essays* (1909), p. 29.

every man who knew him would have turned to him, if it had been possible, "in the hour of death, and in the day of judgment." Is he not a theologian for Churches and Nations and for a world that stand "on the last low verge of life"?

BIBLIOGRAPHY OF WORKS BY
F. D. MAURICE

Use has been made of the following works by Maurice. For a complete bibliography see *Life of F. D. M.*, I, xix–xlii. It has been estimated that Maurice's published writings extend to considerably more than 16,300 octavo pages and contain nearly 5,000,000 words (see Claude Jenkins, *Frederick Denison Maurice and the New Reformation*, p. 23). The works listed here are in the order of their first publication, but the date given in each case is that of the edition to which reference is made in the footnotes. In those cases where a book is referred to in the footnotes by an abbreviated title, this is added in square brackets.

Subscription No Bondage, or the Practical Advantages afforded by the Thirty-Nine Articles as Guides in all the Branches of Academical Education. By Rusticus (1835). [*Subscription No Bondage.*]

The Kingdom of Christ: or Hints on the Principles, Ordinances, and Constitution of the Catholic Church in Letters to a Member of the Society of Friends. 3 vols. (1838). [*Kingdom of Christ* (1838).] The 2nd edition of 1842 was revised and altered, and it is that which has been published in "Everyman's Library." 2 vols. [*Kingdom of Christ* (Ev. ed.).]

Has the Church, or the State, the Power to Educate the Nation? (1839). [*Lectures on National Education.*]

Reasons for not joining a Party in the Church: a letter to the Ven. Samuel Wilberforce (1841).

Three Letters to the Rev. W. Palmer, Fellow and Tutor of Magdalen College, Oxford, on the name "Protestant"; on the seemingly ambiguous character of the English

Church; and on the Bishopric of Jerusalem (1842). [*Three Letters to the Rev. W. Palmer.*]

Christmas Day and other Sermons. 2nd edition (1892). [*Christmas Day.*]

On Right and Wrong Methods of Supporting Protestantism: a letter to Lord Ashley, respecting a certain proposed measure for stifling the expression of opinion in the University of Oxford (1843). [*Methods of Supporting Protestantism.*]

The New Statute and Mr. Ward: a letter to a non-resident member of Convocation (1845).

The Epistle to the Hebrews; being the substance of three lectures delivered in the Chapel of the Honourable Society of Lincoln's Inn, on the foundation of Bishop Warburton. With a preface containing a review of Mr. Newman's Theory of Development (1846). [*Epistle to the Hebrews.*]

The Religions of the World and their relations to Christianity considered in eight lectures founded by the Hon. Robert Boyle. 4th edition (1861). [*Religions of the World.*]

The Prayer-Book considered especially in reference to the Romish System, Nineteen Sermons preached in the Chapel of Lincoln's Inn; and The Lord's Prayer, Nine Sermons preached in the Chapel of Lincoln's Inn in the months of February, March, and April, 1848 (1880). [*The Prayer-Book and the Lord's Prayer.*]

Politics for the People. Edited by F. D. Maurice and J. M. Ludlow (1848).

The Church a Family: Twelve Sermons on the Occasional Services of the Prayer-Book (1850). [*The Church a Family.*]

The Prophets and Kings of the Old Testament (1853). [*Prophets and Kings.*]

Sermons on the Sabbath-Day, on the Character of the Warrior, and on the Interpretation of History (1853). [*Sermons on the Sabbath-Day.*]

Theological Essays. 3rd edition (1871).

The Word "Eternal," and the Punishment of the Wicked: a letter to the Rev. Dr. Jelf (1853). [*The Word "Eternal."*]

Lectures on the Ecclesiastical History of the First and Second Centuries (1854). [*Ecclesiastical History.*]

The Unity of the New Testament: a Synopsis of the first three Gospels and of the Epistles of St. James, St. Jude, St. Peter, and St. Paul (1854). [*Unity of the N. T.*]

The Doctrine of Sacrifice deduced from the Scriptures (1879). [*Doctrine of Sacrifice.*]

The Patriarchs and Lawgivers of the Old Testament (1890). [*Patriarchs and Lawgivers.*]

Learning and Working, Six Lectures delivered in Willis's Rooms, London, in June and July, 1854. The Religion of Rome, and its influence on Modern Civilization. Four Lectures delivered in the Philosophical Institution of Edinburgh, in December, 1854 (1855). [*Learning and Working.*]

The Gospel of St. John: a series of discourses (1885). [*Gospel of St. John.*]

The Worship of the Church: a Witness for the Redemption of the World (1857). [*Worship of the Church.*]

The Epistles of St. John: a series of lectures on Christian Ethics (1881). [*Epistles of St. John.*]

Sermons preached in Lincoln's Inn Chapel. 6 vols. (1891). [*Lincoln's Inn Sermons.*]

What is Revelation? A series of sermons on the Epiphany; to which are added letters to a student of theology on the Bampton Lectures of Mr. Mansel (1859). [*What is Revelation?*]

Sequel to the Inquiry, What is Revelation? in a series of letters to a friend; containing a reply to Mr. Mansel's "Examination of the Rev. F. D. Maurice's Strictures on the Bampton Lectures of 1858" (1860). [*Sequel to the Inquiry.*]

The Faith of the Liturgy and the Doctrine of the Thirty-Nine Articles (1860). [*Faith of the Liturgy.*]

Tracts for Priests and People (1861–62).

Lectures on the Apocalypse (1861). [*Apocalypse.*]

Moral and Metaphysical Philosophy. 2 vols. (1882).

The Claims of the Bible and of Science. Correspondence between a Layman and the Rev. F. D. Maurice on some questions arising out of the controversy respecting the Pentateuch (1863). [*Claims of the Bible.*]

The Gospel of the Kingdom of Heaven: a course of lectures on the Gospel of St. Luke (1893). [*Kingdom of Heaven.*]

The Conflict of Good and Evil in our day: twelve letters to a missionary (1865). [*Conflict of Good and Evil.*]

The Commandments considered as Instruments of National Reformation (1866). [*Commandments.*]

The Workman and the Franchise: Chapters from English History on the Representation and Education of the People (1866). [*The Workman and the Franchise.*]

The Ground and Object of Hope for Mankind: four sermons preached before the University of Cambridge in November, 1867 (1868). [*Hope for Mankind.*]

The Conscience: lectures on Casuistry, delivered in the University of Cambridge. 2nd edition (1872). [*Conscience.*]

Church and State. A series of letters published in *The Daily News* on August 14, 17, 22, 27, September 2, 9, 16, and 25, 1868. (In *Life of F. D. M.* these dates are not given, but it is said that the letters were published in September, 1868.)

Social Morality: twenty-one lectures delivered in the University of Cambridge. 2nd edition (1872). [*Social Morality.*]

A Few Words on Secular and Denominational Education (1870).

Sermons preached in Country Churches. 2nd edition (1880).

The Friendship of Books and other Lectures. Edited with a preface by T. Hughes (1893). [*Friendship of Books.*]

The Acts of the Apostles: a course of sermons (1894). [*Acts of the Apostles.*]

The Life of Frederick Denison Maurice chiefly told in his own Letters. Edited by his son Frederick Maurice. 2 vols. 3rd edition (1884). [*Life of F. D. M.*]

Note.—In the quotations in the text from Maurice's writings the use of capital letters for pronouns referring to God has been made consistent, whereas Maurice himself was frequently inconsistent even in a single passage or sentence.

THE HALE LECTURES

The Right Reverend Charles Reuben Hale, D.D., LL.D., Bishop of Cairo, Bishop Coadjutor of Springfield, was born in 1837, consecrated Bishop on July 26, 1892, and died on Christmas Day in the year 1900.

In his will he bequeathed to Western Theological Seminary, now Seabury-Western Theological Seminary of Evanston, Illinois, a fund to be held in trust "for the general purpose of promoting the Catholic Faith, in its purity and integrity, as taught in Holy Scripture, held by the Primitive Church, summed up in the Creeds, and affirmed by the undisputed General Councils, and, in particular, to be used only and exclusively for . . . the establishment, endowment, printing, and due circulation of a yearly Sermon . . . and . . . of Courses of Lectures."

The subjects of these Lectures were to be:

- (*a*) Liturgies and Liturgics.
- (*b*) Church Hymns and Church Music.
- (*c*) The History of the Eastern Churches.
- (*d*) The History of National Churches.
- (*e*) Contemporaneous Church History: *i.e.*, treating of events happening since the beginning of what is called "The Oxford Movement," in 1833.

The Trustees of the Seminary accepted the generous bequest of Bishop Hale and have endeavored faithfully to carry out its provisions. A full list follows of the Hale Lectures thus far delivered and published.

VOLUMES IN THE HALE LECTURES

WITNESS TO THE LIGHT. By the Rev. Alec R. Vidler, D.D., Priest of the Oratory of the Good Shepherd, Warden of St. Deiniol's Library in Hawarden, Hon. Canon of Derby Cathedral. 1947.

MEN AND MOVEMENTS IN THE AMERICAN EPISCOPAL CHURCH. By the Rev. E. Clowes Chorley, D.D., L.H.D., Historiographer of the Church. 1943.

PERSONALITIES OF THE OLD TESTAMENT. By the Rev. Fleming James, D.D., Ph.D., Professor of the Literature and Interpretation of the Old Testament, Berkeley Divinity School, Affiliated with Yale University Divinity School. 1938.

THE CHURCH IN JAPAN. By the Rt. Rev. Henry St. George Tucker, Bishop of Virginia; Presiding Bishop of the Protestant Episcopal Church; formerly (1912–1923) Bishop of Kyoto. 1937. (Published under the title *The History of the Episcopal Church in Japan.*)

THE PRAISE OF GOD. By the Rev. Winfred Douglas, Mus. Doc., Canon of St. John's Cathedral, Denver, Colorado. 1935. (Published under the title *Church Music in History and Practice.*)

THE SOCIAL IMPLICATIONS OF THE OXFORD MOVEMENT. By the Rev. William George Peck, Rector of St. John Baptist, Hulme, Manchester, England. 1932.

PASTORAL PSYCHIATRY AND MENTAL HEALTH. By the Rev. John Rathbone Oliver, M.D., Ph.D., Associate in the History of Medicine at the Johns Hopkins University, 1932. (Published under title *Psychiatry and Mental Health.*)

CHRIST IN THE GOSPELS. By the Rev. Burton Scott Easton, Ph.D., S.T.D., Professor at the General Theological Seminary. 1930.

NEW HORIZONS OF THE CHRISTIAN FAITH. By the Rev. Frederick C. Grant, D.D., Th.D., Dean of the Seabury-Western Theological Seminary. 1928.

SOME ASPECTS OF CONTEMPORARY GREEK ORTHODOX THOUGHT. By the Rev. Frank Gavin, M.A., Ph.D., Professor at the General Theological Seminary. 1921.

THE ETHIOPIC LITURGY. By the Rev. S. A. B. Mercer, D.D., Ph.D., Professor at Trinity College in the University of Toronto. 1915.

BIOGRAPHICAL STUDIES IN SCOTTISH CHURCH HISTORY. By the Rt. Rev. Anthony Mitchell, D.D., Late Bishop of Aberdeen and Orkney. 1913.

THE NATIONAL CHURCH OF SWEDEN. By the Rt. Rev. John Wordsworth, D.D., LL.D., Late Bishop of Salisbury. 1910.

CHURCH HYMNS AND CHURCH MUSIC. By Peter C. Lutkin, Mus.D., A.G.O., Late Dean of the School of Music, Northwestern University. 1908.

INDEX

Absolution, 151 f.
Adam, First and Second, 51, 52-55, 59, 61 f.. 109, 127
Adderley, J., 72
Ages of the antediluvians. 161 f.
Allegorical interpretation of Scripture, 156, 167 ff.
Anglicanism, 17, 87-93, 207-25
Apologetics, 35
Apostolate, 143 f.
Aristocracy, 195 ff.
Aristotle, 30 f., 76
Articles of Religion, 79, 126-29, 217

Bagehot, W., 7
Baptism, 94-120, 134 f.
Barth, K., 47
Bible, The, 16, 19 f., 29, 40, 45 f., 73-77, 155-82
Bigg, C., 60
Boehme, J., 22 f.
Book of Common Prayer, 17, 81, 130-34, 217
Bride of Christ, 77
Broad Churchmen, 218
Brooke, S. A., 112
Brooks, Phillips, 15, 97, 111 f.

Calvinism, 37, 57-60, 201, 208 f.
Campbell, Macleod, 61
Catholicism, 16, 200 ff., 219 f.
Cavendish, Lady F., 7 f., 47
Chorley, E. Clowes, 39, 97
Christian Socialism, 11, 14 f. 203
Christian Year, 133
Church, R. W., 18 f.
Church, The, 16, 64-90, 163 f., 182
Church and State, 190-94, 198 f.
Clark, Samuel 113

Clayton, J., 72
Colenso, Bishop, 157 f.. 161
Coleridge, S. T.. 32 f., 210
Collins, W. E., 10, 23, 29
Compromise, 223
Congar, M. J., 47
Covenant, 73-77
Creation, 52 ff.
Creeds, 16 f., 122-26

Davies, J. Ll.. 72
Democracy, 194-97
Depravity, 38 ff., 57
Disraeli, B., 26, 157
Dix, G., 49, 96
Dodd, C. H., 48 f. 168
Dods, Marcus, 41

Eclecticism, 21
Ede, W. Moore, 38, 72
Education, National, 198 f.
Election, 57-60, 68, 116
Elliott-Binns, L. E., 23, 72
Episcopacy, 146-50
Erskine, T., 32 f., 61, 71, 172, 176, 220
Essays and Reviews, 157 f.
Eternal Life, 23
Eucharist, 134-41, 151
Evangelicalism, 17, 37, 39, 41, 91 f., 102 ff., 218 f.
Ewing, A., 61, 73

Fall of man, 37-40, 47, 127
Family relationship, 74 ff., 183 ff.
Fathers, The, 32, 46
Forms of worship, 130-34

Garrigou-Lagrange, R., 79
Gladstone, W. E., 7 f.
Gloyn, C. K., 33

Goodwin, H., 9
Gorham Controversy, 94
Government, 185 f.

Hook, W. F., 87, 113
Hooker, R., 210, 222
Hort, F. J. A., 9, 25, 60, 72, 119 f.
Hutton, R. H., 7, 12, 27, 33, 42, 114

Inspiration, 79 f., 162, 174 f.
Israel, The New, 77

Jacques, J. H., 208
Jowett, B., 10, 32
Justification, 61 ff.

Kingsley, C., 97, 114, 208

Language, 185 f.
Law, 75, 185 f., 190 ff., 197, 201
Lee, Bishop, 157
Liberalism, 17, 134, 217 f.
Liddon, H. P., 21, 232
Liturgy, 130–34
Logic, 18 f.
Lubac, H. de, 32, 46, 79 ff.
Luther, M., 62 f., 103
Lutheranism, 37

Major, H. D. A., 156
Manicheism, 44, 65
Mansel, H. L., 23, 177 f., 180
Manson, T. W., 96
Martineau, J., 10, 24, 46, 54, 172
Mascall, E. L., 49
Mason, A. J., 99
Masterman, C. F. G., 11, 24 f., 159
MAURICE, F. D., diverse estimates of, 9 ff.; as a theologian, 11–15, 22; his "system-phobia," 15 ff.; electicism, 21; style, 22, 24 ff.; consistency, 26 ff.; originality, 28 f.; indebtedness to others, 29–33;
ground of his message, 40–45; acquaintance with sects and parties, 89; baptism, 97; attitude to Biblical criticism, 159–63; method of interpreting Scripture, 45 f., 169–75; controversy with Mansel, 177 f.; as a politician, 203; on the calling of the Anglican Communion, 213–25; quest for unity, 225–32
Mersch, E., 50 f.
Method, 19 ff., 40, 127
Methodism, 37
Milton, J., 38
Ministry, 141–54
Miracles, 180 ff.
Monarchy, 195 ff.
More, P. E., 207 f.
Mozley, J. B., 9
Murray, J. O. F., 60

Name of God, The, 12, 16, 40, 44, 67, 75, 110 f., 123 ff., 130, 144, 177, 180, 207, 212, 226, 231
National Churches, 197–201 209, 215
Nationality, 75 f., 183–90, 193 f.
Nature and Natural, 79 ff., 107 f., 110, 178
Newman, J. H., 9
"No party," 90 ff.

Parties, Ecclesiastical, 87–93, 210 f., 217–23
Patriotism, 189 f.
Pattison, Mark, 92
Penido, T.-L., 178
Percy, Lord E., 60
Petre, M. D., 39
Pfleiderer, O., 45, 213
Phillips, G. L., 9
Plato, 15 f., 30 ff.
Plotinus, 31
Popular sovereignty, 194 f.
Predestination, 57–60
Presbyterianism, 208 f., 216

Priesthood, 75, 132, 150 ff.
Progressive revelation, 179 f.
Protestantism, 200 ff.
Pusey, E. B., 106 ff.

Rashdall, H., 8
Rationalism, 17
Real Presence, 137
Religion, 13, 175 ff.
Revelation, 177–82
Rigg, J. H., 32
Robertson, F. W., 111 ff.
Romanism, 17, 153, 200 f., 209, 215

Sacrifice, 137 ff., 150
Sanders, C. R., 33
Sectarianism, 81–93, 198, 223 ff.
Secular, 65 ff., 166, 186 f., 190
Selwyn, E. G., 60
Shorthouse, J. H., 10
Sin, 42 ff.
Socrates, 30, 32
Spirit, The Holy, 20, 36, 78 ff., 98–102, 104 f., 108, 115–18, 163 f.
State, Definition of a, 190
Stephen, L., 10

Sterling, J., 172
Storr, V. F., 32
System, 15–19, 166 f., 208–12, 214–21

Tennyson, Lord, 10
Theologian, task of, 12–15, 35 f.
Theology, meaning of, 11 f.; foundation of, 36–41
Thornton, L. S., 49
Tractarianism, 87, 91 ff., 105–113
Trench, R. C., 130, 183
Tuckwell, W., 97
Tulloch, J., 26 f., 33, 45, 171 f.
Universalism, 61
Universities, 128 ff.

Via Media. 221 f.

Wand J. W. C., 60
Wedgwood, Julia, 33, 232
Westcott, B. F., 47, 72 f.
Westminster Assembly, 127, 216
Wilberforce, W., 39
Wordsworth, Christopher, 157 f.
World, The, 65–70, 110